TRI SINHALA

THE LAST PHASE

1796-1815

TRI SINHALA

THE LAST PHASE

1796-1815

P. E. PIERIS

SECOND EDITION

GYAN

Published by

GYAN

Gyan Publishing House
5, Ansari Road
Daryaganj, New Delhi-110002
Phone: 011-47034999, 9811692060
E-mail: books@gyanbooks.com

Distribution Network
gyanbooks.com
India, USA, Canada, UK, Australia, France

ISBN : 978-81-212-4165-6 (PB)
First Published, Colombo, 1939

2nd Impression 2020

Printed at: Gyan Press, Delhi.

Tri Sinhala
Author: P. E. Pieris

TRI SINHALA

The Last Phase

1796–1815

by P. E. PIERIS, LITT.D.(CAMB.)

CEYLON:
THE COLOMBO APOTHECARIES CO., LTD.
1939

Ehelepola, Molligoda and Kapuvatta
with D'Oyly

See Appendix N.

TO

JUSTIN

IN APPRECIATION OF MUCH ASSISTANCE

THIS BOOK IS DEDICATED

A certain man went down from Jerusalem to Jericho and fell among thieves.

ST. LUKE.

Introduction

For three centuries the Sinhalese had struggled to maintain their independent existence in the face of Western aggression, and the story of their efforts, diminishing pitifully in effectiveness with the dwindling supplies of men and material, has been set out in two previous books—Ceylon, the Portuguese Era, and Ceylon and the Hollanders. When in 1796 the British appeared on the stage they had to deal with a Kingdom crippled in size, negligeable as a military power, and cut off from all access to the sea—with the Ruler, to use Ehelepola's description, "living as fish encompassed by a net." Nineteen brief years had yet to elapse before the Kingship which had lasted for twenty-four hundred years came to an end with the capture of Sri Vikrama Raja Sinha, and this book sets out the true history of that period, stripped of the various cloaks which an active political propaganda, an apathy towards elucidation of fact, and an all too human weakness to accept without reserve anything that savours of sensationalism, have cast over it. The material relied upon is almost exclusively the documents preserved at the Public Record Office, London, supplemented to a very limited extent by those available at Colombo. Due acknowledgment has been made where any previous publication is followed.

Contents

Appendices

CHAPTER I

On the 16th of February, 1796 the Dutch East India Company's military forces evacuated the Fort of Colombo, and the administration of its late possessions in Ceylon was transferred to the British Company, while the Treaty negotiated by Robert Andrews, a Senior Merchant in the latter's service, which had been signed at Madras four days earlier by Dumbara Rala on behalf of Raja Adhiraja Sinha,* the Malabar Prince whom the influence of the then Adikar, Pilima Talavuva, had placed on the throne of Tri Sinhala† in 1782,‡ was left unratified.

At 9 a.m. on the 12th of October, 1798 Frederic North, the thirty-two-year-old youngest son of the second Earl of Guildford, arrived at Colombo by way of Bombay and with due ceremony took the oath prescribed by His Britannic Majesty's Commission as his Governor, Commander-in-Chief, and Captain-General over his Territories in Ceylon, with a further oath of attachment and fidelity to the Honourable East India Company.§ Educated at Eton and Christ Church, an accomplished Grecian and a Fellow of the Royal Society, he had sat in Parliament for

* Ceylon and the Hollanders: P E. Pieris: 2nd Ed. 1924, pp. 171-173.

† The King of Ceylon was always *Tri Sinhala Adhisvara*, Lord of the Three Sinhalas, a title which recalled the original division of the Island into three parts.

‡ Pilima Talavuva to Boyd, Avisaha Vella, 6th Jan., 1800: Secret Diary, Colombo Record Office. The First and Second Ministers or Adikars were known as Palle Gam Pahe and Uda Gam Pahe respectively, after two groups of villages which they directly controlled.

§ North to Board of Directors, 13th Oct., 1798. Record Office, London, C.O. 54/1.

the pocket borough of Banbury, and had also acquired some knowledge of administrative work during the British occupation of Corsica. He found the Sinhalese Kingdom emerging from a serious crisis. The King had died towards the end of 1797 without leaving children by any of his five Queens, and the brother of three of them, Muddu Svami, claiming to have been nominated by him, expected to succeed to the regal power, but three days later he and his sisters were placed in confinement by the masterful Pilima Talavuva, brother* of the late King's Minister, who as Adikar led the Sinhalese party at Court, and under his dictation the son of Venkata Perumal Svami, the late king's one-time Agent in his negotiations with the European powers in South India, an inexperienced young man of eighteen years, was invested with the Sword of State under the name Sri Vikrama Raja Sinha.†

Following the practise of his Dutch predecessors, North hastened to inform the new Ruler of his own assumption of duties by this letter.

To the Illustrious, High and Mighty Monarch who at present Governs the renowned and powerful Kingdom of Candia seated on His Golden Throne.

Illustrious, High and Mighty Monarch,

I take the earliest opportunity of informing Your Majesty of my arrival at this Place as Governor of the British Settlements in the Island of Ceylon and of assuring Your Majesty of the Peculiar Satisfaction which I feel in having

* Not son, as stated by A. C. Lawrie and H. W. Codrington. See Appendix A.

† Muddu Svami to North, 11th Oct., 1799. The English despatches frequently suggest that the late King was deposed, and even killed ; such was not the case.

been chosen by the King, my August Master, to reside so near your Royal Person, that I may strengthen and cement that Amity and Friendship which so happily exists between Him. and Your Majesty and which I trust will last as long as the Sun and Moon endure.

It shall be my constant Endeavour to prove to Your Majesty by my conduct how greatly I rejoice in the auspicious Elevation of Your Majesty and how sincerely I desire to cultivate the mutual confidence which exists between Your Majesty's subjects and the inhabitants of these Settlements.

May all Health, Happiness and Other Blessings attend your Majesty ; what can I write more.

Illustrious, High and Mighty Monarch,

Your Royal Majesty's very obedient Servant,

FREDERIC NORTH.*

Colombo, 29th October, 1798.

This advance was received with such cordiality that the Court's desire for British friendship was not open to doubt,† and in order to avoid all risk of friction North both deported to Tutucorin three important refugees who might be suspected of intriguing against the King from their asylum in Colombo,‡ and also placed under arrest the messenger sent from Tanjore by Ranne Sinha Maha Raja to solicit assistance in securing the throne of Ceylon which he

* Colombo Record Office, Political Diary. Only the English translations of the letters quoted in this book are available.

† North to Court of Directors, 26th Oct., 1798. C.O. 54/1.

‡ They were the son of the late Adikar Gallegodde Rajecaruna Wijewardana Alegiyawanna Wikramasinha Mudiyanse; the nephew of the decapitated Dissava Dennegamuwe Bandara; and Inguruwatte Unanse. North to Captain Davison, 22nd Nov., 1798. C.R.O. Political Diary, Vol. 35.

claimed for himself. He further wrote to the Adikar that even before leaving England he had learnt of his friendliness from General Stuart who commanded the British expedition in 1796, and that he looked forward with pleasure to meeting him before long; while in a third letter addressed to all the Ministers he repeated his hopes of the continuance of friendly relations.*

Simultaneously he advised the Secret Committee of the Court of Directors not to adopt the Treaty in its existing form, but to leave it in abeyance till the question of the future of the Settlements was decided in Europe by a definitive Peace, for some of its provisions, such as those intended to secure a naval base and the cinnamon trade, were founded on erroneous information. The Sinhalese, he reported, did not in fact control any part of the sea coast at the time the Treaty was signed but it was altogether in the hands of the Dutch and therefore would pass to their successors. Nor was it the case that cinnamon could be procured only from Sinhalese Territory; while to concede to the Court the right of direct shipment of that spice would destroy all prospect of establishing a monopoly. Similarly the provision about salt rendered it impossible to build up that control of the supply for which the various European nations in turn had striven, and which was the most effectual means of keeping the Sinhalese in a state of dependence. Besides the Treaty would dangerously facilitate the import of arms within the Kingdom. The Dutch he said had always aimed at securing the entire trade of the Sinhalese and this should continue to be the British policy rather than territorial expansion which he strongly deprecated.†

* 24th Nov., 1798. C.R.O. Vol. 35.

† North to Secret Committee, 26th Nov., 1798. C.O. 54/1.

In February, 1799 an Embassy arrived from the Court ; it was headed by the Adikar himself, an unusual distinction, and with him were associated two other Courtiers ; but as small-pox had broken out in Colombo North proceeded to Avisaha Vella, close to the frontier, where he met them on the 14th at 4 p.m. The ambassadors announced the death of the late King and the accession of the new, at which North ordered a Royal Salute to be fired in token of rejoicing. They next on behalf of the King presented him with a gold chain, a ring set with rubies, and two elephants, after which he ceremoniously sprinkled rose-water on them before they withdrew. A second meeting followed at 7 a.m. the next morning, when they drew attention to the failure to ratify the recent Treaty and demanded the surrender of Tambalagama and the sea coast round Tiru Kona Malai in accordance with what they understood as a promise to that effect made by the English, the Adikar emphasizing the importance of an intimate union between the two Governments and speaking with so much feeling about the Malabars that North suspected some unpleasantness had arisen with the King. On separating he pointed to certain white marks on the hind legs of an officer's* Arab charger and explained that according to Sinhalese lore these were considered of good omen ; North purchased this animal and added it to the recognised presents which accompanied the Adikar on his return home.†

In July after a visit to India, North learnt that his delay in sending a return Embassy was creating an unfavourable impression, while the raising of a Malay Regiment caused

* Major Robertson, D. A. G.; North paid 500 pagodas for the animal.

† North to Secret Committee, 21st Feb., 1799. C.O. 54/1.

so much agitation that many inhabitants of the border Provinces sought refuge among the mountains, fearing an outbreak of hostilities. Two months later Muddu Svami was released and with his wife and children and a few followers escorted to the frontier whence he made his way to Jaffna Patam, where he was lodged by the British within the Fort and granted a small allowance.* He now opened communications with the Governor, offering many tempting concessions as the price of his being placed on the Throne with British help, but received no encouragement. Instead North sent a confidential Sinhalese messenger to explain to the Adikar that he was most anxious for the continuance of the authority of the King and of the Adikar, and would gladly do everything in his power to defend them against foreign and domestic enemies.

In reply the Adikar expressed a desire to meet him again at Avisaha Vella at an early date to discuss certain questions of a very secret nature.† North agreed; his inquiries he said made it clear that the Adikar's object was to establish an intimate and perpetual Union, placing "the Royal pageant whose motives he guides" under the protection of a British force, while securing his own authority on an undisputed basis. In view of this he was not prepared to endanger the success of the negotiations by any over-strictness as to the terms on which such proposals would be accepted, provided that there was a satisfactory guarantee that the necessary expenditure would be covered by supplies of areka, cinnamon, and other like commodities in sufficient quantities to leave a substantial profit. His intention was to send Major-General

* Muddu Svami to North, 21st Sept., 1799; North to Barbut, 3rd Oct., 1799.

† North to Secret Committee, 13th Jan., 1800. C.O.54/2.

Hay Macdowal at an early date to settle the details with the Court: the immediate need was an armed escort imposing enough to prevent any opposition to the execution of his plans. He had asked the Adikar to come with full power to conclude a Treaty, and on 25th December applied to the Governor-General, the Earl of Mornington, for the loan of the 2,500 soldiers who he estimated would be required.*

The meeting took place on the 5th of January 1800. The Adikar who was in poor health, opened the talk by declaring that he was sick not in body alone but in mind as well, for the King had begun to give ear to Malabars and was doing ill. North replied that as it was the Adikar who had placed him on the Throne and who still possessed the real power, he could with little trouble keep undesirable people at a distance and re-establish a more satisfactory state of affairs. But the Adikar was very depressed ; he repeated that the King was ill disposed and he expressed the wish that the English would occupy the country and place him at its head. North answered that he could not depose the King or enter into occupation of the country, but he could take the two under the protection of the British King and of the Honourable Company, and he was prepared to send troops immediately for the purpose : then he would be in a position to maintain the Adikar in power, as well as the King on the Throne ; which latter, he declared, was a necessary preliminary condition to any arrangement.

The First Maha Mudaliyar,† the Sinhalese Official who in the British Settlements continued as the survival of the

* Secret Diary C.R.O.

† Johannes de Saram Wijayasekera Abayaratna, First Maha Mudaliyar, 10th May, 1794—17th Nov., 1809. See Pieris—Notes on some Sinhalese Families. Part III (1911).

Chief Minister of the pre-European Kings of Ceylon, and through whom the correspondence with the Court was conducted, was acting as interpreter along with the Frenchman Jonville; and the Adikar expressed a desire to talk over this suggestion with him at greater length in the morning. Following on this second interview and at the Adikar's request William Boyd, the acting Secretary to Government, who had come out with North from England, and the two Interpreters met him for the third time at 8 o'clock at night,* Boyd being provided with written instructions from North. He commenced by explaining that as the Governor had already recognised the King he was not prepared to question his title to the Throne. The Adikar, while acquiescing, declared that the British already held a large part of the Island and if they so desired they might now become masters of the rest as well: he was anxious to know North's view on the point. The Governor, Boyd replied, desired the continuance of the Adikar's power and undertook to uphold it if he on his part would induce the King to ask for British protection and admit a British garrison within his kingdom; under any circumstances his person and dignity must be safe-guarded; he could continue to reside at the Capital while the Adikar exercised the real authority.

* An account of the interview was left by Jonville in French. The following extract is from a copy on which is endorsed in Sir Alexander Johnstone's writing "This narrative was written by Mr. Jonville and translated by Mr. Tolfrey." "We found the Adikar in the midst of a Thicket, on an eminence the approach to which was by a dozen steps formed by round blocks of granite. The Audience Room was a cube of six feet with no other aperture for light than a door 18 inches wide and 4½ feet high. He was kneeling owing to a Fistula said to be incurable resting on his two hands, his body projecting and his head sunk between his shoulders, a position which added not a little to the expression of villainy legible in his countenance."

On the latter remarking that such an arrangement could not work with the present King and amidst the existing civil dissensions, Boyd urged that it was the one remedy against those very dissensions.

Why was North so anxious to support the King, the Adikar asked; Boyd answered that so far as an attack upon a Prince who was not an aggressor was concerned, the Governor's decision was final. The Adikar retorted that the King was not a friend of the English and inquired how the Governor would act in case of an attack by him. The reply was that if the King took the offensive and attacked the English, they well knew how to defend themselves. The Adikar explained that though it was owing to his own influence that the King was on the Throne yet he had always had an intention of placing the country under the British provided that the supreme power was conferred on himself, and he expressed his great disappointment that his proposal did not find acceptance with the Governor. Boyd then announced North's intention to send Macdowal as Ambassador, but he must have an escort of not less than 800 men and for this the King's permission was needed; such a step he assured the Adikar would lead to a continuance of his own power. The Adikar replied shortly "Send such an escort if such is your pleasure." The meeting ended at 10 p.m. with mutual expressions of regret that matters must continue as before.*

At 9 o'clock the next morning Pilima Talavuva waited on North to bid him farewell and again expressed his disappointment at the Governor's decision. The latter pointed out that it would be infinitely less dangerous to exercise power under British protection, and as for the

* Boyd to North, 6th Jan., 1800. Secret Diary.

difficulty arising from a division of authority, once there was a British garrison at the spot, the Minister could get rid of his enemies by deporting them to the Coast and issue his orders in the King's name. Pilima Talavuva answered that the idea pleased him but inquired if the King's consent was essential before troops could be sent. The Governor replied that it was and that the Minister must persuade him to apply for a force to protect him from his enemies. Pilima Talavuva was doubtful as to his ability to bring this about ; if that were the case, said North, no force could be sent but he intended writing to the King that Macdowal would come as his Ambassador bringing rich presents with him, and in the disturbed state of the country a person of his importance would need an escort of not less than a thousand men. On the Adikar asking why so great a person was selected, North explained that it was intended for the greater honour of the King, and further he wished Macdowal to enter into such Treaties as might serve to build up a future union. Pilima Talavuva was not very satisfied and wished to be enlightened as to the nature of the proposed Treaty ; and in spite of the Governor's evasive answer that it would be one advantageous to both sides, insisted that he did not see the need for the General's mediation, as the two of them could deal with the matter on the spot, though he had to admit that he was not vested with the necessary authority to enter into a Treaty. He finally inquired whether the escort would return with the Ambassador, and was told that the permanent residence of a strong garrison at the Capital would be provided for in the Treaty. After this Pilima Talavuva started on his journey home.

On the 10th of January, North again wrote to Mornington to inform him of what had passed. He would secure for Pilima Talavuva, he said, any authority he desired short of the Royal, if only he would persuade the King to ask for British protection, arguing that if the Minister could bring this about, either his power was already so great that the King would lose nothing by the new arrangement, or else both of them were in such a state of fear that they were prepared to sacrifice their independence as the price of safety. He described the country as being in a condition of most hopeless weakness, torn by a thousand factions, and exhausted by an administration which was radically defective. "Though it may not be today or tomorrow" he continued, "the time I trust will shortly arrive when we shall be put into the effective possession of Candy without opposition and without a crime." In fact all the rival factions at Court had approached him with offers to make their country tributary to his Government.* It will thus be seen that thirteen months had brought about a notable change in his views regarding territorial expansion.

* Secret Diary, C.R.O. Also North to Secret Committee, 13th Jan., 1800. C.O. 54/2.

CHAPTER II

In a few days the Adikar returned and on the first of February had a six hours' interview with Boyd, in the course of which he agreed to the King's person and dignity being safeguarded and Macdowal despatched as Ambassador in the manner proposed, but as he brought no authority to ask for a resident garrison, North refused to act till the King's consent was obtained. The Adikar was nettled. He did not think the English had been so particular and sensitive in their dealings either with the Dutch or with Tippoo Sultan,* he said. Boyd explained that the latter had entered into an alliance with the French to drive out the English, while the King was not an aggressor—an explanation which led to a discussion as to what would be considered sufficient aggression to induce the Governor to take military action.† North was not prepared to act on Pilima Talavuva's bare assurance and insisted on forwarding to the King a letter, which was first corrected by the Minister, explaining the nature of the proposed Embassy. If the King so desired, the force which would form the escort could be placed at his disposal and the Governor would be sincerely happy if its presence would ensure the security of the King's Sacred Person and Dignity against any attempts by the numerous Malabar pretenders to the Throne. The Ambassador would also be authorised to discuss the terms of a Treaty.‡

* Seringa Patam was captured in 1799.

† Boyd to North, 1st and 2nd Feb., 1800..

‡ North to King, 17th Feb., 1800.

Pending the arrival of a reply Boyd remained in close contact with the Adikar who demanded a guarantee that the army while on the march would respect the religious prejudices of the people and not cause damage to their places of worship or dismantle the old guns which were mounted at some of them, or slaughter the sacred cattle which were kept there ; he displayed particular anxiety about an ancient sword which was preserved at the Capital and regarded by the Sinhalese as an object of great sanctity; even though the King as a Malabar might like to get rid of it, there must be an assurance that it would not be sent out of the country. Finally, the rank and privileges of the two Adikars, of whom the second, Migas Tenna, was married to his daughter, must be secured to them for life. The Adikar also expressed his hope that in view of Macdowal's high position the King might be induced to excuse him those irksome formalities to which Andrews had been obliged to submit during his embassy.*

North was exultant at the results of his diplomacy and reported to the Secret Committee that he expected Pilima Talavuva to hand over the entire revenue enjoyed by the King while he guaranteed any form of Government which the Adikar set up as best likely to secure the effective power for himself : the King, he said, appeared to be kept in complete ignorance of all that passed and the real power was with the Minister.† To Mornington he protested that his object in sending a force was to prevent a conspiracy, and he was acting with the consent of the person from whom the conspiracy was feared ; his great anxiety

* Boyd to North, 3rd Feb., 1800.

† North to Secret Committee, 1st Feb., 4th Feb., 4th April, 1800. C.O. 54/2. North to Boyd, 4th Feb. Secret Diary.

was to save the country from the horrors of a Civil War. Macdowal he said was instructed to see that no compulsion was brought to bear on the King; but so long as the King's life was safe he would support any Government which he found established in the Kingdom.* The Adikar had expressed doubts as to the feasibility of taking guns over the Sinhalese roads, which were generally narrow tracks,† and North suggested that if the Minister joined the Ambassador in person it would be an impressive gesture of the cordial relations existing between the two Governments.‡

A reply was soon received from the Court, approving of the Ambassador selected but making no reference to his escort; this was signed by Pilima Talavuva and North pressed him for the King's express consent, adding that Boyd would wait on him to discuss terms.§ The Adikar explained that the reply was prepared at Court and sent to him for his signature and to be sealed with the King's seal: apparently the Governor's letter had not been fully understood, but permission to bring the troops was granted. As for meeting Boyd at his own house, this could not be done without the King's permission and he wished to know for the King's information what was the nature of the questions which Boyd would discuss with him.|| North repeated that his anxiety was firmly to establish the Minister's authority and with that in view he desired the terms settled on which the British power could be utilised

* North to Mornington, 11th Feb.; to Lord Clive, Fort St. George, 16th Feb.

† Boyd to North, 5th Feb. C.R.O.

‡ North to Adikar, 7th Feb., 1800; C.R.O.

§ North to Adikar, 23rd Feb., 1800. C.R.O.

|| Adikar to Maha Mudaliyar, Feb., 1800. C.R.O.

for the purpose ; he was therefore sending a copy of his proposals and if the Adikar would return the document with the King's signature, a duplicate signed by the Governor would be sent in exchange and the British force would be at his disposal. In the meantime the Maha Mudaliyar would attend at the frontier to give any further explanation which might be required.*

Under the suggested terms His Britannic Majesty and the East India Company guaranteed to the King his Throne against all enemies, and in order to render the guarantee effective a British garrison would be stationed within his Dominions to carry out his orders as conveyed by the Adikar and by no other agency. The right of the British to the territory possessed by the Dutch was acknowledged, and they were given the privilege of sending their men to any part of the Kingdom to peel cinnamon and fell timber, while all Customs duties at the frontier were abolished and the legal status of the subjects of the two parties defined. Commissioners would be appointed to assess the King's revenue, which would then be allotted for the maintenance of the Royal dignity, the British garrison, and the Civil Administration ; till the amount available was ascertained the cost of the garrison would be met by contributions of areka, coffee, pepper, rice, cattle and cardamoms up to an agreed amount. The two Adikars were to hold office for life and be supported therein by the British ; all claimants to the Throne and other similar suspects were to receive the King's pardon and be handed over to the British, while any forts which were required for the defence of the Kingdom would be built by the King and manned by the British garrison. Finally, the

* North to Adikar, 27th Feb., 1800. C.R.O.

national religion, temples and priests were to be treated with all respect and consideration.

Boyd was sent to continue the conversations. The Adikar pointed out that letters were never signed by the King but by the Minister, who also sealed them with the King's seal ; though Boyd insisted that under the special circumstances the King's signature was essential, North after an examination of the Archives accepted the procedure which had been followed as sufficient. The terms were examined clause by clause and were declared generally acceptable, but Pilima Talavuva would not undertake to supply goods to the value of two and a half lacs of pagodas,* the figure named by Boyd, to cover the expenditure of the garrison. The questions involved were so important he said, that he desired all the Ministers to discuss the details with North at the spot ; if they accepted the terms the document could be sent for the King's signature and on its return would be signed by the Ministers and North. He inquired further what would happen if the King declined to sign, and was assured that there would be no resort to threats or force.†

North, however, refused to meet the Ministers, and suggested an alternative proposal with regard to the expense of the garrison, which the Adikar accepted. He also warned the Minister that he would be held responsible for the King receiving the Ambassador, and on that assurance the embassy would start without delay. Pilima Talavuva frankly told Boyd that he had not completely given up his ambitions about the Throne ; that, North commented, could not but be suspected by the King,

* An Indian gold coin worth approximately eight shillings.

† Boyd to North, 13th March, 1800.

who would therefore be encouraged by the arrival of the force to arrange for the continuance of British protection; indeed, it might become the Adikar's turn to look to that protection for the preservation of his own life. Then would be the time for Macdowal to negotiate with the Ministers, for his position would be much stronger than North's could be at Sitavaka. He would never, he protested, intimidate the King into concessions; the presence of a foreign force in a Prince's Capital would generally be regarded as intimidation, but that was not so in the present case, where the force would only serve to give courage to the King. On the other hand, he argued, to employ the Minister for the purpose of obtaining the King's signature, would undoubtedly be intimidation.

Boyd made it clear to Pilima Talavuva that hostile action against the King would not be considered, whereupon he enquired what would constitute aggression sufficient to provoke hostilities—would the irruption of 3,000 men into British territory be such aggression?* It would, replied Boyd, but in such a case the Minister would be regarded as the instigator and could not expect British support: he therefore stood to gain much more by agreeing to North's proposals. The Adikar assented and promised his cordial support, but he could not agree to the revenue clauses.† He was urged to sign to the terms so far as he approved of them in order that they might form the basis of a Treaty which the King could ratify, but he would not do so without first consulting the other Ministers, and he could give no assurance of their acquiescence. In any case, what would be the result, he inquired, if the King finally

* North to Boyd, 4th March, and 5th March, 1800.

† Boyd to North, 4th March, 1800.

refused his consent? That contingency would not arise, Boyd replied, if the Adikar were in earnest; but he continued to urge that North should meet the Chiefs at that spot: if their approval were secured, then they could all accompany Macdowal on his mission. He was pointedly asked whether in such an event he would guarantee that the King would remain at the Capital to meet Macdowal: but to this he either could not or would not give an unequivocal answer.

Both North and Boyd were satisfied that the Minister's power was really supreme, and the latter suggested that the King might be persuaded to take up his residence at Colombo with a fixed allowance.* North approved of this as likely to gratify Pilima Talavuva and thought that such a condition might be embodied in the Treaty, with the preamble that the state of the King's health rendered a change of residence to the seaside imperative; but at the same time he instructed the Maha Mudaliyar to find out a method of direct communication with the King and the Court faction opposed to the Adikar.† The Ambassador was ready to start and Pilima Talavuva while undertaking to be responsible for the King's safety promised himself to conduct Macdowal to his presence.‡ North requested him to meet the General at the frontier and to take measures to prevent the inhabitants from being terrified by the sight of the army,§ whereupon he issued orders to clear the roads, erect halting places, and collect provisions all along the route which would be followed.||

* Boyd to North, 5th March.
† North to Boyd, 6th March.
‡ Boyd to North, 6th March.
§ North to Adikar, 7th March.
|| North to Governor-General, 15th March.

North's instructions to Macdowal as Ambassador Extraordinary and Commissioner Plenipotentiary make curious reading. The objects to be kept in view, he wrote, were summed up in the terms of the proposed Treaty and of these the most difficult to achieve would be the preservation of the King's life : knowing as he did the Adikar's ambitions he considered it his imperious and moral duty to save that life, and in the fulfilment of that duty the observance of diplomatic forms and generally accepted usages could be ignored. That, he explained, was the reason why he had no scruple in agreeing to terms which he admitted he should not otherwise feel himself justified in proposing to or accepting from the Minister of an established and independent Monarch. The Adikar had been offered the reality of power on condition of the King's life being preserved and instead of availing himself of that offer he had over-reached himself by "allowing us to march to the Capital without any stipulation in his own favour, whatsoever." If as events developed he proved helpful in securing the King's signature, then he might be rewarded by being confirmed in his office for life ; otherwise Macdowal should support the party which appeared most likely to favour the British. Under any circumstances the control of the revenue must somehow be secured, and liberal terms should be offered to the Dissavas in exchange for the rights in regard to it which by custom they enjoyed. A fort should be built near the Capital to serve as the headquarters of the British army and a secret method of direct communication with the King established ; if found necessary all Pilima Talavuva's transactions might be revealed to him. There were also directions for the Ambassador's guidance in case of the King's flight from his Capital,. his deposition by his

Ministers, and his death. North realised that his proceedings were not easy to defend, and the apprehensions which he declared he entertained that they might invite the censure of " a world to whom the whole of this delicate business must appear extremely doubtful and mysterious,"* were justified.

On the morning of the 12th of March Macdowal set out from Colombo Fort under a salute of seventeen guns, accompanying the letter intended for the King which was carried under a canopy on the heads of Appu Hamis with all the punctilious reverence insisted upon by the Court and escorted by 1,100 men—British, Indian and Malay—who with their four six-pounders, two howitzers, baggage carriers, and carts laden with rice, arrack and the General's personal belongings resembled an invading army. Seven days later he crossed the river into Sinhalese territory and was received by Pilima Talavuva, who took charge of the thirty-two cases of presents, which included a state coach to be drawn by six horses,† but strenuously objected to the presence of the guns. Macdowal however suggested to North that this was a pretence intended to mislead the Court officials who accompanied him, as he must have known that the guns were essential for the success of their plans, and North instructed him to insist on their retention, as well as to urge the Minister even at this late stage to sign the draft treaty and forward it for the King's ratification, and not to allow him to leave the camp till the Capital was reached. He should also endeavour to get back the Malays who from time to time had deserted to the King, by letting it be known that they would receive

* North to Governor-General, 15th March, 1800.

† Appendix B.

a pardon.* However to appease the Minister, three thousand of whose men were reported by the spies to be occupying the roads in front, the firing of the morning and evening guns was discontinued and the artillery covered with white cloth and relegated to the rear.†

Other difficulties now began to present themselves. The carriers were drawn from the class who held their lands on the tenure of serving for fifteen days only and at the expiry of their term they insisted on returning home and relays were not forthcoming to take their place. Heavy rain made the roads almost impassable. The spies employed by the Maha Mudaliyar and Jonville could gather but little information and nothing of value could be elicited from the Adikar, who also expressed his displeasure at Macdowal's displaying his flag in spite of an undertaking given by Jonville that this would not be done.‡ There was a rumour that the Minister had again incurred the King's displeasure and North was prepared to take full advantage of such a contingency: "If the power of that Minister be not absolute" he wrote, "it must be in a short time perfectly destroyed, and I will certainly not interfere to preserve any part of it. His conduct towards us has been nearly as iniquitous and treacherous as that towards his Master."§ Captain Macpherson, the Secretary to the Embassy whose diary has been preserved, was sent to Ruvan Ella to meet Pilima Talavuva, who objected to every unguarded utterance of his in the course of a long conversation being recorded. He still insisted that the

* Macdowal to North, Galbokki Wela, 20th March; North to Macdowal, 21st March.

† Macdowal to North, 21st March.

‡ Macdowal to North, 23rd March.

§ North to Macdowal, 24th March.

guns should be left behind, while Macpherson begged for a supply of coolies, whom the Adikar could not easily provide as his men were only liable to serve from one stage to another. As to the report which had arrived that the King had left his Capital in alarm, he explained that it was customary for him to spend two or three nights at a time at the Palace of one of the Queens.*

Macdowal at length reached Ruvan Ella and from the King's Garden there he wrote of a story which had reached his ears that the Adikar when Dissava of Saparagamuva had enticed a Dutch Governor into an adventure similar to his own, which owing to his treachery had ended in utter failure ; he was referring to the narrow escape from destruction of Colonel de Meuron with his Swiss Regiment in 1791, which was the only result of Governor Van der Graaff's intrigues with this Minister,† and the knowledge had a depressing effect on his mind. "He is a strange and mysterious man" he wrote, "and I freely confess that I have not the means of ascertaining a thorough knowledge of his character or what his object is, except by conjectures." The appearance of the army had alarmed the inhabitants who were abandoning their villages in fear.‡ The decision was now taken to leave the cannon behind and proceed with a small escort of Sepoys and Malays making a total of 200 firelocks, a reduction against which the Adikar strongly protested ; every man in the King's

* Macpherson to Macdowal, 23rd March.

† "Ceylon and the Hollanders," p. 153.

‡ Macdowal to North, 25th March. The true views of the Adikar are shown in a series of 13 letters : he desired 1,500 troops sent with the Ambassador and a stronger force kept ready to be rushed up by forced marches as soon as he reached Gannoruva ; and also two cannon taken under concealment. Secret Diary, 31st July.

country, he explained, was a soldier and had arms, except the goldsmiths, tailors and drummers.*

North in the meantime was secretly attempting to open communications with the King through Levuke Rala, Dissava of Uva, who was believed to be hostile to the Adikar, and if the need arose he was even prepared to enlighten the King regarding his Minister's misconduct.† Once again the Ambassador took the road ; the mountain paths were in a terrible state and it was only with much tugging and many falls and bruises that the horses could reach the top of Balane Pass,‡ and the sight of the *Tanayama* or Rest House at Gannoruva, which was to be Macdowal's home for the next few weeks, was hailed with delight.

* Macpherson to Macdowal, 27th March.

† North to Macdowal, 29th and 30th March.

‡ Macdowal to North, 6th April.

CHAPTER III

On the 9th of April the King received the Ambassador in audience at the *Magul Maduva* adjoining the Palace. Every incident connected with the ceremony, which according to invariable custom took place at night, was regulated by a ritual almost ecclesiastical in its elaboration, devised to impress foreign representatives with the greatness of the Ruler whom they were privileged to behold. It was half past four in the afternoon when the summons to appear was received and it was nine o'clock before the presents were all sent across the river, when Macdowal and the Dissava who had been deputed to escort him started hand in hand from the *Tanayama*. Within two hundred yards of the Palace Gate he rested for his dinner, moving forward at midnight to where Pilima Talavuva received him in state and led him stage by stage through numerous courts to where the raising of seven successive curtains revealed the King. Little of the exhausting ceremonial usual on such occasions was omitted, Macdowal falling on his knees three times whenever he approached or retired from the Throne. The letter which he carried in both hands at the level of the eyes was received by the King himself, and a formal conversation followed, rendered wearisome by its passage through two Ministers and two Interpreters before it reached the listener. Refreshments were served to the Ambassador in a separate room after the interview ; they consisted of Sinhalese sweetmeats, fruit and water, and it was five o'clock in the morning before the exhausted man started on his way back.*

* Details of the reception have been published by Cordiner. (Description of Ceylon, 1807). Percival's account is marred by mis-statements of facts within his knowledge (Account of the Island of Ceylon, 2nd Ed., London 1805). *Supa Sastre*, a very rare palm leaf book in Sinhalese verse, deals with the preparation of food for use at the Palace.

The examination of North's proposals was next commenced at Gannoruva, the King being represented by the Adikar, Levuke and the Dissava of Matale. The knowledge they displayed of British secrets was disconcerting to Macdowal, as when they questioned him about the despatch of light artillery from Colombo to Ruvan Ella; much more mortifying was their incisive and logical criticism of the proposal to maintain a garrison within the Kingdom. Indeed the General found his position so embarrassing that he protested he had not come to supplicate for favours but to offer the protection of a powerful nation, and he threatened that if the Governor found himself thwarted over a treaty on which he had spent much time and labour, he would withdraw his friendship and protection and leave them to look after themselves.* North, who was being kept in close touch with all that happened, was fain to admit that the Ministers' attitude was not unreasonable, and he therefore suggested as an alternative that some territory should be ceded to the British the revenue of which would pay for the military force to be maintained for the King's service.†

On the 15th Macpherson at a secret interview with the Adikar discussed the possibility of winning over Levuke but met with little encouragement. Pilima Talavuva lamented his initial mistake in not himself mounting the Throne, for the King was unfriendly; indeed the turbanned escort armed with swords and targets which accompanied the Adikar on state occasions was made up of the King's confidential Malabar Guards. North meanwhile was bringing pressure to bear in his own fashion by letting it

* Macdowal to North, 14th April, 1800.

† North to Macdowal, 16th April.

be noised about that he was not prepared any longer to keep the various pretenders to the Throne in confinement or out of the country.* He was also anxious to recover the letter he had written to Levuke who however did not appear willing to part with it. Jonville on instructions was carrying on secret inquiries regarding river transport while Macdowal was busy studying other possibilities; to a British soldier the military power of the Sinhalese appeared "truly contemptible" yet as he pointed out their ancestors when led by their Chiefs had fought bravely and the conquest of the country would be very expensive.† He impressed on the Adikar that the contemptuous disregard of the proposed terms would highly exasperate the Governor,‡ who for his part was still nursing his plan to reveal the transactions of his Minister to the King.§

On the 17th Macdowal was definitely told that the Ministers would not recommend the Treaty for the King's acceptance as in their opinion it was one-sided and only safeguarded British interests while giving no fair equivalent in return. He angrily demanded whether they considered the protection of the country by the presence of a British garrison of no value; they retorted that in their opinion that constituted the most objectionable feature of the proposals. Macdowal blustered; he would not, he declared,

* North to Macdowal, 17th April.

† Macdowal to North, 17th April, 1800. Cf. Dom Affonco de Noronha to Dom Joao IV of Portugal, 27th Jan., 1552. "I assure your Highness that in crossing a river at the base of the mountain where he tried to stop us, the fidalgos and some soldiers effected this with a degree of labour and peril that it was not possible to undergo as much with Turks or Moors of Spain." (Pieris and Fitzler; Ceylon and Portugal. Leipzig 1927).

‡ Macdowal to Adikar, 17th April.

§ North to Macdowal, 19th April.

alter one line of those proposals. The Ministers who bore themselves with much dignity and gravity, expressed their readiness to produce their counter proposals* and North while admitting that he was not surprised at their attitude directed that these should be carefully examined.† They were presented three days later and Levuke, in reading them out clause by clause from his *talpat* notes, explained that they were only in draft form and subject to amendment. They provided for mutual amity, respect for religion, the collecting of cinnamon within the Kingdom on the King's account, certain shipping rights for the King and the yearly exchange of embassies. Macdowal who had worked himself up into a rage as the details were being explained declared that he was not only extremely displeased but disgusted and that he would start back for Colombo as soon as the King's permission was granted. The Ministers replied " You frighten us when you use such strong language " and went away to make their report.‡

While North expressed his approval of Macdowal's attitude towards the " wanton and childish folly "§ of the Ministers, the Adikar, who avoided all further confidential communications, announced that the Treaty could not be signed and the General would receive his final audience. Macdowal anticipated that in a few months he would precipitate hostilities and advised the Governor to weigh the claims of the various pretenders and make his own preparations ; the legal heir, he said, might well be placed on the Throne and further advances by Pilima Talavuva

* Diary of Embassy.

† North to Macdowal, 20th April.

‡ Macdowal to North, 20th April.

§ North to Macdowal, 22nd April.

rejected with disdain. Levuke had shown himself very loyal to the King and had fearlessly championed the liberties of his country, but should a crisis arise the General was still hopeful that he would support the British.*

On the 21st Macdowal presented himself for his farewell audience, but the King was sincerely anxious for a settlement and before he was received a long discussion with the Ministers took place. They were prepared they said to concede everything asked for, with the reservations that it was for the King to decide where the troops were to be stationed, that no fort was to be built except at his request and there would be no interference with his revenue. They wished further to reduce the strength of the garrison to 200 men in place of the 800 proposed by Macdowal.

The Governor was very gratified with this change in the situation† and by the 25th there remained unsettled only the questions of the strength of the contemplated garrison and the site of the fort, whether Gannoruva as demanded by the British or Iddamalpana which the Ministers preferred. So hopeful was the outlook that at their request a fair copy of the Treaty was prepared for the King's signature, with the figure alone left blank pending his consent,‡ but North while yielding on the choice cf the site, continued to insist on the larger number.§ The final audience came on. The Ministers expressed their willingness to pay for 800 men provided that only 200 were stationed within the Kingdom, but Macdowal was obdurate and after several messages had passed

* Macdowal to North, 22nd April.

† North to Macdowal, 24th April.

‡ Macdowal to North, 25th April.

§ North to Macdowal, 25th April.

between the Ministers and the King, the document remained unsigned, and the Ambassador, who was presented with an elephant and a gold chain, given permission to depart, the Adikar being unable to conceal his emotion at the outcome of the long struggle.*

The General started to return and at Attapitiya was met by fresh instructions from North to re-open negotiations, offering the Ministers the choice of one of three courses—to receive a garrison of a thousand men of whom only four hundred would be paid for by the King, or to purchase the right to demand military help whenever needed by surrendering all territory within thirty English miles from the sea, or finally, to concede to the British the privilege of opening warehouses within the Kingdom, to be protected by a garrison not exceeding 400 in number. If a settlement was not reached he threatened to send for Muddu Svami who had already come to an understanding with the other refugees at Tutucorin and Colombo.† The Adikar should receive no further support and if the Treaty was signed the troops could be employed to arrest him and his adherents and deport them from the country, if the King would make such an order, while overtures should be renewed to win Levuke to the British side.‡

Macdowal therefore re-opened communications, and was curtly informed that the native soldiers of the Island had at all times proved a sufficient guard for their King, while it was the business of the English to defend the Coast against all enemies; § the third suggestion was ignored.

* Macdowal to North, 24th April.

† North to Macdowal, 26th April.

‡ North to Macdowal, 29th April.

§ Ministers to Macdowal, 29th April. Macdowal to Ministers, 29th April. Adikar to Macdowal, 1st May.

North was indignant at the reply : he said he had no doubt that a serious crisis at Court was fast approaching and through the Maha Mudaliyar he warned the Adikar that if he dragged the country into war, hostile action would be mainly directed at him as the party against whom there was just cause of complaint in consequence of his " direct and notorious breach of faith."* He also informed Mornington that the time had come to take Muddu Svami's claims into serious consideration.†

On the 14th of May, Macdowal once again re-entered Colombo. North would have been more than human if his failure did not fill him with bitter resentment ; his facile pen had led Downing Street to indulge in pleasant anticipations of the transfer by treaty of the military and financial control which would enable him without disturbing popular prejudices to take on himself the real direction of affairs within the Kingdom and to build up a liberal and enlightened policy.‡ He now had the task of explaining away the disappearance of his sand castle, and he put on a brave face, while he did not mince his words.

It was true, he admitted, that he had failed to effect a union with " a man whose profligate and perfidious ambition had announced views which we could not countenance with Honour " but in its place he had obtained valuable inner knowledge regarding the Court and the nobles there. The object of the Adikar was, he was convinced, to start a war, in the hope that during the ensuing confusion he could secure the royal power after which he would make terms with the English. Migas Tenna was dominated by

* North to Macdowal, 3rd May.

† North to Mornington, 3rd May.

‡ Dundas to North, 13th March, 1801. C.O. 55/61.

him ; Levuke, young and ambitious, favoured the exiled claimants and was friendly towards the English : while the majority of the other nobles followed Pilima Talavuva. The Captain of the King's trusted Malay Guard had declared that but for the fact that their families were hostages in the King's hands, they would all join the English at any moment : they would never, he was assured, fire on a British force.

He revealed the fact that he was in correspondence with several Chiefs, who had their own agents in Colombo, but he would not enter into an intimate connection with any one of them unless the Adikar's " insolent silence " forced him to break with him, when he would have recourse to " threats, favour and force " to drive him out of the country. He was making ready for war and had ordered elephants to be trained for hauling the cannon : hunts had been organised in the Matara District and the Vanni to secure the necessary animals : once they were available he would be ready at the shortest notice to take advantage of any event within the Kingdom which would appear to justify his interference : in the meantime he would not commit himself to any one line of action or place himself in a position where he could profit only from one train of events. Active propaganda was being carried on to secure the goodwill of the people through whose villages he would have to move, so as to induce them to remain passive in case of hostilities. Saparagamuva had responded favourably and he was also unostentatiously encouraging Muddu Svami to press his claims. But his main anxiety, he protested, was to preserve the King's life and authority ; nevertheless in view of the " selfish and infatuated men " who for their own ends had prevented him from imposing his authority to maintain peace and order among them, he would adopt a "firm and vigilant neutrality, ready to interfere on every occurrence which may allow of interference" as being what strict justice as well as sound policy recommended.*

But Pilima Talavuva had not given up hope. "Will every thing end here ?" he wrote to the Maha Mudaliyar,† "If the Governor will make any new attempt, it will be well." The reply was that in the light of recent events the Governor could not re-open negotiations with him till satisfied of his friendliness and sincerity, and a commercial treaty had been approved by him.‡ Communications were next started with Moratota,§ who as Maha Nayaka Unanse was the head of the priesthood and had the right of unrestricted audience with the King ; the agent employed was a priest of the Galle District with a great reputation for sanctity who was visiting the Capital to be invested with certain spiritual authority over the temples in British territory. It should be remembered that though a Ganinnanse, as a priest was called, could be ordained within British Territory, yet he could not attain the higher status of a Therunnanse without the intervention of the Chief Priest at Court, and that the Nayaka priest who exercised ecclesiastical jurisdiction over the entire priesthood in the Littoral received his appointment directly from the King.|| The Adikar treated this envoy with much kindness and presented him with a village

* North to Secret Committee, 19th May, 1800 ; to Mornington, 30th May, 1800.

† Recd. 26th May.

‡ Maha Mudaliyar to Adikar, May, 1800.

§ Moratota Rajaguru Dhammakkanda Unanse, Head of the Poya Malu Viharaya.

|| Appendix C.

for the maintenance of his temple and he was also received by the King, who expressed his great desire for friendly relations. Indeed, Moratota suggested that he might come in person as the King's Ambassador, and that if a Treaty were entered into he and North should meet at the Frontier and each set up a stone in memory of the great event.* Two priests were sent by him to continue the exchange of views but nothing substantial resulted:† the Minister was informed that the Governor demanded the restoration, to the subjects of both sides, of the concessions determined by the Treaty of 1766‡ but replied that that Treaty needed modification.

There was a strong undercurrent of excitement; Galagoda at Palam Kottai, Muddu Svami from Jaffna, the refugee princes at Colombo, and Levuke, were all entangled in the web, while the natural son of the late King had also come § with his mother the beautiful Dugganna Unnehe, Chandra Rekava; but North had to move warily, for the Governor-General in Council had not only warned him

* S. D: North to Marquess Wellesley, 4th August, 1800, C.O. 54/2.

† Maha Nayaka Unanse to Maha Mudaliyar, recd. 22nd July, 1800.

‡ Adikar to Maha Mudaliyar, recd. 19th Aug., and reply.

§ Letter to Candian Princes at Colombo, 28th Nov., 1800.

The following explains itself:

Kandy, Nov. 9th, 1815.

Received from the Provincial Court of Colombo the sum of four thousand three hundred and twenty-two rix dollars two fanams and two and a half pice deposited in the General Treasury being the balance of the Estate of the late Chandra Rekawa, a Kandyan woman, administered under the order of the said Provincial Court and which sum is transferred to my Judicial Disposal in further administration to those entitled as her Legal Representatives.

J. D'OYLY,

Resident.

against taking any step which might "expose the British character to the hazard of any invidious reflection," but had also expressly forbidden him to proceed to hostilities without previous sanction.* No one, declared North, entertained a more lively sense of horror with regard to such invidious imputations than himself,† but communications with the courtiers had become so frequent he said that the veil which had hitherto covered the affairs of the Kingdom was now entirely torn away.

Early in 1801 the King married a Princess of his own blood, the daughter of an inveterate enemy‡ of the Adikar who was recalled to Court from the village where he had lived in enforced retirement, and a rupture between the King and his Minister was again anticipated.§ But this expectation was ill-founded. Pilima Talavuva's devotion to his religion was a noteworthy side of his character, and in order to acquire merit he had at great expense built a new Viharaya at Asgiriya. Its chief glory was an image of Buddha, twelve Sinhalese cubits in length and recumbent on its couch, both chiselled out of one great boulder of granite. On its completion the King with his two Queens visited the building and was so pleased with what had been done that he dedicated several lands for the maintenance of the establishment and on his orders this offering was recorded by an inscription on the same rock.‖ This year the Administration of the British Settlement

* Gov.-Gen. in Council to North, 28th May, 1800.

† North to Gov.-Gen., Caltura, 23rd June, 1800..

‡ Gampola Deviyo, first cousin of Kirti Sri Raja Sinha; his two daughters married the King.

§ North to Secret Committee, 2nd March, 1801.

‖ Lawrie's Gazetteer, I. 74. He is however in error in speaking of Ehelepola as one of the Adikars at the time.

was changed, the authority given to the Company being resumed and a new Commission and Royal Instructions issued to North, while the responsibility for its management as a Crown Colony was transferred to the Secretary for War and the Colonies.*

The arrival of fresh troops at Tiru Kona Malai had excited the interest of Pilima Talavuva and while answering his demand for an explanation the opportunity was taken to convey to him that North was willing to resume negotiations.† However no further communication was received from the Court and there were rumours that a French emissary had made his way there, but in spite of this it was manifest that there was a sincere desire for friendly relations, and the volume of trade was steadily increasing. North was not inactive for he was satisfied that not the Adikar only, but the majority of the courtiers were prepared to sacrifice the King to their "profligate ambition."‡ At length on the last day of the year a message arrived from Court repeating its desire for amity and suggesting a conference to discuss the terms of a Treaty, whereupon North requested that an Embassy should be sent for the purpose.§

Early in February, 1802 this arrived headed by Migas Tenna whom North found "very young and open." On the 5th of the month he and his two companions were received by the Governor with much distinction, the three being conveyed from their lodgings in three Dutch carriages the doors of which were left open in deference to their

* Secretary of State to North, 13th March, 1801. C.O. 54/5 and 55/61.

† Maha Mudaliyar to Adikar, Jan., 1801.

‡ North to Hobart, 5th Oct., 1801.

§ North to Hobart, 31st Dec., 1801.

objection to being locked in like prisoners. At a secret interview Migas Tenna attempted to re-open the Sitavaka conversations, urging that the King had made himself disliked by destroying the houses and trees of his subjects, and by interfering with the privileges regarding dress enjoyed by certain classes under the sumptuary customs of the country, but North refused to discuss any proposals except those which Macdowal had taken with him. Migas Tenna pressed for the restoration of the districts which the Dutch had unjustly withheld, and the return of which had been the subject of yearly discussion with them, but North roughly brushed the demand aside as an impertinence and a piece of folly. Instead he put forward his own proposals which included the maintenance of 1,800 men, European and Asiatic, who would be at the King's service when demanded, and towards the cost of whom the King should contribute yearly four lacs of rix dollars.

These terms were minutely discussed by the Ambassador along with Boyd, who insisted on a final decision within ten days. This was refused, much to North's annoyance, and his resentment found expression in strong language. The object of the two Adikars, he declared, was to irritate him against their sovereign, in furtherance of their own nefarious designs; and so long as they remained in power no Treaty was likely to result; the explanation was to be found not in the unreasonableness of his demands but in "the pernicious influence of those profligate Ministers": he was considering therefore the possibility of placing a Minister friendly to the English at the side of the Throne. There was a feeling at Court, he had heard, that the Adikar was seeking to start a quarrel with the British, and this opinion he would not discourage, for he thought its constant repetition might in a little time bring about his overthrow. North's irritation further showed itself in a curious exhibition of pettiness. In order to avoid the expense of the great retinue which should accompany an Adikar, Migas Tenna had appeared in his character of a Dissava ; on his departure therefore North presented him with a silver hilted sword, which was less than was proper for an Adikar, asserting that he had dropped his dignity as a slight to the Governor and with the intention of diminishing the consequence of the Embassy.*

Pilima Talavuva was still anxious to negotiate : he sent his suggestions regarding the road across the Kingdom to Tiru Kona Malai which North was desirous of securing, and expressed his wish for another interview at Sitavaka. North however was anticipating an early change of Ministers, and if the King were deposed he had decided not to recognise the successor nominated by them but to support Muddu Svami's claims with all the force at his disposal ; he therefore replied that as two treaties proposed by him had been already rejected, he considered himself released from every obligation to protect the King or to prevent any other Prince of the Royal Blood from asserting title to the throne.†

* North to Hobart, dated Aripo, 16th March, 1802. C.O. 54/6.

† Maha Mudaliyar to Levuke, 28th June, 1802.

CHAPTER IV

North had fared badly in the contest of wits and what was worse he had been made to look ridiculous ; no doubt he was feeling that someone should suffer for this when in July, 1802 news was received that two bands of Moormen from Puttalama who according to their custom were engaged in purchasing areka nuts within the King's dominions, had been deprived of the stock, stated to be 292 *ammunams*,* which they had collected. North immediately addressed a remonstrance to the King; his duty, he declared, was not only to defend the people subject to his Government, but also to uphold its honour and dignity which had suffered in the persons of those individuals. While emphasizing his own respect for and attachment to the King, and his anxiety always to preserve the best understanding with the Court, he expressed the earnest hope that the unfortunate incident would induce His Majesty to regard the terms of amity and alliance which he had frequently offered with greater favour than he seemed previously inclined to do ; he concluded by demanding compensation for the wrong which had been done. His letter, dated the seventh of September, was accompanied by another from Robert Arbuthnot, the Chief Secretary, to the Adikar, to the effect that delay in giving satisfaction and making amends for the injured dignity of the British Government would result in other steps being taken.

North was quick to realise the possibilities of the incident and three days earlier in a secret despatch to Hobart he

* An ammunam varied from 24,000 to 30,000 nuts.

explained his decision, in case of delay, to cut off the supply of salt which was essential for the existence of the King's subjects and to follow this up, if required, by moving his army to the frontiers. He was not in favour of agreeing to Pilima Talavuva's secret proposals, he said ; if the King on his Minister's instigation had recourse to extreme steps, he would support Muddu Svami's claim to the throne ; he had reason to believe that there was a powerful faction at Court opposed to Pilima Talavuva and this he would back with all his available forces.*

Any interruption of the existing peaceful relations was what the Court least desired, and in spite of the provocative tone of Arbuthnot's letter, the Adikar sent an immediate and courteous acknowledgment,† followed five days later by the results of his inquiry. The Renter of the areka nut farm, he said, admitted the confiscation but claimed to have acted within his rights in accordance with former practice ; moreover as by his present contract he was liable for a larger supply than previously, he could not permit any interloping : he had only received 132 ammunams and 3,668 nuts, and the balance claimed by the traders had been left by them at various centres of collection. Nevertheless, the Minister continued, since the purchases were made prior to the Renter's visit to the districts concerned, it was considered equitable to restore the nuts, which would be done on demand being made at Kekunavala where the seizure had taken place.‡ North expressed his satisfaction at this but both insisted that the traders'

* Secret Despatch, North to Hobart, 4th September, 1802 with enclosures. C.O. 54/6.

† Letter of 28th September, 1802. Enc. to S.D., North to Hobart, 21st Nov., 1802. C.O. 54/7.

‡ Letter of 3rd October, 1802. Enc. to Idem.

figures should be accepted, and that good fresh nuts should be substituted for those seized, which by now would be damaged.* The Court was anxious to avoid any ground for complaint and on the 14th of November Levuke wrote to point out that no one had yet appeared to take delivery, adding that if fresh nuts were desired it might be possible to supply them in a couple of months.†

The King had taken North's reference to a Treaty very seriously to heart and by his special directions a letter signed by all his Chief Ministers and dated the 28th of September was forwarded to the Governor. In this they declared that their Master praised him as a fortunate and wise person who endeavoured to win Royal favour, and invited him in his great wisdom to submit such proposals as would ensure the continuance of amity so long as the Sun and Moon shall endure.‡ This was followed by a a request for the despatch of a confidential Agent,§ whose report together with the Ministers' suggestion of a meeting|| were then placed before North. To his dazzled imagination the great opportunity had arrived and he felt confident of securing a highly favourable bargain, for the Sinhalese excluded as they were from the sea, had to depend on the British for the prime necessaries of life. He decided not to consult his Council or his legal adviser, the Advocate Fiscal, but to act on his own responsibility and enter into a

* Arbuthnot to Adikar; 12th Oct., 1802. Encl. to Despatch, North to Hobart, 2nd Feb., 1803. C.O. 54/10.

† Levuke Ralahami to the Maha Mudaliyar, 14th Nov. Enc. to S.D. of 21st Nov., 1802. C.O. 54/7.

‡ Conjoint Ministers to North, Enc. to Despatch, North to Hobart, 14th April, 1803. C.O. 54/10.

§ Levuke to Maha Mudaliyar, 22nd Oct., 1802. Enc. to Idem.

|| Levuke to Maha Mudaliyar, 14th Nov., 1802 as above.

Convention binding for three years, till a final and considered decision could be received from London.* His objectives were military control, the direction of foreign relations, representation on the King's Councils, a roadway between Colombo and Tiru Kona Malai across Sinhalese territory, authority to regulate arrangements on the frontiers, the abolition of frontier duties, and the exclusion of all Europeans who did not hold his Passport. Such were the terms he had suggested to Migas Tenna, and only if these were accepted in principle would he send a Commissioner to settle details.

The Ministers however had not forgotten the abortive treaty which was the only fruit of the time, labour and money expended on the negotiations with Andrews, and to this they drew pointed attention in their reply ; their Archives they said contained the records of many other treaties as well : all these they would consult and frame their own proposals for the Governor's consideration.† Offended vanity aggravated North's disappointment at this further failure to achieve the easy and spectacular triumph which he anticipated : the Ministers, he retorted, could send any document they liked, but he would enter into no contract except on his own terms ; he wanted no further proposals but would immediately take such action as he considered necessary to safeguard the interests of his Government.‡

Although on the 21st of November North had reported to Hobart that the areka nut incident was satisfactorily

* Despatch, 21st Nov., 1802 : also Maha Mudaliyar to Levuke, 21st Nov., 1802. Encl. to Despatch of 14th April, 1803.

† Levuke to Maha Mudaliyar : 7th Dec., 1802.

‡ Maha Mudaliyar to Levuke : 7th Dec., 1802.

settled, it still held useful possibilities. The Puttalama traders who had at last presented themselves before the Sinhalese Officials had returned with the news that their nuts had been sold—not altogether an unreasonable course to adopt under the circumstances—and they had been told that if they came back in January with a correct statement of accounts, and the season rendered it possible, they would be given fresh nuts. Arbuthnot now wrote to the Adikar that the Governor insisted in the most peremptory manner that the full quantity of 292 ammunams of fresh nuts should be delivered at the King's expense to the Governor's Agent at Puttalama within one month after receipt of the letter, which was dated the 24th of December. In addition to this demand, the satisfaction of which, for practical reasons, could hardly have been anticipated, the letter continued " His Excellency would be willing to suppose that the equivocal conduct of the Court of Candy had proceeded from some mistake, did not the recent rejection of the terms which he has proposed for a Treaty with that Court convince him of the insincerity of their declaration and inimical nature of their intention." The more deeply to impress the Court with a sense of his indignation at the injustice done to the traders, he placed an embargo on the sale of salt,* and threatened that further insults to British

* At the time there was at Puttalama a convoy of 130 bulls with 70 ammunams of areka nuts, come to purchase salt and salt fish : the owners ran away when the embargo was announced but it was soon discovered not only that it was impossible to prevent smuggling through the five entrances into the King's territory, but also that the stoppage of the supply of foodstuffs from there would soon create famine conditions in the town, as the stocks in the market were only sufficient for four days' consumption, chiefly owing to the fact that so far only two vessels laden with grain had arrived from the Coast. A. Johnston to Arbuthnot, Puttalam, 28th December, 1802. C.O. 54/10.

subjects might result in other action to assure their safety and uphold British dignity.*

Unruffled by this truculence Pilima Talavuva replied that the question of the areka nuts was already disposed of by the correspondence which had passed, while the Treaty proposals had been advanced in order not indeed to displease the Governor but to establish a friendship which would lead to the increased welfare of both parties.† Somewhat sobered, in language at least, by the reproof North said he would send not the traders but a subordinate of the Maha Mudaliyar, the Padikara Mohandiram, to take delivery, and if this were not perfected by the 21st of January, then it must be done at Puttalama : should these conditions not be fulfilled he would consider amicable relations at an end and would take action to enforce his just claims.

Though the crop was not yet fully ripe urgent orders‡ were issued to the Madige headmen who were accustomed to purchase the nuts on advances made from the Treasury, which had to be repaid with interest,§ and on the 22nd of January seventy ammunams were tendered to the Mohandiram with a promise of the balance or its value at the Colombo rates at the time of the seizure within twenty days ; the amount of the balance however was in dispute, and that the King's Officer was willing to leave to the Governor's decision after hearing evidence on both sides.||

* Arbuthnot to Adikar.

† Adikar to Arbuthnot, 5th Jan., 1803.

‡ Adikar to Arbuthnot, 16th Jan., 1803.

§ D'Oyly's Diary, p. 116. Ed. by H. W. Codrington : R.A.S. Ceylon, 1913.

|| Abraham Perera Mohandiram to Maha Mudaliyar, 23rd Jan., 1803.

Concession was met by increasing the stringency of the demands, for a peaceful settlement was not what North desired ; he had already secured the assent of his Council to military action and on the 13th of January, 1803 Lieut. Colonel Barbut left Jaffnapatam to assume command of the 1,200 men who were available at Tiru Kona Malai, while Macdowal busied himself with the 1,700 at Colombo. These, the Governor informed Hobart in a private letter of the 15th January in which he subscribed himself as "your most faithful and affectionate servant," would be ready by the 1st of February, protesting at the same time that the Court was intentionally creating delay in order to discredit his Government with its subjects.* He was full of confidence in his military plans and without waiting to ascertain the result of the Mohandiram's mission, he sent to the Adikar another specious offer to accept cash payment for any shortage of the 292 ammunams provided it was tendered by the end of January ; otherwise he said negotiations would cease for he had made extensive preparations to enforce his rights, and he was bound to consider any further delay as calculated only to protract a final settlement till the season favourable for military operations was passed. He had learnt, he added, that armed men were assembling on the borders of Matara and he would not discontinue his preparations till these were dispersed.†

The Minister promptly replied that as settlement by the end of the month was insisted upon, delivery could be made at Batu Gedera by that date. Further if men were assem-

* C.O. 54/10.

† Arbuthnot to Adikar, 21st Jan., 1803. Enc. to Des. of 14th April, 1803.

bling on the Matara border that was probably in view of the movements within the British territory and would be stopped immediately on the cessation of the latter.* It was true that men were being moved in Saparagamuva but Arbuthnot himself had offered the explanation that this was connected with the King's visit to Kataragama Devale,† and by the 24th of January everything was reported to be normal with only the usual guards on the frontiers.‡ As for the nuts, North declared he knew they were not available at Batu Gedera. Possibly he was not aware that, as pointed out by Levuke, in Saparagamuva the nuts could be gathered up to the month of *Navam* (February) and he ignored the substantial additional advantage of the water transport available between that Province and Colombo.§

Everything was ready according to North's schedule, and on the 29th of January many fateful documents were signed. One addressed to the Adikar, after extolling the exemplary patience and moderation with which North claimed to have borne himself, continued that his sense of what he owed to the dignity of his Government and the welfare of the people committed to his charge rendered it impossible for him to submit to any further evasions and refusals, and he had given orders for his troops to enter the King's territory ; his intention was not indeed to molest the peaceable inhabitants or interfere with the Religion, Laws or Customs of the country, but to oblige the Court to make reparation for the injury sustained and the expense

* Adikar to Arbuthnot, 24th Jan., 1803. Encl. to Idem.

† Arbuthnot to Lewis Gibson, Agent at Matara, 21st Jan., 1803. Enc. to Idem.

‡ Gibson to Arbuthnot. Encl. to Idem.

§ Report of the Appuhamis. Encl. to Idem.

of military preparations and to obtain security against the repetition of such an incident.* In a second, which was addressed to the King, North lamented that the aggression of the Court compelled him to send armed forces to obtain redress. As an unequivocal proof of his desire to restore lasting friendly relations, he submitted the terms of a Treaty for the consideration of the Ministers ; if they were signed as accepted and sent to the British General who by then would be within the King's territories with his army, further hostile action would cease.†

These terms were grouped under sixteen heads ; compensation for the merchants' loss and payment of the costs of the expedition were to be secured by the cession of Sat Korale ; ‡ the right of the British to everything which the Dutch had possessed, to control foreign relations and the entry of Malays and Europeans within the Kingdom, to a roadway from Colombo to Tiru Kona Malai, river transport and timber from the King's forests, and the cinnamon monopoly was to be confirmed. The status of the King would be recognised and British troops supplied when demanded to maintain it at his expense. All duties at the frontiers would be abolished and his subjects granted the right to trade and purchase salt in the British Settlements. There were also provisions for the administration of Criminal and Civil Justice.

North's gratification at the development of his plans found expression in his communications to Lord Clive, the Governor-General in India, and to Hobart.§ His ultima-

* Arbuthnot to Adikar. Encl. to Idem.

† North to King. Encl. to Idem.

‡ *Sat*, seven ; hence usually spoken of by English writers as Seven Korles.

§ Dated 30th Jan. and 2nd Feb. respectively. C.O. 54/10.

tum he described as "creditable to the moderation of Great Britain." He impressed on them that the settlement of the areka nut dispute had broken down "in consequence of the illusive and unjust conduct of that power, or more properly of the insidious designs of the Minister who directs its motions, whose wish has been to drive us into a war with his country for the purpose of overthrowing by our means the Sovereign whom he has exalted and of raising his own authority on the ruins of his Throne." The Chiefs, he declared, had already sounded him on the possibility of making personal arrangements regarding themselves, and he did not think the inhabitants were disposed to offer any resistance.

His secret instructions to Macdowal betrayed a curious indecision. While Pilima Talavuva was to be held up as the instigator of the war yet if it was found that his power was sufficiently great to endanger the success of the expedition, then he should be vested with full authority, to be exercised however in the King's name and under North's control. Further he should be stimulated to bring pressure to bear on the King to accept North's terms by being told that the Governor was inclined to favour Muddu Svami's claims. As for the other Ministers, Migas Tenna was expected to support the Adikar and Levuke to lead the King's party which was opposed to him; at the same time there was reason to believe that under certain circumstances he might side with Muddu Svami, who North was satisfied had a numerous and powerful following. If the King withdrew from the Capital and would not return at Macdowal's invitation, then Muddu Svami should be proclaimed in his place, but this must be so staged as to appear the spontaneous act of the Chiefs themselves.*

* C.O. 54/10.

On the 31st of January the two British armies took the road and seventeen days later the Appu Hamis who had conveyed the letter to the Court returned to Colombo; they had heard they said a whisper among the King's subjects that their Ruler was blessed by God and that the divinities of the Hatara Dewala,* the four Hindu temples at Kandy, had appeared to him in a vision and declared that if his enemies crossed the mountains within the week, they would be destroyed.†

The reply which they brought was signed by all the Ministers and after reciting the King's gratification at North's expressions of devotion to his person, emphasized the fact that from the time the English first arrived at Tiru Kona Malai and sent the Governor of Madras' Ambassador with his letter, the Court had kept faith with them. The exchange of yearly embassies provided the opportunity to discuss all outstanding questions and their resumption would greatly facilitate diplomatic relations. The Ministers expressed the hope that in view of the existing friendship with the King of Great Britain, the Governor in his wisdom would see that an equitable settlement was reached.‡

The suggestion that the proper procedure would be through the yearly embassies which bore the "tribute" to the King and which North had discontinued, coming at a time when British armies were on their way to the King's Capital, incensed the Governor, who saw in it "so flagrant an instance of an intention to persist in hostility"§ and the

* Dedicated to Natha, Vishnu, Kataragama and Pattini.

† Report of the Appuhamis. Enc. to Idem.

‡ Ministers to North. 12th Feb., 1803. Enc. to Idem.

§ North to Hobart, 25th Feb., 1803. C.O. 54/10.

next day his obsequious Council, consisting of the Chief Justice and Arbuthnot, agreed that further negotiations were useless and that a Treaty should be immediately entered into with Muddu Svami.

The Court was anxiously watching and once again the age-old strategy of the Sinhalese, already so well tested against two Western nations, was brought into play. The Court disappeared among the mountains of Uva, and on the 21st the combined British armies were permitted unopposed to occupy the abandoned Capital with its magazines empty and the palace within the great square which recalled Seringa Patam, on fire; the smouldering remains of the coach which he had once accompanied were left to remind the General of his previous visit.*

The scene of desolation can be well pictured from the following brief reference left by a priest who at great risk smuggled away the copy of the *Mahavagga Vinaya* which had been offered to the Brotherhood at Mal Vatta five months before : " On the day in the month of Navam of the year 2345 of the Buddhist Era on which the English people entered Nuwara, when thieves removed the goods and cloths of the Poyage and stole the bags and wraps in which the books were encased, in my reverence for this book and for the service of our religion I, Rambukkana Sobita Unanse, took the same and carried it away safely across the Hantane forest. It is proper that anyone looking into this book should give the merit to me."†

* For a contemporary description, see Appendix D.

† This volume is now in the Colombo Museum Library : the relevant passage is mistranslated in its new Catalogue of Palm Leaf Manuscripts (W. A. de Silva : 1938).

Muddu Svami had been brought to Kantalai in good time and on the 7th of March was escorted to the palace under a royal salute and much military pomp. Macdowal proceeded to discuss North's suggested terms with him, to find to his disappointment that the Prince was less pliant than had been expected. He was willing to pay for British help by the cession of Sat Korale, the richest of the Provinces, yielding as it did a fourth of the King's revenue, which did not exceed a lakh of pagodas, as well as the grant of commercial privileges ; he would also give a safe conduct to Sri Vikrama and guarantee to him a pension so long as he lived within the British Settlements ; but he too had a touch of that regal spirit which had made the continental prince, Kirti Sri, so truly one with his Sinhalese subjects ; he refused to take the oath of allegiance to the British Sovereign, or to cede Saparagamuva, the Province which contained that Foot Print sö venerated by those who would look to him to defend their Faith. Should he consent to such a betrayal, his name would for ever be held up to execration, he declared.* The terms were modified in accordance with his wishes and Macdowal was instructed to hand over to him all the territory which was not ceded to the British, and to settle the constitution of the force needed for his support. The document after being signed by the Prince was forwarded to North on the 14th of March, but the General was getting nervous : his armies had achieved nothing worth recording, the rains were due shortly, and increasing sickness was causing anxiety. He therefore decided to leave behind a strong garrison under

* This should settle any doubt as to the political division within which Sri Pada lies. On my Report dated 25th Jan., 1913. Government ruled that it lay in Saparagamuva. (Sessional Paper 36, 1913).

the command of Barbut and withdraw with the rest of his men before the 25th.*

North's enthusiasm for his puppet was also fast cooling and he pointed out that since under the terms of the Convention as finally settled he did not guarantee Muddu Svami's throne, he could not undertake to support him with military aid till he was furnished with precise information as to what force the Prince could raise and what effective party he had in the country. Indeed he did not hesitate to declare that so far the alliance with him had led to nothing but inconvenience and unpopularity.† Macdowal frankly expressed his opinion that the campaign had already become a hopeless undertaking: food was running short, the transport coolies were deserting in large numbers, Muddu Svami's expected partisans had failed to declare themselves and not a man had joined him, while the King's authority seemed more firmly established than ever before.‡ North seized on this news to send a remarkable reply. The co-operation of a party at Court, he said, was an essential part of the agreement and its absence absolved him from all obligations based on that expectation; he could not undertake to place Muddu Svami on the throne and the General was directed to advise him against being formally proclaimed. He never desired to conquer the country and had adopted that Prince's pretensions solely in order to find a legal and established Government from which to claim an indemnity for the injury which had been received. Those pretensions having proved entirely delusive, could no longer be supported,

* Macdowal to North, 9th March, 1803.

† North to Macdowal, 19th March, 1803.

‡ Macdowal to North, 18th March, 1803.

and consequently the object with which the war with the King was originally started, was revived.*

However on the very day this letter was written, the General had proclaimed Muddu Svami King and publicly announced that his enemies would be the enemies of the British King and be dealt with accordingly.† His letter conveying this news crossed North's instructions to him to send back the Tiru Kona Malai division except those selected for the resident garrison, and recommending the Prince's return with them ; he himself, he said, had again entered into communication with the Court.‡

Acting on the King's orders Pilima Talavuva had written§ to ask why the English were acting as they did when there was no enmity between the two Governments, and attached to the palm leaf missive was a secret message on paper to remind the Maha Mudaliyar of what had passed with the Governor and stating that the Adikar was awaiting help. In reply he was informed that the moment was favourable for giving effect to his scheme as the Governor was now both less inclined towards Muddu Svami and also greatly distressed at the sufferings of the people ; if he would deliver the King over to the British they would provide for his future maintenance while he himself could continue at the Capital as the First Personage in the Kingdom.||

The result of this advance was that on the 28th Migas Tenna entered the town with his firelock and match

* North to Macdowal, 23rd March, 1803.

† Macdowal to North, 23rd March, 1803.

‡ North to Macdowal, 25th March, 1803.

§ Adikar to Maha Mudaliyar, Secret Diary, 9th April, 1803.

|| Maha Mudaliyar to Adikar, 26th March, 1803.

wrapped in white muslin in token of peace* and the next day had a conference with Macdowal. The English, he observed, had obtained possession of the country and the King had fled ; under those circumstances, and with the knowledge they had of Pilima Talavuva's views, he could not understand why they had set up another King. To the General's question whether the Adikar could govern in the absence of a King, he replied that the English would know best. Macdowal admitted that he did know, but it was for the Minister to advance his own proposals. Migas Tenna answered that he could do so, but wished to know what would satisfy the British. Macdowal significantly remarked that it must be unpleasant for the Sinhalese to have a Malabar for their King, because all positions of importance in the country would be filled by people of his race. That was a subject he dared not discuss, said Migas Tenna ; the English were fully capable of regulating the Government but he repeated that he was anxious to know what it was they desired. Macdowal thereupon said that as the Governor would shortly visit Sat Korale he felt no doubt that he would give Pilima Talavuva an interview there. Migas Tenna answered that he would have great pleasure in going there to meet him but he must first communicate with the Adikar, and this Macdowal requested him to do and to inform him of the result.

At night a secret messenger came to the General to state that a letter would follow asking for an interview as suggested and that the reply should be worded in such terms that it could be submitted to the King whose permission had first to be secured.† Migas Tenna left under a salute

* Cordiner ii. p. 196.

† Secret Diary.

of nine guns and on the first of April the General started for Colombo with the bulk of the troops, several hundreds of whom died before long of the fever which they had contracted. After some exchange of letters it was arranged that North should meet the two Adikars at Dambadeniya at the end of April.*

It was a very disillusioned Frederic North who on the 14th of April forwarded his elaborate apologia to Lord Hobart. The areka nut incident, he protested, had been engineered by the machinations of the First Adikar to serve as that act of aggression which would impel the British to have recourse to arms, as hinted at on the 2nd of February, 1800 ; but it was now established beyond question that the power really was with him. Muddu Svami had no following, and, what was worse, no personality. Levuke, from whose alleged jealousy of Pilima Talavuva much had been expected, continued staunchly loyal to the King. The results so far achieved by the military effort were negligible. Sickness was raging and the loss was dreadful, while British escorts had been harassed within sight of the Capital. A speedy termination of hostilities was imperative and could only be effected by arrangement with the Adikar. Fortunately a truce relieved the immediate anxiety regarding the safety of their communications, and important developments were expected from the approaching interview. As for the war, he pleaded somewhat nervously " It has not been provoked by me, but on the contrary I have endeavoured to avert it by every measure compatible with the national honour, the independence of the power which I represent, and the security of the people entrusted to my care."

* Macdowal to North, 29th March. Adikar to Macdowal. Macdowal to Adigar, 11th April, 1803.

Muddu Svami on learning of the contemplated meeting, sent a pressing invitation to North to visit him at the Capital ; North replied that he doubted the possibility of making the necessary arrangements to do so, but the Prince could rest assured of his own sincere desire to promote his interests ; he concluded with the prayer that his prosperity might continue so long as the Sun and Moon endured.* Muddu Svami thereupon asked for permission to meet the Governor at Dambadeniya : if this could not be granted he expressed his desire to send Barbut there as his representative.†

* North to Muddu Svami, 28th April, 1803.

† Barbut to North, 23rd April, 1803.

CHAPTER V

At ten o'clock on the morning of the third of May, Pilima Talavuva appeared at the bungalow at Dambadeniya where North was lodged and was received with an impressive military display ; but he was a sick man and the terrible epidemic of fever which was sweeping through the country and from which many of the courtiers were suffering, prevented the attendance of Migas Tenna, greatly to North's disappointment. After minutely scrutinising the Convention in seventeen paragraphs entered into with Muddu Svami, the Adikar agreed to accept it subject to certain variations to which that Prince's consent was needed, and the following day three copies, signed and sealed by North, were taken to him and received his signature.

These variations were substantial : under them Muddu Svami as King would hold court at Jaffna, while the administration was to be entrusted to Pilima Talavuva with the title of Sri Astana Kumarayen. The latter guaranteed an allowance of 30,000 rix dollars a year to him, and another to Sri Vickrama who would reside at Negumbo or some other part of the British Settlements ; payment would be made through the British authorities and be secured by the yearly delivery of 20,000 ammunams of areka of 24,000 nuts the ammunam, at the rate of six rix dollars each payable in copper coin. Members of the late royal family who were under confinement were to be released and a general amnesty proclaimed for all political suspects. The fort which the British had built at Gangavila with the help of the Moors of the district, the only people who had taken their side, and was named after Macdowal himself, was to be substituted for Girihagama which had been promised to them under the Convention. The various provisions were to come into operation as soon as the person of the King was surrendered to the British and not till then, and in the interval the truce between the parties was to be maintained.

On the same day North wrote with much satisfaction to inform Hobart of the success of his diplomacy. He had, he said, effectively driven a wedge between the Adikar and his sovereign and the former would be compelled to play into his hands as everything depended on the surrender of the latter. Muddu Svami, judging from his character as it now stood revealed, would no doubt be very pleased to exchange his precarious prospects for royal status and an assured income combined with safety; he had some fears as to whether the Prince would consent to the title with the challenging royal *Sri* which the Adikar desired, but the latter was persuaded to agree to the more modest designation of *Utum Kumarayen*, Exalted Prince. As to the payment of the allowance, in view of the fact that areka nuts fetched 14-18 rix dollars the ammunam at Colombo—to which figure had to be added an export duty of ten rix dollars—the arrangement would certainly not result in a loss. Gangavila was excellently situated for controlling an important Province and was intended to be the headquarters of the Malay Regiment. Finally, it was not to be overlooked that there was no provision as to what was to happen on the Adikar's death, and in his present state of health anything was possible. In case of such a contingency arising, with the rival claimants living under British control, there might be further developments.

While expressing his opinion that the conditions were "inferior to the just pretences of Great Britain" he concluded his illuminating despatch as follows : "I was drawn to war by premeditated injury and systematic insult ; I have been obliged to carry it on with an inadequate force and an empty Treasury ; and you will, I think, scarcely be of opinion that in the present state of affairs I ought to venture on a second campaign in hopes of further advantages."*.

Barbut had returned to Colombo, only to die of the terrible fever, and on 16th May Macdowal himself set out in order to secure Muddu Svami's signature, taking with him a watch and a betel box with its fittings as a present to him from North ; it was left to his discretion whether or not he should co-operate with the Adikar in capturing the King, but he was instructed not to get drawn into a campaign.† There appeared to be good reason for North's complacency ; Barbut had reported that the food situation was eminently satisfactory, and that in his opinion the Malay Regiment with a proportion of European Artillery was fully adequate not only to defend the station but also for active operations in the field ; it was sufficient to march over any part of the country, he confidently asserted.‡ The road to Tiru Kona Malai was open ; Sat Korale and Fort Macdowal were strongly held ; finally, as the surrender of the King's person was a necessary preliminary to any demand by the Adikar for assistance, a combination of circumstances which could disturb the peaceful enjoyment of the expected acquisition or render

* North to Hobart, 4th May, 1803. C.O. 54/11.

† Instructions, 9th May, 1803.

‡ Barbut to North, 22nd April, 1803. C.O. 54/11.

a further campaign imperative, was in the highest degree improbable.*

Macdowal however did not find the reality very much to his taste. Sickness was still raging and Muddu Svami was one of the victims, but the drastic treatment of the surgeon, Holloway, soon cured him, though it left him with a very sore mouth. His attendants too were sick, and only five or six "squalid and famished wretches" remained in attendance upon him. The General was anxious to meet the Adikars before obtaining the Prince's signature to the amended agreement, but they failed to appear. Money was so scarce that when the Prince asked him for 300 pagodas, he wrote to North declaring that he might as well have asked for the mines of Peru, for he believed that the Paymaster could not raise five. Some coiners were set to work and out of the metal obtained from temple vessels they struck a few pice† but could proceed no further; they either fell sick or appeared to be under a charm. The General found them in a deplorable condition, and they declared that the gods whose brass vessels they had demolished and profaned had driven them out of their senses.‡ At the end of ten days he wrote "There is indeed nothing here to detach one's mind from gloomy reflections. The scene is painted deep black, with scarce a streak of light."§ He was anxious about the sufficiency of the available

* North to Hobart, 17th May, 1803. C.O. 54/11.

† A pice was the same as a stiver, being the forty-eighth part of a rix dollar, which latter was only a coin of account.

‡ Macdowal to North, 28th May. A similar story has been preserved by Joao Ribeiro about the guides commandeered by the Portuguese to lead their raiding bands to the Dewale at Kataragama. See his Historic Tragedy of Ceilao, tr. P. E. Pieris, Colombo, 1925, p. 87.

§ Macdowal to North, 29th May, 1803.

stores and ordered a careful survey to be held. By the 3rd of June he was ill in bed, though twenty-three grains of James powder taken with rhubarb every two hours and followed by a hot bath somewhat revived him. The Adikar had written to say he could not come without the King's permission for which Macdowal should apply, but the General was so annoyed at his "perfidy" that he would not do so.*

North in the meantime was busy conducting a separate correspondence with Levuke and advised the General to do the same, but as secretly as possible. To that Dissava he expressed his disappointment that the Ministers had not prevented the Adikar from bringing about the war. There were now, he said, two powers, the King and the Adikar, and as the latter had offered very fair terms, he intended to support him with all his forces unless the King agreed to make peace on the conditions set out in his letter.† Meanwhile Major Adam Davie, a Scotsman from Edinburgh, had been appointed to succeed Barbut; Macdowal considered him a very gallant officer and well-meaning man,‡ but he shrank from the responsibility and begged for permission to resign because he was convinced that as matters stood, the "utmost attention, activity and circumspection" would not enable him to avoid discredit and blame.§ So bad was the health of the troops that for three months the 19th Regiment had not furnished a single man for duty. The Malay Regiment was in hospital without proper medical aid and suffering both from the

* Macdowal to North, 3rd June, 1803.

† Maha Mudaliyar to Levuke, 7th June, 1803.

‡ Macdowal to North, 1st June, 1803.

§ Davie to Macdowal, 31st May and 1st June.

lack of their opium, the effects of living on rice from immature grain, and excessive hard work, while their pay was in arrears for two and a half months. Macdowal had authorised an allowance of two drams each of ghi and arrack and one day's beef in the week, but this could not be continued owing to lack of stores.

Persistent efforts were being made to seduce the Malays and on the 7th Captain Nouradin Goah, their Adjutant, received a letter from his half brother Sankelan, who commanded the King's Malays, inviting him and his brother to kill or drive away the English and join the King who would reward them highly.* The invitation was ignored and Nouradin's fidelity was rewarded by the gift of a hundred pagodas and a *kris*, which was, in North's words, "a plain one, as befits a soldier, but the first which was made in London for the service of our King."† The King had sent four letters to Macdowal ; in one he complained that some trees in his palace grounds had been felled. These revealed the fact that he was being kept in ignorance of what was taking place‡ and was anxious to ascertain the terms on which peace could be restored.§ On the 11th the General, his bowels weakened and his mouth affected by the large doses of mercury which he had been obliged to swallow, started back for Colombo after informing Davie of his decision to recommend the evacuation of the town.||

North realised that a crisis was very near and that his only chance depended on his finding the King more com-

* Sankelan to Nouradin, Hanguranketa, 3rd June.

† North to Nouradin, 17th June.

‡ Davie to Robert Arbuthnot, 10th June.

§ King to Macdowal, 7th June.

|| Davie to Arbuthnot, 17th June.

plaisant than his Adikar. He had arranged to reinforce the garrison with 250 Malays and Sepoys, and he was also sending a priest to Levuke to reveal the Adikar's proceedings and to impress on the Minister his own sincere desire for friendly relations ; but the continued occupation of the Capital was the only effective weapon which he held. " It may be difficult " he wrote to Macdowal* " but it cannot be more disastrous than another campaign which is otherwise inevitable—every nerve must be strained to preserve Kandy till we hear from the King." To Migas Tenna who was reported to be raising troops in Sat Korale he sent a threat that if he did not desist, the King would be informed of his share in the Adikar's proposals.† Levuke replied that he was prepared to lay any proposals before the King, while Pilima Talavuva sent word to Davie that he himself was in disgrace as the result of his dealings with the Governor and urged him to send 500 men to occupy Hanguran Keta.‡

During the month 47 Europeans and 506 Asiatics were reported as available for duty, and though the sick numbered 192 and 231 respectively, they were being steadily evacuated and *doolies* for the conveyance of all the bad cases were on their way from Tiru Kona Malai, accompanied by a strong Malay escort.§ But desertions were rapidly increasing, though it was hoped that the arrival of fresh stocks of food and opium would check them.|| On the 17th of June Davie sent word that the Sinhalese troops were being called out and batteries erected on the Han-

* North to Macdowal, 11th June.

† Maha Mudaliyar to Migas Tenna, 15th June.

‡ Davie to Arbuthnot, 13th June.

§ Abstract of the Garrisons in Ceylon. C.O. 54/11.

|| North to Hobart, 1st July and 8th July. 54/11.

guran Keta road ; he anticipated that his communications with the coast would be soon cut off and he himself attacked by the King's Malays and he urgently asked for instructions regarding the evacuation which the General had foreshadowed. On the 20th North addressed a letter to the King declaring that he had been driven into war by the aggressive action of the King's Ministers, but that he was always anxious for peace and was now sending the conditions on which a settlement could be reached. If these met with the King's approval the Capital would be immediately handed back to him and friendly relations re-established. His terms were similar in principle to those previously advanced, with further conditions for the release of Muddu Svami's relatives and the right of unrestricted trade in rice and salt.

His letter was sent to Davie for delivery, with instructions that if the terms were agreed to he should forthwith evacuate the town and withdraw to Tiru Kona Malai, after despatching Muddu Svami and his relatives with a suitable escort within British territory.* That Prince was not unnaturally nervous about his own safety and asked to be conveyed to Colombo. To this request North replied that the intervening forests were so unhealthy that he would not expose His Majesty's person among them but had instructed Davie to convey him to Tiru Kona Malai. Further, as the Adikar had not fulfilled his engagements, it was no longer necessary for him to sign the revised Convention, he added, but whatever arrangements were made with Sri Vikrama, all possible attention would be paid to the safety of his kinsfolk.

* North to Davie, 20th June, 1803.

Two days later, on the 25th, North instructed Davie that the flooded condition of the rivers rendered it impossible to despatch troops, provisions or medicine; he was gravely alarmed by the increasing desertions and fully appreciated the critical and dangerous situation of the garrison; under the circumstances he judged it necessary and proper to evacuate Kandy with the least possible delay. His orders were worded as follows: "You are therefore upon the receipt of this letter to take measures for the purpose of taking proper precautions for the security of the sick, which I trust the number of doolies lately sent from hence and from Trincomale will enable you to effect. The artillery, ammunition, and stores of all kinds must be destroyed as completely as possible, the cannon spiked or broken up, the powder consumed and the shot thrown into the river, in short, the whole to be rendered totally useless. A proper escort must be furnished to the Rajah Mootoo Swamy." If however there was a probability of the King agreeing to the Governor's proposals, then action was to be delayed, though only for a few days.*

Davie's appeal for instructions was received by North after this was written, and was followed on the 28th by a definite command to evacuate as soon as facilities for transporting the sick were available.† But it was already too late and with deep despondency North on the first of July wrote to Hobart: "I have this day received the dreadful intelligence that Candi was taken on the 24th ultimo, owing, as I have too much reason to believe, to the defection of a great detachment of His Majesty's Malay Regiment,‡

* Arbuthnot to Davie, 25th June.

† Arbuthnot to Davie, 28th June.

‡ The letter books of Admiral Peter Rainier, preserved at the National Maritime Museum, Greenwich, afford side-lights of North's opinion about this. (D. No. 3).

which formed the principal force of that Garrison."* It appears that on Friday the 24th of June, after a secret warning from Pilima Talavuva, the King's forces commenced an attack and after a short resistance Davie hoisted the white flag and asked for terms; the details are not known for certain,† but about five o'clock in the evening the garrison, estimated at 30 European officers and men, 300 Malays, 12 Bengal Lascars and 30 Indian Pioneers,‡ started on the road to Tiru Kona Malai, taking their arms with them, only to be brought to a halt after two miles by the flooded condition of the river. The next morning a message was received demanding the surrender of Muddu Svami, a demand which after some parleying was complied with. By Sunday morning the flood had not abated and the Malays and Indians were steadily deserting to the Sinhalese, who were seen all around, though no attempt was made to molest the troops; Davie now decided to return to Kandy and after proceeding a short distance gave

* North to Hobart, 1st July, 1803. C.O. 54/11.

† Milhanage Johannes, a Sinhalese Lascarin who chanced to be with the garrison, claims to have read the *pus kolaon* which the terms of surrender were recorded, but this is in the highest degree improbable. The words in his deposition as recorded are "which he himself read"; it might be possible to understand these as implying that Davie read out the writing to the garrison, were it not for the fact that there is no reason to think that Davie could read the Sinhalese language, or that many of the garrison understood it. Of his evidence, which was given on the 6th of July, North expressed the opinion "Every particular of the narrative may not be true." Encl. to Despatch of 8th July, C.O. 54/11. Greeving, a Dutch assistant Surgeon with the army, also purports to give the terms but his narrative is so marred by grossly untrue statements, *e.g.*, as when he speaks of the death of Davie nd the impalement of Muddu Svami—as to be valueless where a oubtful point is involved. C.O. 54/12.

‡ Evidence of Mohammed Gani, recorded on 11th July. Pioneers were employed to clear the road ahead of the army.

orders to ground arms.* Further on the passage was found occupied by the King's forces and apparently on directions received the Malays were separated from the Europeans and marched ahead, while Davie, Nouradin and his brother were summoned before the Adikar who sent them on to Kandy followed by two of the English Captains. About eight other officers and nearly a score of the rank and file remained; the latter were led aside two by two and executed with the sword, while the former were either shot or put an end to their own lives with the pistols which they had concealed when they surrendered their other arms; the European sick left behind in hospital had already been slaughtered.

These few facts seem to be established with reasonable certainty and it is foreign to the purpose of this work to enter into an analysis of the conflicting evidence, such as it is, in order to ascertain the exact details of these sanguinary incidents.† North on the 8th of July summed up the position as known to him thus: "I therefore hope that the effects of the horrible atrocity will be reduced to the loss

* Greeving states that the troops had not been permitted to take any ammunition with them, but none of the others who were present mention this important fact, which if true would hardly have been omitted by Corporal Barnsley, a statement from whom was recorded by Capt. Madge on 27th June (C.O. 54/11). North writing on 8th July could not believe that Davie would have evacuated Kandy and started for Tiru Kona Malai except with arms and ammunition, and that being so he could not understand why he consented to surrender the arms. The most reliable account is Barnsley's as recorded by Alexander; see Appendix E.

† Four years after the event Cordiner wrote: "As no English officer who was present at the fall of Candy has yet appeared to give an account of the causes which led to it and the subsequent disasters, they are still involved in much obscurity: and a circumstantial and authentic detail of the transactions is rather to be wished for than expected."

of about a hundred invalids." The King appears to have been informed that the death of the British soldiers was the result of an attempt to avoid surrendering Muddu Svami,* an explanation creditable to Davie of which more might have been made by his apologists. Friendly relations with the British was what the youthful King earnestly desired, and the Court had a lively appreciation of the potential value of every European prisoner; his directions to preserve the lives of the white troops arrived too late and he expressly declared that what had occurred was without his order and against his will. His Gabada Nilame wrote by his authority as follows: "When the King demanded the surrender of Muddu Svami, who was a wicked man to both nations, the English who were in Kandy refused. They also disobeyed other orders, which determined the Chiefs of the Court who were there to kill them. This is the only cause of their death."†

The Adikar will always remain suspect, for his position was so delicate, in view of North's threats of exposure, that he might well have endeavoured to prove his unshaken loyalty to his Master by destroying the luckless tools of his fellow-conspirator. Davie in his captivity wrote with bitterness: "I hope the Governor will not this time allow the troops to be puppetted about to their destruction by following the advice of the Adikar. The First Adikar was the person that did everything at Kandi; the night before the attack he sent a friendly letter to blind, and in the morning was the person that conducted it. It was at his

* Peradeniya to D'Oyly. Encl. to Secret Despatch, North to Camden, 11th Jan., 1805. C.O. 54/16.

† North to Hobart, private, 19th July, 1804. Also, Reports of Talgama Unanse; Gabada Nilame to Maha Mudaliyar. Encl. to Secret Despatch, North to Hobart, 30th Sept., 1804. C.O. 54/14.

desire also that the Malays so basely and treacherously left us to be murdered."*

According to the Adikar, the responsibility was with Pusvelle Rala, to whom Muddu Svami was surrendered; his words as englished by the Government translator, were are follows: "He is the very person who went to kill the English, and as soon as I was informed of his departure, I have laid many reasons or causes before the King and went to deliver them from being killed. Then I found the soldiers were already destroyed and they were killing the officers who were at different places by sending for them; since I have arrived at the spot I have delivered the lives of three English and two Malay officers."†

Copious vilification formed the smoke-screen raised for North's protection and strong language has been freely employed in discussing this unhappy incident; nevertheless his successor in office, Thomas Maitland, deliberately rejected the word "massacre." "I have determined to drop it totally" he wrote to Camden‡ "from a deep conviction arising out of the total ignorance we are in not only of who were the perpetrators of it and in whom the sovereign power rests, but also out of the nature of the thing itself." Whatever may be the truth of the version submitted to the King, it is certain that out of the four

* Encl. in Maitland to Earl Camden, 22nd Nov., 1805. C.O. 54/18.

† Adikar to Maha Mudaliyar, Secret Diary, 15th July, 1804.

‡ 18th Aug., 1805. C.O. 54/18. Maitland seems to have taken an extreme view of the responsibility of the Malays: "You will however perceive that in his (Davie's) first letter he, the Commanding Officer of the time, attributes the massacre of Candy entirely to the Malays, which indeed I am sorry to say was thoroughly known and believed here at the time." Maitland to Camden, 28th Feb., 1806. C.O. 54/21.

prominent actors in the tragedy, it was not he* who played the rôle of villain.

As for Muddu Svami, he was led by the Adikar before Sri Vikrama, who demanded from him at whose instigation he had ventured back into his kingdom. Muddu Svami indicated the Minister, whereupon the King exclaimed "That is not true. My Adikar is incapable of such an act. You say this because you desire him to accompany you on the road which you will now take." Muddu Svami stood convicted of the greatest crime known to law, one of which no one could take cognisance save the King, and his life was forfeit ; nevertheless as a Prince he was entitled to be executed by the sword without the degradation of the halter; that privilege was not denied to him.†

* The King's own version was recorded by William Granville, who accompanied him on the voyage from Colombo to Madras :

King on 18th Feb., 1816 : "Do you or do you not visit the evil administration of public affairs upon your King's Ministers ? In that business I was not concerned. Let Pilima Talavuva bear the blame. I was too young a Prince to influence the conduct of my first Adikar. I heard of the event only when it was over. I saved Major Davy's life. . . His party were in the hands of the Adikar and perished. Major Davy received every mark of favour from me. I gave him land and as much as he wanted to eat and drink. He was allowed wives. The laws could grant no more. Did I make those laws ? " Granville's Journal, reprinted in Ceylon Literary Register, Series iii, Vol. iii.

† Reports of Talgama Unanse, 25th June and 27th August, 1804. Encl. to North's Despatch, 30th Sept., 1804. C.O. 54/14. For a jewel given by the Prince to a British officer, see Louis Kornitzer : The Bridge of Gems, pp. 225-6, London 1939. Nouradin and his brother were said to have been executed in August after twice refusing to enter the King's service. See Lieut.-Colonel Doody to Castlereagh, 21st July, 1805. C.O. 54/19.

CHAPTER VI

On the 27th of July a verbal message* was received from Pilima Talavuva. Single-handed, he said, he had been helpless against the body of Ministers. He had given timely warning at Dambadeniya that the British force should be strengthened, but only the General had been sent. About a hundred Asiatics and two English had deserted to the King and during the fighting the Malays had fired only one round. He himself had been dreadfully ill. He revealed the fact that the King had given orders for invading the British territory and was expected to descend in person from Kanda Uda after the Perahera, the great religious festival of the year which lasted for a fortnight in August. He claimed that the lives of the three officers were spared as the result of his own intercession with the King, and ended with a request that all letters written on paper previously sent by him should be burnt.†

Active hostilities were now inevitable and the Adikar's levies, though ill-armed and undisciplined, poured into the Matara district and created so great a panic that Tangalla was hastily evacuated and preparations made to abandon Matara Fort.‡ Chilaw was threatened and for three days Levuke, supported by the guns and Malays obtained from Davie, was engaged in the unfamiliar task of attacking

* By Tepulangoda Mudenneka Rala.

† Secret Diary, 29th July.

‡ Writing from Galle on 29th April, 1809, Maitland referred to Major Beaver's "essential services in restoring the District of Matara after it had been unpardonably deserted by our Troops and was in complete possession of the Kandians." C.O. 54/36.

the petty fort of Hanvella. In this he was unsuccessful: the Malays fired high and ended by going back to the British, and the responsibility for the failure was laid on him ; his dallying with the English was known and he was charged with conspiring to deliver the King over to them;* he was sentenced to be executed with the sword, while his men were set to open a rice field of two thousand acres, as being a task for which they were better qualified.† North availed himself of the opportunity to forward bombastic despatches about his military successes for the edification of the Secretary of State‡ but it was impossible thus to gloss over his discomfiture, and in October he asked to be relieved from his office as early as possible, explaining that he felt himself incapable of carrying on much longer the complicated business of his responsible post in a satisfactory manner.§

Months would elapse before this could be done and in the interval he would not discuss peace, he asserted, till the King was deposed and Pilima Talavuva captured and punished ; he even charged the former with "atrocious conduct in the massacre of the English," a charge which he did not attempt to justify. He was preparing for a campaign in July which he intended to be final and decisive, after which he would retain the whole country by right of conquest. The plan for changing the dynasty from the Malabar to the Sinhalese race, he said, would fall with its author the Adikar, who alone was capable of carrying it

* Puskola by Ehelepola: Board Papers, 1815-1828. C.R.O.

† Report of Talagama Unanse.

‡ Despatches of 31st Aug. and 15th Sept., 1803. C.O. 54/11. *Ceylon Gazette*, 24th and 31st Aug., 7th and 14th Sept. Proclamation of 29th Aug.

§ North to Hobart, 6th Oct., 1803. C.O. 54/11.

through, while the only legitimate Pretender had been cut off in the person of Muddu Svami. Transport, however, was likely to prove a serious problem as more than a half of the coolies employed by Macdowal had died of fever and the epidemic was still raging throughout the country with unabated fury ; to meet the difficulty he was hiring the necessary labour from South India. He did not expect the campaign to last more than three months and he fervently asserted that he considered it his duty to set in motion every engine of violence and policy which circumstances would present to him and morality allow.* In furtherance of this decision he arranged to purchase Kaffir slaves in Mozambique and Goa who as soldiers were expected to be peculiarly effective in striking terror into the minds of the Sinhalese.†

Major-General Wemyss, however, who arrived at this juncture to relieve Macdowal, was less optimistic ; he would need, he reported, 8,000 effectives and 20,000 coolies for such a campaign while all that he found being done was to send detachments in every direction with orders to seize the cattle, to burn and destroy towns, villages and stores of food, and to act in every manner that would cause the enemy most annoyance.‡ Shocking atrocities, perhaps unrivalled since the days of Jeronymo de Azavedo, were being committed, and the disgusting record of one officer's activities in the course of a week, drew from the Commander-in-Chief, the Duke of York, the criticism that it was "extremely disgraceful to His Majesty's arms."§

* North to Hobart, 3rd March, 1804. C.O. 54/14.

† North to Hobart, 1st Jan., 1804 and Appendix F.

‡ Wemyss to Hobart, 26th March, 1804. C.O. 54/14.

§ J. W. Gordon, Horse Guards, to E. Cooke, 15th Nov., 1804. C.O. 54/15. The officer in question was Captain Robert Blackall of the 51st Regt., who signed his diary on the First of April, 1804, at Negombo.

This will be the less surprising when the conditions of military life are realized, and Alexander Alexander, a Scotsman from Ayrshire who arrived at Tiru Kona Malai on the 22nd of June, 1803 and served there for eight years, has left a record* of his experiences which cannot be lightly ignored. According to him the health of the soldiers was normally very bad, they suffered greatly from ulcers and swollen legs, and their sufferings were aggravated by the wretched condition of their barracks. They were poorly fed, for the hostilities with the King had put an end to the supplies which used to be received from his dominions. Their mid-day meal consisted of meat, usually from old and diseased cattle, and loathsome to sight and smell. This was filthily prepared as curry and eaten out of earthen *chatties* with rice of an inferior quality which was boiled without any attempt to rid it of the dirt with which it was mixed. Breakfast and supper was made up of rice cakes and jaggery with a little fish or liver, and a quart of arrack was allowed daily for each five men. Under these circumstances it is not surprising that the flux or dysentery was rampant, and the medical officer in charge, or "surgeon" as he was called, had only two remedies for all diseases—Glauber salts for flux and mercury for liver and other complaints. Alexander himself suffered very severely and only began to recover his health after he married a native woman who looked after his food. At times the mortality was so heavy that assistance had to be obtained from outside for burying the dead.

The garrison he described as "a sink of sin and profaneness." No form of religious worship was observed and

* The Life of Alexander Alexander, written by himself and edited by William Howell, London and Edinburgh, 1830.

the officers, who headed the revolt against religion, converted the old Dutch church into a place of amusement, while they left the village mongrels to dig up the bones of their dead from the graves in the over-crowded cemetery. They took little or no interest in their men who were thus left at the mercy of unprincipled and ferocious non-commissioned officers. Flogging of appalling severity was of daily occurrence, often for nominal faults, and aggravated by circumstances calculated to gratify the sadistic propensities of some of those in authority : one was described as jumping about in ecstacy at the sight of its infliction. A sentence of five hundred lashes with the cat was not rare, and accustomed though Alexander was to the shocking brutalities practised on male and female slaves in the West Indies, in which he had himself taken part, the soldier's lot in Ceylon, he declared, was much worse. Comparing these men with the Company's Indian troops, warriors who did not use spirituous drinks, among whom punishment was rarely needed, he expressed the opinion that from the point of view of morality, conduct and sense of duty, they were "in every respect superior to the Europeans." "The longer the European troops remained in this wretched place, which I may call the gates of death and hell, the more immoral and depraved they became."

Early in February, Macdowal had sent the Adikar a secret letter by the hands of a Moorman who had an interview with him at Denavaka. He revealed the King's plans for an invasion and advised North to threaten another advance on Kandy as the best method of immobilising the army. If peace proposals followed, he said, he should insist on all the Ministers meeting him and entice them to the frontier, where he could take them prisoner and thus be able to compel the King to do as he wished.* The suggestion was rejected by North ; there would be no talk of peace, he declared, till the murders were avenged, and it would be the Ministers that the British army on its next campaign would capture.† Pilima Talavuva hastened to defend himself against any suspicion of complicity ; he had nothing to do with the incident, he protested, while ascribing it entirely to the King's curelty ;‡ he had been faithful to his word, he said ; he further inquired whether the Governor would consent to his residing in Saparagamuva, as the last expedition had ruined his lands ; and he concluded with a cryptic reference to what could be achieved "this time."§

Migas Tenna also made verbal approaches with a view to peace, but North while insisting on a written communication declared that there would be no peace till either the King was deposed or those responsible for the murders were surrendered.|| His anxiety was to force the Court to assume the attitude of the penitent, and through the Maha Mudaliyar he sent word to the Maha Nayaka Unanse and the Gabada Nilame to the effect that the Governor was very angry and would soon wreak a terrible vengeance: the only method of appeasing him would be for the King to express his contrition through an embassy of his chief Ministers and throw himself on the Governor's mercy.

The answers received, which were written on the King's directions, did not afford North much consolation. The

* Recorded by R. Plasket, 15th Feb., 1804.

† Macdowal to Cadogan, 27th Feb., 1804.

‡ Adikar to Macdowal, recd. 4th May.

§ Adikar to Macdowal, recd. 6th May.

|| North to Hobart, 25th May, 1804.

Maha Nayaka, as befitted his calling, after recounting the past history of the country, pointed out that "Buddha and Four Gods watch over the Island, and every foreign Power that may wish to conquer the country will fail in the attempt. If foreigners desire to obtain any advantage from Ceylon they must employ peaceable measures and not violence—of the truth of which the fate of the Dutch is a Proof." The Gabada Nilame's language was less suave; "as to Ambassadors, there may be one on each side, if the Maha Mudaliyar can arrange the peace; but till then there can be no ambassadors. The English have long since attempted to come to Kandi—they have been there and we have received no detriment from them. We are ready to receive them and await there arrival."*

The appearance of large reinforcements at Tiru Kona Malai provided the psychological moment for once again sounding the Court but in view of the rumours of British entanglements with French, Dutch and Maharattas† no perturbation was displayed there. It was said that the King's brothers and uncle who were at Viliachery in the Tondiman's country were maintaining a correspondence with the French on his behalf.‡ Pilima Talavuva was in such high favour that the King had himself provided the *Kotahalu Mangalya* festival to celebrate his daughter's attaining womanhood, and also appointed his son, who was still a boy, to be in charge of Udu Nuvara. The King's active participation in the administration and his

* Encl. in North to Hobart, 30th Sept., 1804. C.O. 54/14.

† Cf. Admiral Rainier to North, Cananore Road, 27th Feb., 1804; Madras Road, 17th July and 15th August, 1804. (Greenwich Marine Museum).

‡ North to Lord William Bentinck, 14th July, 1804.

sense of responsibility towards his subjects* is well illustrated by the fact that in spite of political anxieties, he did not hesitate to degrade three of his Dissavas for oppressing the people, while the lake which at this time he began to construct will remain as his lasting contribution to the abundant charms of his capital.

North therefore turned to his elaborate plan of campaign, under which numerous detachments operating from various points were to concentrate on Kandy, but this was vetoed by Wemyss, who did not consider his resources sufficient for the task. In the result three marauding columns starting from Colombo, Negumbo and Tiru Kona Malai ravaged the adjoining districts ; a fourth was allowed to make its way from Batticalo to the capital unopposed but fortunately the Commander, Captain Johnstone, discovered in time the error he had committed and hurriedly effected his escape, though with 145 casualties.†

* Dr. S. Paranavitana has drawn my attention to a *Sittu* issued by Pilima Talavuva to some Patabendas of the Panawal Korale in Korale Tuna which records a stern censure by the King on certain officials who had oppressed the villagers, and bought up their holdings by lending money at usurious rates of interest. They were deprived of their offices and the lands regranted to the original tenants to be held in perpetuity. The document is dated Esala 1727 Saka (A.D. 1805).

† North to Camden, 8th Feb., 1805. C.O. 54/16. A lurid picture of the incidents of this flight—for that is what it was—has been left by Alexander Alexander who was at Tiru Kona Malai at the time it took place, and this might be compared with advantage with Johnstone's own more reticent narrative of his Expedition to Kandy, 1804. (New Ed., Dublin, 1854). The tactics employed by the Sinhalese were identical with those used against the Portuguese in the xvi and xvii centuries and the results were similar. In Alexander's words "And thus they at length reached Trincomalee . . . forming an assembly of the most miserable looking men it is possible to conceive . . . All had to go to hospital . . . few, very few, survived."

On the 14th of March, Parliament had passed a Resolution to present an humble Address to the King praying that the correspondence "relative to the causes and circumstances which gave rise to the hostilities which have taken place between His Majesty's Government in that country (Ceylon) and that of the King of Candy" may be laid before the House,* and this could not fail to be disconcerting to North. Hobart had expressed his views of the Governor's proceedings in language which could hardly be misunderstood. "I was much disappointed" he wrote "at finding you unexpectedly engaged in a War which I have observed with deep concern has been attended with consequences of a most disastrous nature."† Accepting North's assertion of Pilima Talavuva's responsibility for the first act of aggression, the violation of the truce, and the subsequent murders, he instructed him not to enter into negotiations to end hostilities so long as that Minister wielded the uncontrolled power which he was found to enjoy, while the return of the British prisoners must be a necessary preliminary. Once British honour was satisfied by the fulfilment of these conditions, and provided all the territory ceded by the Batavian Government were retained, the acquisition of further territory was not an object which should stand in the way of an early settlement. The wisest policy to follow was that adopted by the Dutch as the result of their long experience, and the Cabinet was agreed that the Treaty of 1766 should form the basis of negotiations with the Court..

North's secret despatch to Hobart of 5th October was subdued in tone : the prospect of peace was still distant

* C.O. 54/15.

† Hobart to North, No. 16 of 29th March, 1804. C.O. 55/62.

and the Adikar's authority seemed undiminished : nevertheless he thought that the misery arising from the blockade which he was maintaining was so great, that a revolution was quite possible. If terms could be arranged, the control of the salt supply would be a sufficient curb on the Sinhalese while the roadway across the country, to which so much importance had been previously attached, he now considered unessential, in view of the unhealthiness of the terrain through which it would have to be traced.*

Secret communications were also opened in order to induce the Court to make the first advances, so as to save British prestige. Galagoda Bandara of Saparagamuva was sounded through his father-in-law Bandara Nayaka Appuhami, an influential resident of the Giruva Pattu : the Governor, he was informed, desired not acquisition of territory but satisfaction for "the cruel and perfidious murder" of his countrymen, and that involved the punishment of the Adikar by banishment or preferably by surrendering him to the British.† The reply was not encouraging : from the start the King had been anxious for friendly relations and it was the conduct of the British which had created the present situation. If British troops were killed on the retreat from Senkadagala Nuvara,‡ they were themselves to blame, because their attempt "by false and deceitful excuses not to deliver Muddu Svami who was the enemy of our Lord the King's Crown"

* C.O. 54/14.

† Arbuthnot to D'Oyly, 24th Oct., 1804. Encl. in S. D. North to Camden, 11th Jan., 1805. C.O. 54/16. Galagoda would seem to be the son of Gallegoda Dissava of Uva, who lived at Matara for some years and was known as Peradeniya. Lawrie: Gazetteer i, p. 247.

‡ The Sinhalese name for the Capital.

exasperated the King's men "and such mischief happened to some of the soldiers," but the prisoners who were still alive were receiving the Royal favour. If the British were anxious to resume friendly relations they should make that clear as early as possible.*

Migas Tenna was next approached with dire threats to ravage the country from end to end unless Pilima Talavuva was removed from office and the captives restored,† but his reply, prepared under the King's directions, was no more encouraging and deserves quotation. "To ruin the country by burning houses and by doing other acts of mischief to unarmed and peaceful people is only worthy of such mean, foolish and cruel robbers as plunder villages or on the high roads, who have no understanding of what this world is, and what the next: what is good and what is evil: but a wise person who governs a country will never permit such outrages." He himself entertained no doubt as to the wisdom of the Governor, and was convinced that what had occurred was the result of the ignorance and recklessness of the troops engaged. "Our troops too" the letter continued "can step over the frontiers and plunder and burn the houses of the people in the country below, but this has not been done because we did not give them permission to commit such atrocities." As for restoring the officers, that would be considered as soon as friendly relations were resumed and the blockade lifted.‡

* Peradeniya Dissava to D'Oyly, encl. to idem; the writer is described as Rajakaroene Wijeyekoon Pandita of Peradeniya and Mudliyar of the Gate.

† Maha Mudlr. to Second Adikar, encl. to idem.

‡ Dumbara to Maha Mudlr., 3rd Jan., 1805.

North considered this answer unsatisfactory and sent word to Galagoda that he was preparing for an intensified campaign which must inevitably end in the total ruin of the King's dominions,* for he had reached the conclusion, as he explained in a secret despatch, that what was of importance was not the negotiation of peace but the humiliation of the Court and the destruction of its influence among the inhabitants of the Settlements.† But he was a broken man; "I have felt my Force gradually diminishing for the last year, and have been for this month past labouring under a derangement of the nervous system" he wrote to Camden on the 8th of February, 1805.‡ "I must repeat to your Lordship that nerves, shattered and unstrung as mine are, are not formed to encounter the fatigue and disgusts of such a Government as this."

Two letters both dated the 13th of February which were received about this time were not calculated to soothe those frayed nerves. The first, addressed by Galagoda to the Maha Mudaliyar, after referring to North's threats, continued "Therefore if the Governor who is lacking in wisdom and does not know what will happen for the future, will cause such things to be done, without looking before and behind, without considering what is of service and what is not, what is good and what is evil, what is approved by religion and what is forbidden, it is manifest that steps will also be taken by the Principal Chiefs to crush and destroy the envious English people but not including the Cingalese people of the country below. Nor is this all; God who has diverse powers and who is the protector of

* Maha Mudlr. to Galagoda.

† Secret Despatch, 11th Jan., 1805, ut supra.

‡ C.O. 54/16.

religion, will also put them in great fear. It is better to consider all this."

The second was addressed by Pusvella Mudiyanse to Illangakon Mudaliyar at Matara:* as the British had abandoned their attitude of friendliness and were acting contrary to the King's interests his armed forces under his various Dissavas were preparing to take the field, and he summoned the people of the Littoral to rally to his standard, as they had done in the past against the Portuguese and the Hollanders.†

In view of such "extravagant pretensions and habitual insolence" North expressed his determination to commence a "decisive campaign," for he was sure that "no sufficient opening will be made for the negotiation of a Treaty till the Capital and King's House be again captured and destroyed by our Troops and His Person brought into imminent danger."‡ No action, however, was taken in furtherance of this resolution. A famine had broken out within the kingdom, aggravated by an outbreak of small-pox to which the King himself fell a victim,§ a calamity which was said never before to have happened to a Ruler of Lanka, and was regarded as a token of divine displeasure. The Adikar hastened from his Province, Saparagamuva, and took direct control of affairs; military preparations were suspended while the Dissavas busied themselves with the collection of the areka, a commodity for the export of which peace conditions were needed. At the same time in answer to a cautious approach from the Court, the Maha

* Pieris, Notes on Some Sinhalese Families, Part iv, Colombo.

† Encl. to Secret Despatch of 21st Feb., 1805. C.O. 54/17.

‡ Secret Despatch as above.

§ North to Camden, 13th April, 1805.

Mudaliyar was instructed to reply that peace could be established immediately if a proper apology were tendered, and the prisoners restored; North no longer attached importance to the other terms on which he had long insisted.

The capture of the Indiaman Brunswick by European enemies off the coast of Galle appeared to have stiffened the attitude of the Court. Shortly after Pilima Talavuva's son was married to a daughter of Raja Adhiraja Sinha by one of his junior wives;* her status was such that the connection was regarded as violating the customs of the country, while the almost regal ceremonies with which the event was celebrated throughout Yati Nuvara, the chief centre of Pilima Talavuva's authority, appeared to point to loftier ambitions. The King was displeased and banished the son from Court, whereupon it was reported that the Adikar retired in disgust to his house and tore off the cap, which an Adikar alone was entitled to wear.† But North was not to take advantage of these discords, for Thomas Maitland,‡ brother of the Earl of Lauderdale,

* North to Camden, Confidential and Secret, Talai Manar, 4th August, 1805. C.O. 54/18: "not indeed entirely legitimate but of a rank which according to the customs of the country would not have allowed her to marry the son of a simple nobleman, however high in office." Davy (p. 317) appears to refer to this incident as follows . . . "The minister expressed a wish to unite his son to the natural grand-daughter of King Kirtissere" and fixes a much later date. He is followed by Codrington who gives the date as 1811, six years after North's Despatch. Davy is obviously in error.

† No doubt the head-dress of green velvet which the Adikars alone could wear. See D'Oyly's Diary, 18th June, 1811. Ed. by H. W. Codrington, R.A.S., Ceylon, Vol. XXV.

‡ In an Act of 5th April, 1809, Maitland described himself as "The Right Honourable Thomas Maitland, Captain-General and Governor-in-Chief in and over the Island of Ceylon and the Territories and Dependencies thereof." C.O. 54/58.

relieved him of his duties on the 18th of July. "With whom could I treat at any time but with the two Adikars, who have both during five years solicited ineffectually my assistance to depose their Sovereign" he wrote in the bitterness of his heart as he waited at Talai Manar to cross over to India. He was convinced that the King and his Minister regarded him with malignant hatred, and that his effigy, dressed in a uniform of blue and gold, which they pricked with pins and fired at with pop guns, was the constant object of their magic spells.

Whether the avowed antipathy to any idea of territorial expansion contained in North's Despatch of the 26th of November, 1798 addressed to the Secret Committee of the Honourable Company was a candid expression of his views at the time or not, he had by the 25th of December of the following year developed a very different policy of military and financial control of the Sinhalese Kingdom to the stage at which the military assistance needed for its successful execution had to be secured. All this was antecedent to the Avisaha Vella meetings with the Adikar, who was not the only Minister he had in view as a suitable tool. To lay the odium of the conspiracy on Pilima Talavuva, as some writers have done in an attempt to shield North, is to misrepresent facts. Had North's plans been crowned with success, his violation of the rules of conduct observed by men of honour would have been drowned in the plaudits that hailed the Empire Builder; they miscarried, and it was left to another successfully to replace his vision of a Protected State by a more forceful design.

CHAPTER VII

"Abstracted from every Principle of Justice, there does not appear any Principle of Policy which ought to induce Great Britain to wish the entire subjugation of that Island, as the advantages derivable from such a Possession could not be commensurate with the expense of maintaining it ; but when the Principles of Justice are combined with those of Policy (and on all occasions they ought to be inseparable), I feel satisfied that there is no ground for our desiring greatly to extend the territory we acquired by just rights from the Dutch, and that so long as the Court of Candy should have agreed to the peaceable possession of our rightful acquisitions, we ought to have refrained from all encroachments on their limits."*

In these words Earl Camden laid down the lines of policy which Maitland was to pursue, adding that the war had been unnecessarily protracted, and that the sacrifices demanded by North for the restoration of peace were greater than it was expedient to insist upon. Besides reasons of policy and justice the fear of a possible attack by the French on the British East Indian possessions† rendered very desirable an early settlement of the trouble in Ceylon, where their spies were believed to be well organised and acting in concert with the Court. Maitland found military affairs in so chaotic a condition owing to Wemyss'

* Camden to Maitland, 21st Feb., 1805. C.O. 55/62.

† Camdon to Maitland, Secret Despatch, 4th June, 1805. C.O. 54/18.

incapacity and inability to work in harmony with North* that in his opinion the results of a French invasion would be disastrous, and in such an eventuality he planned to abandon Galle after blowing up the fort and to concentrate on Colombo and Tiru Kona Malai.† He was hopeful that the change of Governors would of itself help to restore friendly relations but he would make no immediate advances for fear of encouraging the Court.

His criticism of North's opinions and actions was severe:‡ his political conduct did not appear to be based on any well-grounded opinion as to the party in whom power was vested. No proposition was ever advanced that gave a chance of restoring peace. The military operations of which so much was made resolved themselves into attacks on a couple of advanced posts, in retaliation for which some

* Maitland to Camden, 19th July, 1805. C.O. 54/18. The first part of the Colonial Establishment consisted of a corps of Malays (Champagne's) most of whom had been in the Dutch service. An effort had been made to raise a regiment of Sinhalese (Ramsay's) but this had completely failed as the men were found to be totally unfit and incapable of executing the functions of military duty; consequently it was changed into a regiment of Coast Sepoys. The third corps (Baillie's) consisted of 800 Caffrees from Mozambique, Goa, etc. And finally there were the Lascars from Bengal and Chittagong attached to the Royal Artillery. (Maitland to Castlereagh, 19th Aug., 1808. C.O. 54/29). As to the Sepoys and Malays Maitland thought that they were "of no use as an efficient military force, but useless as they are in this point of view, we still must carry on the appearance of having a certain number of soldiers." (Ditto, 9th March, 1808. C.O. 54/28). Major Mac Nab in his Memorandum of the 27th Jan., 1808 recommended that the Malays and Sepoys should be replaced by Africans "on whom a stronger reliance may be placed than on the capricious Malay or the prejudiced and superstitious Sepoy." As the abolition of the slave trade had closed the supply from Africa he suggested obtaining them from St. Salvador and St. Sebastian with the sanction of the Portuguese Government of Brazil. (C.O. 54/30).

† Maitland to Castlereagh, 9th March, 1808. C.O. 54/28.

‡ Maitland to Camden, 18th Aug., 1805. C.O. 54/18.

miserable huts were burnt and a few cattle driven off.* He could find no reason to believe that the Sinhalese were hard pressed or were anxious for peace, while it was ridiculous to talk of blockading their country. Adopting language which recalled that of the Duke of York and the King of Ceylon he declared that the military operations "if strictly analysed, I much fear, would not be found of a description and character highly favourable to His Majesty's arms." He proposed to commence by demanding the restoration of the prisoners, after which commissioners could be appointed to discuss peace on the basis of the Treaty of 1766. With this object he was communicating with Moratota, employing as his mouthpiece John D'Oyly,† a member of the Civil Service, who had acquired a good knowledge of Sinhalese, instead of the Maha Mudaliyar, for Maitland distrusted the high native officials, and throughout set himself to destroy their influence and power.‡

* On 13th Dec., 1811, Maitland wrote from Bolton Row, London; "I indeed heard on my arrival that it had been a practice in some instances for officers to sell as Prize cattle stated to be captured from the enemy—in my opinion a most improper and unwarrantable proceeding." C.O.54/41.

† For information about him see Letters to Ceylon 1814-1824. Pieris, Heffer, Cambridge, 1938. "One of the best informed and humane men under Government." Maitland to Castlereagh, 25th Jan., 1809. C.O. 54/31.

‡ This attitude is well revealed in his Instructions to Thomas Eden, printed in Notes on Some Sinhalese Families, Pt. iv, pp. 134-139. Also, his instructions to William Montgomery, Agent of Revenue, Jaffnapatam, Encl. to Despatch of 28th Feb., 1807. C.O. 55/25. "From the first hour of my arrival up to the present moment I have ever been of opinion that the wisest measure of Policy that could be adopted was to diminish by every possible means the overgrown authority of the Mudaliyars. Upon this principle I have consistently acted." Maitland to Castlereagh, 25th Jan., 1809. C.O. 54/31.

D'Oyly's letter* with its quaint imitation of the Court diction, deserves to be quoted in full.

" Invested by the Great Supreme King of Great Britain, His Master, with the highest authority both in Civil and Military Affairs, His Excellency the Governor, General Maitland, is arrived in Lankawa. Tho' War has been his habit from early youth, it hath entered into the considerations of His Excellency, whether it were possible to carry into effect the benevolent intentions of the Great Supreme King of Great Britain, His Master, to give peace to all nations after having spread his victories in every region by the valour of his mighty fleets and armies. Therefore, ere he despatches his armed forces into the field, it hath pleased His Excellency the Governor to declare, that if all the English officers and soldiers now resident in the territory of the King of Kandy be restored, then shall negotiations commence in order to open the barriers for the commercial intercourse of the subjects of both Powers, and to conclude a Treaty of Peace, which may endure as long as heaven and earth shall endure.

In many conversations with His Excellency the Governor having learnt these his sentiments, I make known the same to thee, the Chief of Priests and Lover of the World's and Religion's Good, in order that you may communicate them to the Great Gate† in a happy hour."

Moratota replied‡ that the King throughout ardently desired peace with the English and in spite of its violation

* Dated 5th Sept., 1805. Enclosure to Most Secret Despatch. Maitland to Camden, 19th Oct., 1805. C.O. 54/18.

† An erroneous rendering, descended from the Portuguese and Dutch, of the Sinhalese expression usually employed to indicate the King—*Maha Vasala.*

‡ Moratota to D'Oyly, 24th Sept., 1805. Encl. ut supra.

by North regarded with satisfaction the wish of the wise new Governor for its re-establishment; the other matters could be disposed of when this was settled. He continued "In former times when a Governor arrived at Colombo, a suitable *Keydapana** is despatched in a respectful manner to render that event acceptable to the happy lotus-like mind of the Divine Supremely Great King, the Ruler of Tri Sinhala. Ere this takes place it is impossible to think that the subject matter of this secret letter can have stability. Because heretofore there was not a Governor thus wise and just, many persons suffered loss of property and loss of lives. We have thought it a sentiment proceeding from Sense and Wisdom that the present Governor making mutual enquiry, negotiates for peace before the occurrence of such loss of property and loss of lives. If contrary to this hostile acts are committed, we shall make the necessary preparations."

With the best of intentions Maitland failed to appreciate the etiquette of the Sinhalese Court when a newly-appointed official assumed the duties of his post; in his eyes the demand for the submission of a formal *Keydapana* reporting the event was only a proof of "the stupidity of the Candians" who could not understand that the representative alone and not the Government had changed, nor why he, a new-comer, should not begin exactly as if no unfriendly feelings existed.† Moratota was informed that while the Governor was most anxious to show all due respect to the Court in accordance with ancient usage, yet he was prohibited by his Sovereign's express commands as well as the custom of nations from negotiating any

* A missive addressed to or by the King himself.

† Most Secret Despatch ut supra.

Treaty so long as English officers and soldiers were held prisoners in Sinhalese territory. However in proof of his sincerity he was prepared to send an officer with a flag of truce to treat about an exchange of prisoners only: after that was effected peace negotiations could be formally opened.*

The Court, however, was adamant: the establishment of peace must precede the discussion of any other question,† while Maitland was equally firm about the preliminary restoration of prisoners.‡ A condition of stalemate was reached and with a sigh Maitland replied "If it be unsuitable to the dignity of the Illustrious Great Gate, the Happy Ruler of Lanka, to consent to the equitable proposal before communicated, it is also impossible for His Excellency to controvert the commands of his Sovereign and the prevailing customs of all nations. Now though the evil fortune of both prevent the accomplishment of the good he desires, His Excellency is willing at any future period to appoint a proper officer to confer on the matters which are requisite to the establishment of friendship." While thanking Moratota for his pious endeavours for the good of the World he said that he would be happy to recognise them by a present of any rich commodity which the British territory afforded.§ Moratota briefly replied that the ancient practice must be observed|| and was informed that whenever the King's Commissioner fixed a

* D'Oyly to Moratota, 3rd Oct., 1805. Encl. ut supra.

† Moratota to D'Oyly, 24th Oct., 1805. Encl. to Despatch, 13 of 28th Feb., 1806. C.O. 54/21.

‡ D'Oyly to Moratota, 12th Nov., 1805. Moratota to D'Oyly, 23rd Nov., 1805. Encl. ut supra.

§ D'Oyly to Moratota, 15th Jan., 1806.

|| Moratota to D'Oyly, 27th Jan., 1806.

date for his arrival at Sitavaka, a British representative would be sent to discuss terms.*

The position was slightly ridiculous. For all practical purposes everything was as secure as if peace had been signed† and there was no reason to suspect any hostility at Court ; but in view of the feeling which had been excited in England the Cabinet was anxious to be able to announce a formal settlement. North's cruel methods of warfare and the tone of his letters had excited resentment and left an evil heritage to his more scrupulous fellow-countryman, who could not avoid repeating his expression of opinion regarding the former's policy and conduct : "A policy that I hope, however, I may be permitted to say, no thinking or reflecting man could justify, a conduct I am sorry to say very wide indeed of the humanity and moderation which has generally characterised the measures of His Majesty's Government. The effects of such a line of policy and conduct were not to be counteracted in a day, nor was the inevitable hatred and animosity arising out of our conduct to be annihilated by the signature of any parchment."‡ But in view of the peaceable attitude of the Court he also declared " I shall enter into no foolish expeditions. I will not throw away the lives of His Majesty's subjects by disease in burning and destroying the defenceless huts of innocent natives. I will be perfectly satisfied in protecting what is confided to my care."§ He did not feel the smallest degree of satisfaction, he said, in being nominally at war with a so-called Power which to

* D'Oyly to Moratota, 11th Feb.

† Most Secret Despatch, 19th Oct.

‡ Maitland to Camden, 28th Feb., 1806. C.O. 54/21.

§ M. S. D. of 19th Oct.

him was " beneath all contempt "* but he did not hesitate to have recourse to a weapon which, effective with every race, was likely to be peculiarly so in the case of the poverty-stricken Sinhalese. The Gabada Nilame† known to be in great favour with the King, had already accepted British gold and was expected before long to become their tool, and Maitland was confident that " by underhand means and very little money " he would soon obtain a more complete hold over the King's subjects than he could expect to secure by any war.‡

His chief preoccupation was about the release of the prisoners. Davie was the only officer known to be alive though there was also the Dutch soldier Thoen at the Capital who was allowed considerable freedom§ and set to make gun-powder, about which he knew nothing. It was the tradition with Sinhalese Kings to treat captured officers with much consideration,|| chiefly in the hope of enlisting them in their own service, and as Peradeniya had stated the British prisoners had received the King's favour. Davie was kept under close guard at a house near the

* Maitland to Camden, 28th Feb., 1806.

† Pusvelle Rajakaruna Vaidyaratna Attanayaka Sriranga Narayana Bamunu Mudianse.

‡ 22nd Nov., 1805. C.O. 54/18.

§ Talagama Unanse's Report. The renegade Englishman Benson, of the Madras Artillery, who used to swagger about in British uniform with a gold chain around his neck and a silver hilted sword, both given him by the King, had died of a wound received at Hanvella. Thoen's Narrative, appended to "The Wanderer in Ceylon" by T. A. Anderson, London, 1817.

|| When the Dutch garrison of 500 men was captured by Raja Sinha at Pannara in 1645, Saar records that "To the Lieutenant, as a courageous German soldier, he presented a horse, an elephant and a thick gold chain, and he always made him ride by his side, which astonished everyone." Johan Jacob Saar, 1647: tr. by P. Freudenberg, R. A. S. Cey. XI. p. 274.

Palace and in December he was summoned to the Royal presence. One of the Bengal Lascars was sent to shave him, and dressed in the uniform of a British officer with nankeen pantaloons and his old hat, but without shoes, he was led by some officials to where the Sinhalese troops were drawn up in front of the Palace. The King appeared borne in his palanquin about thirty yards from where Davie stood and after being greeted with prostrations spoke in Malabar to a Dissava in attendance and inquired if the captive were in health or in distress. This was passed on by the Dissava in the same language to another of the Indian prisoners who interpreted the message into English for Davie. He replied that by the favour of the King he was in health. The King then expressed his wish that Davie should go and fight for him, to which he answered that if ordered he would do so. He was next told that it would be to Colombo he would have to go, whereupon he explained that if the English caught him, he would be put to death. The King conversed for a time with his officials and sent the Dissava with a gold chain which he put round Davie's neck and also presented him with a sword, some Sinhalese money and silver rupees, after which he was taken back to his lodgings.*

* Evidence of Mohamed Saib of Trichinopoly; Panavula of Bengal; and of Kar Bocus of Batavia, of 5th March, 1805. Encl. to Despatch North to Camden, 6th March. C.O. 54/17. "Pannela Unanse adds that the King has given clothes to the Sepoys. (He) sent for one of the three English officers who were in Candy, gave him many things and two women, and sent him to Doombere where he is well off, and that the two other prisoners are dead: That an officer lately taken in Candy had been cured of his wound. and was doing well." Encl. in Despatch of 11th Jan., 1805. C.O. 54/16., Thoen had heard that Davie received from the King "valuable presents consisting of silver plates, gold and silver chains, a silver hilted sword, different brass articles, etc. The King it was said also gave him three servants and allotted him two women at different times."

He was subsequently transferred to Karaliyadda, fifteen miles from the Capital, and two letters written by him from there have been preserved. They form a pathetic record of the lonely man's despair at the omission of his Government to take effective action for his restoration to liberty, when "with one hundred men (not Malays) I would bid defiance to the whole Kandian force, as long as we had meat to eat." He sent his advice as to the plan to be adopted in case a campaign was undertaken, and for this he considered five hundred men sufficient. He was steadily carrying on pro-British propaganda among the Sinhalese, holding before them the advantages they would receive from that Government, and was confident many sympathisers would be found in case of hostilities.* His place of confinement was frequently changed and the accounts of the Secret Service expenditure† give interesting details of the persistent efforts—occasionally successful in spite of the vigilance of the King's officers—to maintain contact with him. With all his anxiety to re-open negotiations Maitland resolutely declined to send an embassy which he regarded as a mark of humiliation and likely to be represented at Court as an acknowledgment of inferiority ; the stalemate therefore continued and though D'Oyly conveyed a hint to the friendly Gabada Nilame that the difficulty might be overcome by giving the prisoner a chance of escaping, it led to no result.‡

Maitland's revelation of the true state of affairs had been an unpleasant surprise to Downing Street§ but Windham

* Encl. to Despatch of 22nd Nov., 1805 ut supra.

† Encl. Maitland to Windham, 28th Feb., 1807. C.O. 54/25. Twenty-five star pagodas was paid for conveying one letter.

‡ Despatch of 21st May, 1806. C.O. 54/22.

§ George Shee to Maitland, 8th May, 1806. C.O. 55/62.

approved of the attitude which he had taken up* though he remarked that the propriety of adhering to or departing from points of etiquette depended on the particular State one was dealing with, and in the case of the Sinhalese Court expediency was the main consideration.† At last the Governor gave way; he agreed to send the embassy, but in order to uphold prestige demanded that commissioners should first meet at the frontier and settle on the manner in which the ambassador would be received, the mode and time of surrendering the prisoners and general preliminaries. He was met by a curt refusal; ancient procedure must be followed and no variation could be permitted. Maitland, however, persisted‡ on the specious plea that he might be deceived and thus find himself in a worse position than before, but in reality in the expectation of being able to effect Davie's escape by the power of money Valuable presents of horses, dress fabrics, mirrors and similar articles were being given to the Chiefs who were thereby kept not only friendly but in a state of expectation; this was a better investment for the money he thought than sending yearly presents to Court, though he was fain to admit that the procedure was "the most unpleasant that could be adopted." Some persons had undertaken to abduct Davie for a heavy reward but so great was the terror inspired by the possibility of detection and punishment by the King that half way through they abandoned the attempt. Maitland therefore increased the figure to two thousand pounds.§

* William Windham succeeded Viscount Castlereagh on 5th Feb., 1806.

† Despatch No. 4 of 10th May, 1806. C.O. 55/62.

‡ Despatch of 20th Sept., 1806. C.O. 54/22.

§ Despatch of 28th Feb., 1807. C.O. 54/25.

At Downing Street, Castlereagh* was gratified that war had been avoided and a state of neutrality bordering upon peace secured.† Maitland had fully acted up to his Instructions which represented the views of His Majesty's Ministers and was directed to continue the same policy of abstaining from acts of hostility and to show a desire for peace and friendly intercourse "the better to promote the Interest and happiness of their respective subjects." Taking into consideration the climatic difficulties and weighing the benefits likely to accrue from a conquest, no invasion even if successful would compensate for the loss which was inevitable. He concluded his despatch with these words "Upon this view of the subject I trust that the Candian War may be considered as in fact at an end, hostilities having ceased and no disposition, at least on our part, to renew them."‡

But the Court was too strong for Maitland. Davie could not be abducted and he reconciled himself to sending an embassy as the only possible means of rescuing him, though even so he was not confident of success.§ The ambassador was to take costly presents and the only question was as to the nature of his escort. So far as the King and the Ministers in general were concerned there was no doubt about their friendly disposition and an honorary guard would be sufficient to ensure his safety, but the attitude of Pilima Talavuva, from whom no communication had

* Castlereagh succeeded Windham on 25th March, 1807.

† Castlereagh to Maitland, Despatch 1 of 14th April, 1807. C.O. 55/62.

‡ Castlereagh to Maitland, No. 2 of 11th June, 1807. C.O. 55/62.

§ Maitland to Castlereagh, 1st Dec., 1807. C.O. 55/26; and to Windham, 31st Aug., 1807 idem.

yet reached Maitland, had still to be ascertained. A letter was accordingly addressed to him but his reply caused a disagreeable surprise; there would be no difficulty about releasing the prisoners, he said, as soon as the embassy had been conducted in strict accordance with ancient custom, but before amity could be re-established the maritime districts which had been among the subjects dealt with by the unratified treaty must first be restored.*

Maitland emphatically refused to enter into a discussion on this subject: the possessions of the British Sovereign, he said, originally acquired by the valour of his armies from his enemies the Dutch, had since been confirmed to him in perpetual Sovereignty by the Treaty of Amiens. His Majesty had at no time entertained views hostile to the Ruler of Happy Lanka, but just as he had no desire to encroach upon the territory of others, neither could he permit the slightest encroachment upon his own. The embassy could only be proof of the Governor's respect for the Sinhalese King, and of his anxiety to secure peace and tranquillity, and at the same time it would afford the King an opportunity to display his own friendliness by restoring the prisoners; it was ready to start, he said, but first there must be a clear understanding that its mission was limited to these objects.†

The embassy was not sent but relations continued perfectly amicable and the King set at liberty the British prisoners, consisting of about 300 Malays and Sepoys, though he would not release Davie.‡ His fondness for

* Maitland to Castlereagh, 9th March, 1808, and enclosure, Adikar to Maitland, 11th Feb., 1808. C.O. 54/28.

† D'Oyly to Adikar, 23rd Feb., 1808.

‡ Maitland to Cooke, Galle, 27th April, 1809. C.O. 54/35.

horses set the fashion to his courtiers and the Governor was quick to assume control of the supply as also of other foreign luxuries, appreciating its value as a political engine.* Maitland's health, however, had broken down; only the constant use of mercury afforded him relief against "repeated attacks of a bilious complaint"† and on the 15th of March, 1811 he embarked at Colombo on the Grenville which three days later set sail from Galle. Had he borne in mind Windham's advice and recognised what was expedient in dealing with an Oriental Court, his strong feeling for the prestige of his own country would have been less of an obstacle to the usefulness of this English gentleman.

John Wilson now took charge of the administration as Lieutenant-Governor.‡ A close watch was being kept on the Court, for anxiety about French intrigues had not lessened and D'Oyly's Diary throws some light on this obscure period. Pilima Talavuva was still continuing a secret correspondence with him and did not hesitate to express his dissatisfaction with the King on the ground that he was repressing the Chiefs§ and depriving them of their wealth; he was so unpopular, he said, that a nominal

* Maitland to Castlereagh, 25th Jan., 1809. C.O. 54/31.

† Maitland to Liverpool, 15th Dec., 1810. C.O. 54/38.

‡ Wilson to Liverpool, 16th July, 1811. C.O. 54/40.

§ The King always championed the cause of the poor against the oppression of the great. On the 28th Nov., 1817, Hardinge Giffard, Advocate Fiscal, in a letter to his brother-in-law, J. W. Croker, in speaking of the changes brought about by the British occupation, said "The people were not long in discovering that they had made an exchange for the worse. The tyranny of the King had not reached them and it had controlled that of the Headmen, but now they were delivered up to fifty tyrants avaricious, unprincipled and remorseless." This letter has been kindly furnished by Lady Evelyn Giffard.

force was all that would be required to seize his capital. He also revealed the names of the King's agents at Puttalama through whose means he kept up communications with the French and expressed his own disapproval of the attempt to force the British to restore a portion of the coast. He had great faith in the protection of the gods and was convinced that the one sure means by which the British could obtain and hold possession of the country was to win the *beylma* or favour of the gods by rendering worship and honour at their Hatara Dewala. He had also confidence in the efficacy of English medicine and was anxious for liniments with which to alleviate his own bodily pains.

Ehelepola who had succeeded as Uda Gampahe Adikar on Migas Tenna's death in 1808 and who was married to Pilima Talavuva's sister's daughter, was also exchanging messages with D'Oyly. It was therefore hardly surprising that serious internal troubles, of which details are not available, broke out and kept the King fully occupied. Wilson's intervention was solicited from many quarters but he was resolute in his determination to adhere to Maitland's policy of abstaining from every act which might be construed into even an appearance of hostility. Stern action soon re-established a semblance of order ; Pilima Talavuva himself was executed and the same fate awaited several other courtiers ;* Asana, the Mohundiram who was the Chief of the King's Malays, and who had figured prominently in the Davie incident, escaped with sixty compatriots and their families to the British, though

* Wilson to Liverpool, 16th July, 1811. C.O. 54/40.

his brother was killed during the flight. He had throughout been close to the King's person and as his intimate knowledge of the royal places of refuge was considered likely to be of value in certain eventualities, provision was made for his proper maintenance near Negombo.*

* Wilson to Liverpool, 29th Sept., 1811.

CHAPTER VIII

Ehelepola was appointed in Pilima Talavuva's place and rumours of hostile preparations received from all parts of the island were so ominous, that Wilson was apprehensive of a rupture though he was resolved that nothing but an actual attack would induce him to have recourse to measures of force, " the ruinous effects of which, to the inhabitants, the revenue, and every plan and measure of improvement, I am deeply sensible of" he wrote.* Though two of his letters still remained unanswered he was anxious to provide every opportunity for discussing any alleged grievances and on the 29th of September he sent another letter to the King himself. He pointed out how the tension which existed between the two Governments at the time of Maitland's arrival had steadily relaxed in consequence of his just and moderate policy, with the result that unhampered trade had been resumed to the material advantage of every one and there was hope of a friendly understanding being established before long. This happy condition had been recently interrupted by rumours of military activity within the King's dominions, which coupled with the failure to send a reply to Maitland's last letter, rendered inevitable the suspicion that action hostile to the British was in contemplation and obliged him to adopt precautionary measures, including the opening of a military roadway along the boundary from Kalutara to Chilaw.

* Wilson to Liverpool, Jaffnapatam, 11th Sept., 1811.

In his anxiety to prevent his own action being misunderstood, he now earnestly appealed for a frank discussion, solemnly disclaiming in his King's name any aggressive intentions, and promising the fullest explanation of any circumstance which might have been capable of being misunderstood. His Britannic Majesty's power was so overwhelming that the Court would not suggest that his attitude was the result of fear ; on the other hand there was reason for him to believe that the French were striving to avoid that total destruction of their authority in India which was inevitable, by stirring up the Eastern Princes against the British—to their own ultimate ruin, as tragically illustrated by events in the great Empire of Mysore and the death of Tippoo Sultan. The decline of French influence was not confined to India, but was manifest throughout the world. In language which no doubt recalled to the Sinhalese Ministers what the Portuguese had to say about the Hollanders, he declared " In Europe where they are best known they are universally considered as the disturbers of the world and the enemies of all nations, sacrificing the treasures, the people, and the Government of every country where they are admitted to their own unsatiable ambition and rapacity."*

The Court he was convinced " would not hesitate whether to prefer empty promises, a helpless alliance, and ruinous association with people of that description or the friendship of a Monarch equally renowned for his justice and good faith as for his power." If, however, the Court's attitude

* " Subjects and rebels of the King of Portugal, well-known pirates in the whole of India, hated by all Indian Kings and Potentates, and driven out of their lands." Diego de Melo de Castro to Vijayapala, 21st Nov., 1637, Pieris, Portuguese Era, ii, 203.

continued unaltered, it might become necessary to treat it as unfriendly. His Britannic Majesty's European forces were at hand in all parts of the world, and there were also available in his West Indian colonies Caffrees similar to those who formed the two battalions on duty in the Island—"men trained to war, habituated to the woods and indifferent to climate or fatigue"—and, he hinted, His Majesty might consider these the proper troops to employ if an invasion of the Sinhalese territory became necessary. In view of the horror with which these savage black soldiers were regarded in the Island, the threat, scarcely veiled, was a curious piece of guacherie which could not fail to irritate.*

This letter was accompanied by one from D'Oyly to the Adikar who replied to it at great length outlining the historical incidents on which the custom of the Court was founded. Vijayo was the first to colonise the Happy Island of Lanka, after expelling the Yakkho who occupied it and making it a fit residence for human beings. Of the Kings who succeeded him Deveni pe Tissa "a noble Bodhisatva Avatara, bringing relics, painted figures, and images of the Omniscient" established 84,000 religious edifices and endowed them so as to continue for 5,000 years. Later as the island grew in material prosperity the Seydi Demalu landed at Jaffna and by offering presents obtained permission to reside and trade on the sea coast, but after a considerable time they assumed a hostile attitude and by war seized on a few districts till they were destroyed by Dutu Gemunu. After another long interval there followed invasions by Malabars from the Soli Karai which were

* Encl. to Despatch, Wilson to Liverpool, 29th Sept., 1811. C.O. 54/40.

successfully repelled. The prosperity of the country was maintained, as for instance under Kalikala Sahitya Pandita Parakrama Bahu of Polonnaruva, Mahalu Parakrama Bahu of Dambadeniya and Sri Parakrama Bahu of Kottai who sent armies across the seas and imposed tribute on many foreign Rulers. All this was achieved without foreign aid.

When Dharma Parakrama Bahu was reigning at Kottai the Portuguese arrived in Lanka and on offering presents were allowed to remain at Kolon Tota* keeping guard and rendering tribute to the Rulers of Lanka and from there they carried on trade till fired by evil ambitions they in turn made war and seized some territory. But when Raja Sinha succeeded to the throne he destroyed them utterly and since he needed guards at Kolon Tota and other coast towns, he selected from among foreign nations the Dutch people, whom he caused to be brought and placed in charge ; and they continued in obedience and tranquility performing faithfully the services which were imposed on them and yearly presenting offerings and gifts. When Kirti Sri Raja Sinha was King they through evil counsel assumed a hostile attitude whereupon war began and it was decided to replace them by the French. Learning of this the Hollanders made urgent representations that the French should not be trusted and promised to abandon their unwise attitude and to continue to perform the customary duties as of old, and thus enmity was appeased.

Once again in the time of Sri Raja Adhiraja Sinha the Hollanders showed themselves somewhat perverse whereupon English officers and men arrived at Tiru Kona Malai

* The Sinhalese name for Colombo, *tota* meaning port.

and Andrews came as ambassador offering to perform the established services and duties. The Hollanders in consequence wrote a series of letters which were preserved in the royal Archives, vilifying the English and declaring that "good did not happen in any country which was friendly to the English: that the English are people of crooked dispositions, fitted to injure their master, to injure their Friend; that they have seized on many countries by crafty deceit, skilful only in speaking falsehoods." They mentioned the cases of two Rulers who had hired the services of the English and ended by losing their thrones, but this vilification was not allowed to prejudice the King's Ministers. Andrews was received with distinction, his proposals discussed and ambassadors sent to Madras to settle terms; further a promise was made that no assistance would be given to the Hollanders in case of hostilities with the English and this promise was faithfully kept.

D'Oyly's statement of the Governor's desire to maintain friendly relations had caused great satisfaction, but as to his complaint that indications had been noted adverse to Peace and Friendship, the Court too had means of judging how the change had come about, and no doubt D'Oyly could form his own conclusions after studying them. The Court was unable to admit any hostile attitude on its part, whereas the English without proper inquiry had accepted the words of wicked reprobates, and allowed themselves to be dragged into war for which the Court was entirely free from blame. One thing was certain: no foreign foe, be it English, Hollander, French or Caffree, might conquer Lanka, through the protection of the four gods,* the Guardians of its Religion, and the Merit of the King;

* Vishnu, Sumana, Kartika and Vibhisana.

for five thousand years no foe may continue to reside there, and the Governor could ascertain the truth of this from the wiser among the people of the Littoral. He should also reflect on what had happened when last the English attempted an invasion.

Besides this the Governor's *Keydapana* contained certain matters so unbecoming that so far from their being submitted to the King they might not be listened to even by the Adikar ; the copies preserved at Colombo of the *Keydapan* which the Dutch Governors used to send should be consulted to ascertain in what the impropriety consisted. The preliminaries adopted in the case of Andrews' mission for settling the wording of that *Keydapana* and the procedure for its presentation might be studied with advantage, and there would be Mudaliyars in Colombo familiar with the Dutch *Keydapan*. The Court raised no impediment to the establishment of permanent friendly relations ; as soon as the customary embassies were exchanged and the coast districts surrendered the objects which the Governor desired could be accomplished.*

As Wilson pointed out, what the British Government described as friendly presents the Court with its tenacity of forms treated as acts of homage which formed a necessary preliminary to any talk of reconciliation. Though D'Oyly pressed for a reply to the main points of his letter the Adikar would not yield ;† the shortcomings he had

* Dated 27th Nov., 1811. Encl. to Despatch, Wilson to Liverpool, 26th Feb., 1812. C.O. 54/42. In the absence of the original of this valuable exposition of the Sinhalese point of view an attempt has been made to form a co-herent narrative in spite of the deficiencies of D'Oyly's translation.

† Adikar to D'Oyly, dated Batugedera, 8th Feb., 1812, Encl. to Despatch, Wilson to Liverpool, 26th Feb. C.O. 54/42.

indicated, he said, prevented the despatch of an answer. Those demonstrations of respect and honour which the Seydi Demalu had initiated constituted the Customary Prooedure; it had been followed by other foreign nations who came to the Island and was continued unchanged by the Portuguese and Hollanders. It might be all well to speak of these last as "a Company of Traders," but Andrews after careful inquiry adopted their practise both in the form of the *Keydapana* and the manner of its presentation. In times past also enemy Chiefs had been captured in war and their release obtained by proper application made through suitable representations, accompanied by the offering of presents. For instance the Dissava of Colombo* and two other officials had come with gifts on an embassy to Kirti Sri Raja Sinha and obtained the release of the Dissava of Matara who was a prisoner. If ancient custom were observed the same result would follow with regard to the English officers: but the coast districts must also be surrendered.

Meanwhile the endeavours to rescue Davie were not relaxed and Asana himself was sent on a mission to abduct him but was no more successful than the others.† Some of the notes received from the unfortunate man were singularly moving. "Gr. Wilson: O be expeditious in saving me. Is there any question that my wishes are to be released hence without delay—sick unto death. Without money or clothes or food. Please send a little opium and laudanum to alleviate my pains—12 months unable to rise from my mat. A pen knife, a bottle wine, gin, or

* The Company gave this name to its officer at Colombo.

† Wilson to Liverpool, 26th Feb., 1812. C.O. 54/42; also D'Oyly's Diary.

brandy and laudanum." And again "My anguish . . . body is insupportable. I see but imperfectly—My dear friend—no paper—do send laudanum."* "For heaven sake send quickly laudanum and opium my torture is indescribable—also a monthly Army List I wish to know my now rank that I may settle affairs."† His condition was not the result of ill-treatment for he seems to have received much consideration, and besides being provided with servants was even appointed to a post in the Madige department.‡ When a letter from him was intercepted though the messengers were punished yet no blame was attached to him, for the King, who presided at the inquiry which followed, pointed out to his Ministers that under the circumstances Davie's action was a very natural one.§

So friendly were relations in general that at D'Oyly's request Ehelepola sent him botanical specimens from the mysterious forests round Sri Pada,|| a shrine which the former was anxious to visit; he asked for permission for Hooker, the botanist, to conduct a scientific expedition there and sent the Adikar a present of some geese for which he had expressed a wish, promising at the same time

* Laudanum seems to have been a very popular sedative in Europe at this period, and in November, 1811, the Prince Regent took as much as 700 drops a day to relieve the pain caused by an injured ankle.

† Original received through Pannala Unanse, on 6th Jan., 1812. Encl. to Despatch 2, Brownrigg to Liverpool, 29th March, 1812. C.O. 54/43.

‡ D'Oyly, p. 11.

§ D'Oyly p. 92. Another well authenticated instance of the King's kindliness is recorded by Thoen; when captured he was brought before the King who on learning of the sufferings he had undergone remarked "that after all I had suffered no one but God would kill me and that no one should ever do me harm."

|| See Letters to Ceylon, pp. 29, 112.

to obtain from abroad fan-tailed pigeons which also he desired.* The King took much pleasure in his *Kurullan Maduva* or aviary where in addition to birds native to the country there were others which talked various languages, and Ehelepola's offering of a *Rana Girava*, or Golden Parrot, which was purchased at Colombo for a heavy price, gave him great satisfaction.†

D'Oyly was able to secure the good offices of Pusvella Dissava to send Davie a few luxuries like wine and tea, together with some articles of clothing; these were forwarded to the Dissava's brother, the Gabada Nilame, by whom they were first submitted to the King who expressed the opinion that the dried dates were musty and retained four bottles of Madeira for himself. D'Oyly at the same time intimated to the Dissava his anxiety to meet him on the frontier but was told that this could not be arranged without the King's permission, and he was urged in the interests of peace to exert his influence to re-establish the yearly embassies.‡

He had also opened communications with several chiefs of the Adikar's Dissavani, Saparagamuva, and three of the Nilames, Varigama, Elapata and Eknelligoda, showed themselves not only sympathetic, but willing to consider the possibility of a British occupation of their Province.

* Adikar to D'Oyly recd. 18th March, 1812. D'Oyly to Adikar, 22nd March, Encl. in Despatch of 29th March. C.O. 54/42. Though Hooker was mentioned in D'Oyly's letter as already in Colombo, he did not in fact visit Ceylon. The Sinhalese words used for "geese" and "fan-tailed pigeons" were *Pattayo* and *Lakori* respectively.

† D'Oyly's Diary.

‡ D'Oyly to Pusvella, 14th March, 1812. Encl. in Brownrigg to Liverpool, 29th March, 1812. C.O. 54/42. Pusvella to D'Oyly, 29th March. Encl. in Brownrigg to Liverpool, 13th April, 1812. C.O. 54/43.

Ehelepola himself had his headquarters at the Royal Village of Batu Gedera from where he was enforcing various social reforms to which the King attached importance. The use of arrack which was prohibited by the religion of the country, was forbidden ;* and the slaughter of animals as well as the rearing of pigs was discouraged. Measures were introduced to prevent the exposure of infants in the forest, a practice which, along with that of infanticide, was not uncommon especially in the case of female children where the family was considered too large for the parents' means, or the child's planet had been declared unlucky.† At the Capital the construction of the bund of the lake still occupied all the available tenants who were subject to such service. At the same time the King maintained a strict supervision over the administration of his officers and charges of oppression if well established were swiftly followed by dismissal. His kindness of heart was well illustrated by his treatment of the traitor Pilima Talavuva's son who had been banished from Court ; he was sent for and asked what he desired, to which he replied that his only desire was to worship the Danta Datu, the Tooth Relic of the Buddha, which was preserved at the Maligava adjoining the Palace, whereupon the King

* With the British came a change. In the Journal of Brownrigg's Tour round the Kingdom occurs the following :—17th April, 1816. Stopped at Kundasale where I had the pleasure to see a Plan of Mr. Sawers in full Progress of a distillery of Arrack, which he has planned and executed, thus turning one of the King's Gardens to a most important benefit, in saving the carriage of this indispensable article of military supply. Despatch 144 of 5th June, 1816. C.O. 54/60.

† D'Oyly's Diary, pp. 80, 81, 86. The Foundling Hospital of London was incorporated by Royal Charter in 1739 on the petition of Captain Thomas Coram "to prevent the frequent murders of poor miserable children at their birth, and to suppress the inhuman custom of exposing new-born infants to perish in the streets."

appointed him Diyavadaṇa Nilame, in charge of that august shrine , this generosity, however, did not prevent his entering into a treasonable correspondence with D'Oyly and discussing the possibility of deserting to the English.*

Robert Brownrigg, an Irishman from County Wicklow, whose public service had been hitherto exclusively on the military side, relieved Wilson on the 10th of March, 1812 when he arrived in His Majesty's ship Africaine as Governor and Commander-in-Chief, and he did not fail to assure Liverpool of his determination to continue Maitland's pacific policy in his dealings with the Court.† He also sent a *Keydapana* to inform the King of his assumption of duties, expressing his pleasure that it occurred at a time when the friendly intercourse subsisting between the subjects of the two Powers was a happy augury of future tranquility. Its formal establishment, he said, was being delayed only by the unwillingness to release Davie, and he noted with regret that " whilst other powerful Sovereigns of the Earth deem essential to their Glory and the Dignity of their Crowns the immediate restoration of Prisoners, unfortunately captured in War, there should arise in the Breast of Your Majesty just causes for withholding this purest Token of pacific Disposition." He concluded by expressing his hope of the speedy establishment of a steadfast peace, in accordance with the benevolent wishes of his own Master‡ This letter was accompanied by another from D'Oyly in which, referring to the Adikar's letter of the previous February, he announced the Governor's

* D'Oyly, pp. 92, 140.

† Despatch, 29th March, 1812.

‡ Encl. in Despatch, Brownrigg to Liverpool, 12th June, 1812. C.O. 54/43.

readiness to send an Ambassador with the customary presents, if upon that condition alone Davie would be restored : the surrender of territory, however, could not be discussed.*

The Court was sincerely anxious for friendly relations and Pusvella urged D'Oyly to represent the true facts to the new Governor " in order that he may understand both the Fruit of living in Harmony and the disadvantage of living in Discord," at the same time addressing Illangakon, the new Maha Mudaliyar, in the same strain and reminding him that the Mudaliyars were only officials belonging to the Great Household of the Great Gate.† D'Oyly took the opportunity to draw the Dissava's attention to the hopes expressed by the Governor and repeated his wish for a personal meeting at the frontier, protesting that no endeavour would be lacking on the British side to establish that permanent tranquillity which both parties desired.‡

Elapata died in May at the early age of 36 years after recommending his sons to D'Oyly's care ; representing as he did one of the highest families among the Sinhalese, his daughter was intended to be the wife of the Adikar's son, and on his death-bed he entrusted to Ehelepola what was his most cherished possession—the cloth stained with the blood of the black leopard which his ancestor Suriya Bandara, the adopted son of Raja Sinha of Sitavaka, had killed with his spear, a feat for which he had been rewarded

* Enclosure ut supra.

† Pusvella to D'Oyly, 29th June, 1812 ; to Illangakon, 10th July, 1812 ; D'Oyly to Pusvella, 14th July ; Pusvella to D'Oyly, 29th July. Encl. to Despatch 23 of 3rd Nov., 1812. C.O. 54/44.

‡ 10th July, 1812. Encl. to Despatch, 23rd Nov., 1812. C.O. 54/44.

with among others the village of Elapata.* The trust was ill-discharged ; the late Chief had left much wealth and Ehelepola's actions in connection with it, and the alleged torture by the King's officers of the Walauwa Kankanamas in order to force them to disclose concealed treasure, created a serious scandal, Eknelligoda protesting that he would prefer the English to come and take it for themselves.

In June it was announced that the King contemplated an early progress through the Kingdom in order personally to examine the administrative work of his Dissavas, redress grievances and generally place the affairs of the country in order. He had issued regulations intended to stop profiteering at the expense of his subjects ; under these the price of commodities like coconuts, salt and rice was fixed at a moderate figure and everyone who had more grain than was needed to meet his own requirements was compelled to sell the surplus at a fixed rate which was followed at the Royal Stores as well. If traders from the Littoral would not part with their goods at these prices, the King undertook to have stocks available at the Capital. The simplicity of life at the time can well be guaged by the fact that the variety of mangoes known as the Jaffna had never been tasted by the King and an application was made to D'Oyly for a few of the fruit. At the same time the sumptuary laws regarding clothes and the dressing of the hair and beard were more strictly enforced, and the distinctions between the various orders of officials clarified by issuing to them head-dresses of varying shapes. The bund of the lake was at length completed ; a square *Kunda*

* D'Oyly's Diary, p. 108. Pieris, Notes on Some Sinhalese Families, Pt. ii, p. 4.

Salava or Pleasure House was erected on an islet which was approached by a draw-bridge and four boats were also prepared for the diversion of the Royal Household on the beautiful sheet of water which was overlooked by the new eight-sided Patirippuva with its gilded finial, from where the King on occasion showed himself to his assembled subjects.*

* D'Oyly's Diary.

CHAPTER IX

Brownrigg's *Keydapana* led to unexpected repercussions; on the 18th of July a request was received from the Adikar for a cover in which a *talpat* from the Court had been wrapped, and a sealed binding cut out of one of them, as he desired to satisfy himself regarding the manner in which they were bound and sealed.* A reply was sent that in spite of a search specimens of these could not be secured in Colombo.† It was then learned that the *Keydapana* contained variations from all previously received whether from the Hollanders or the English, and that serious exception was taken to these. In every former instance, it was pointed out, three seals of wax‡ were affixed on the top of the paper cover enclosing the *Keydapana*, whereas in the present case the paper on which the message was written was headed with a stamp in gold. In its present form it could not possibly be submitted to the King. Further there was a report that it had not been escorted through Colombo with customary ceremony, and that it was only from Gurubevila that it was conducted with drums. There would be Mudaliyars in Colombo who had

* Adikar to D'Oyly. Encl. *ut Supra.*

† D'Oyly to Adikar, 22nd July, 1812. Encl. *ut Supra.*

‡ On the 2nd of May, 1810, at the Court at the Queen's Palace, the King in Council approved the Draft of a Seal for use in the Settlements in Ceylon as follows :

Obverse.—A view of the Town and Harbour of Trincomalie and a Ship entering with this legend underneath

Usque Auroram et Gangem

and this inscription round the circumference

Sigillum Regionis nostrae in Taprobane

knowledge of the customary procedure and an explanation was needed of these innovations. It was no excuse to plead that the practise which obtained in India had been followed. " The thing which is done in the countries of Dambadiva suits not to be done in this Happy Island of Lanka. Excepting that the Customary things which have continued from antiquity in this country be done without default, it suits not that they become less or greater." The mere despatch of an Embassy with presents would not be sufficient radically to extinguish the present strained relations, and it was good to bear in mind that previous wars had resulted only in the destruction of lives and property and had failed to secure the objects for which they were started.

Reverse.—His Majesty's arms, Crown, Garter, Supporters and motto, with this inscription round the circumference :

Georgius Tertius Dei Gratia Britanniarum Rex, Fidei Defensor.

C.O. 54/39.

On 5th Nov., 1811, the Secretary of State informed Brownrigg that Sir Alexander Johnstone, the Chief Justice, had been entrusted with the Public Seal made for Ceylon, to be delivered to the Governor. C.O. 54/40. On 29th March, 1812, Brownrigg reported to Liverpool that it was received by him and handed over to the custody of the Chief Secretary. C.O. 54/42.

At the inquiry before the Sub-Prize Committee held on 11th March, 1815, Kapuvatta Second Adikar was questioned.

Q.—The King's property being stated by the Adikar as left in the care of his Ministers to be placed in safety, what is the Seal placed upon it by them ?

A.—The Seal of the Treasury with letters round it or a seal bearing the impression of a Lion or Bird, and they always seal his property with one or other of these seals.

Q.—Could any person who is not in authority under the King use any of those seals which you state to be indiscriminately used by his Ministers ?

A.—Yes, with the exception of the Lion. C.O. 54/56.

When in Raja Sinha's time the Hollanders would not yield up certain districts even while they continued to send their embassies, it was the arrival of the French at that Ruler's invitation which forced them to re-establish friendly relations by surrendering what they had seized. Again under Kirti Sri Raja Sinha the resumption of embassies after the war did not settle the difficulty created by a similar grievance, which indeed continued till the final expulsion of the Hollanders. When a written explanation of these various matters, and unambiguous and straightforward proposals for allaying the existing enmity, were received, then a speedy reply would be forwarded to the Governor's *Keydapana.**

D'Oyly hastened to explain that the blazon to which exception was taken reproduced the arms of His Britannic Majesty and was used in accordance with European custom as a mark of special honour. The *Keydapana* he said had been conducted with the ceremonial employed for the last fifteen years, but if importance was attached to the matter, inquiry would be made to ascertain what the ancient Custom was and this would be followed in future.†

* Adikar to D'Oyly, 15th July, 1812. Encl. *ut Supra.*

In October, 1655, Raja Sinha pointed out to the General of the Dutch forces who were laying siege to Colombo on his behalf, that a letter addressed to him had not been wrapped as usual in white linen and that some of his royal titles were omitted, and that these were formalities the omission of which could not be excused even on account of the hurry of war. Later during the siege he returned unread a letter because it was written on half a sheet of paper. In reply to the humble apology which followed he wrote "If the late Director-General (Hulft) allowed the manner and good customs in which I ought to be served, what trouble is it to your honours to imitate him ?"

Pieris : *Portuguese Era,* ii pp. 407, 437.

† D'Oyly to Adikar, 27th July.

At the same time Pusvella wrote in warm appreciation of the sentiments regarding peace which D'Oyly had expressed. He reminded D'Oyly how the faithful and submissive service of a Dutch Governor had been richly rewarded by Vimala Dharma* who conferred a title on him. The Mudaliyars of ancient lineage to be found in the British territories could enlighten him as to what was proper and what was not, and the new Governor by following the Dutchman's example could win even greater favours and higher honour. As to his meeting D'Oyly, such a course would be without precedent and there could be no innovation except with the King's permission. Nevertheless with the re-establishment of the embassies, it might be possible to arrange this as well.†

But the Ministers would not change their attitude: when a *Keydapana* was forwarded in accordance with

* 1687-1707. The reference is to Lourens Pyl, Governor 1680-1692. In 1688 the Dutch Ambassador to the Sinhalese Court, Alebos, was informed "that the Governor will be honoured with a gold ola conferring on him a title of honour and having engraved on it the grant of a province," (R.A.S. xi, 103). According to the translation of the present letter the title conferred was "Governor Unanse, Prince of Love"; what Sinhalese name is concealed in this it is difficult to say. Further Hendrick Becker was appointed by Narendra Sinha in 1716 to be his Privy Councillor. Marchelis Michielssen Boschouwer, who arrived in the island on the 12th Feb., 1612 as envoy from Holland to King Senevirat, was given the town of Migamuva (Negombo) and was consequently known as Migamuve *Maha Rala*, a title which Boschouwer interpreted as *Prince*. (Pieris: Rise of the Dutch Power in Ceylon, p. 43). A further instance was that of Gerard Hulft of Amsterdam, who commanded the Dutch forces at the last siege of Colombo. Raja Sinha by his *Sannas* of March, 1656, appointed him, "the most trusty servant that ever he had in his life," to be Director-General over all his Dominions. (Portuguese Era ii, p. 428).

† Pusvella to D'Oyly, 29th July. Repld. to, 4th Aug.

ancient Custom and its contents were found to satisfy the requirements of the Court, the Principal Chiefs in the Circle of Ministers would submit it to the King, and receiving the Royal commands pronounced in words " ever speaking the truth " on the crown of their heads, communicate them by a *talpat* to the Governor.* Brownrigg on the 19th of October wrote to express his keen disappointment at what seemed the breakdown of negotiations, repeating his previous offer to send an ambassador provided there was a promise to surrender Davie, but firmly indicating that there could be no cession of territory.†

D'Oyly had appealed to Pusvella that his representative might be permitted to see Davie but was told that though any articles intended for him would be forwarded, yet he was kept under such close guard that an interview was out of the question.‡ As rumours of his death were persistent D'Oyly begged that the Court would permit Davie to send a written communication about the state of his health.§ Pusvella replied that the hopes of the resumption of embassies which D'Oyly had held out seemed to be now in the background while his correspondence related solely to Davie and the last contained " many words which cannot be thought, which cannot be told." Where anything had to be submitted to the King, unless the representation satisfied Court requirements he himself would be exposed to danger.|| D'Oyly retorted that the release of Davie was

* Adikar to D'Oyly, 6th Sept. D'Oyly's translation is not easy to follow and Brownrigg appears to have regarded the letter as settling the difficulties which had arisen.

† D'Oyly to Adikar, 19th Oct., 1812.

‡ Pusvella to D'Oyly, 1st Oct., 1812.

§ D'Oyly to Pusvella, 15th Oct., 1812.

|| Pusvella to D'Oyly, 5th Nov., 1812. C.O. 54/47.

intimately connected with the restoration of friendship, whilst it was natural to inquire after the welfare of one who had so many friends in Colombo ; but if no assurance of his being still alive was received they could only infer from the silence that he was no more and lament his untimely fate.*

In the meantime Liverpool had written warmly commending Wilson's policy of non-interference and expressing his confidence that Brownrigg would continue it, as it had the full approval of His Majesty's Government. If through any cause war became unavoidable the sole objective should be the defence of the existing Settlements and not their extension, and once that was effected friendly relations should be re-established at the first opportunity.† Much concern he said was being felt about Davie and the Prince Regent was prepared to acquiesce in any measure short of a renewal of hostilities which might bring about his restoration to his family and country.‡ Brownrigg had little doubt that he was no longer alive but he was also satisfied that the Court harboured no thought of hostilities ; he gave an emphatic assurance that only an actual attack would induce him to deviate from the conciliatory attitude which he had adopted, though it was ominous that in the same breath he expressed the opinion that if the necessary men could be spared from India " the present would be the moment to emancipate the interior of Ceylon from the oppressive rule of the Kandyan King."§

* D'Oyly to Pusvella, 15th Nov., 1812.

† Despatch 11 of 31st March, 1812. C.O. 54/43.

‡ Liverpool to Brownrigg, Despatch 2 of 23rd Jan., 1813. C.O. 54/44.

§ Brownrigg to Liverpool, Secret and Confidential. 23 of 3rd Nov., 1812. C.O. 54/44.

In view of events which were soon to follow what he had to say on the 3rd of November, 1812 regarding the attitude of the Court deserves to be recorded in his own words. "Ever since my having assumed the Government the disposition of the Kandyan Court has had more the appearance of a desire to have a footing of friendship than of a renewal of Hostility and I have had no reason to suspect that such has been at any time in their contemplation. I really believe that they are by no means disposed to be hostile." Maitland in his retirement was still so concerned about the well-being of the Island that he impressed on Downing Street how important it was that Brownrigg should follow the policy of Wilson who refused to interfere with the internal affairs of the Kingdom when appealed to by the Adikar and some of the Dissavas.*

Brownrigg was well aware of the undercurrents which were at work. In December the Adikar was summoned by the King to appear at Court and he started accompanied by the officials of the Saparagamuva Dissavani, among them being Eknelligoda. To Varigama he entrusted his Province with the *Vedibet ge* or powder factory and four *Kodi tuvakku*† or small cannon, emphasizing the need of caution in view of the proximity of the English. Varigama led forward and presented his four children, each of whom offered Ehelepola four gold pagodas ; he conferred on the eldest the office of Mohandiram of the Four Kadavat

* Maitland to Peel, 29th Jan., 1812. C.O. 54/45.

† "Their Artillery is only a sort of Muskets, which stand upon a frame with three Feet, of which the hindmost is broad and shorter than the two foremost; Having no Lead they shoot with Iron Bullets. These Muskets, the Nobility, which serve the King, carry with 'em in fights."

Schweitzer, 1676.

or Guard Posts on the frontiers, and presented gold chains to the others.*

Among the very few acts of permanent value with which the Portuguese administration of the districts held by them in the seventeenth century should be credited was the preparation of the Tombo† or Register of Lands which took the place of the Sinhalese *Lekam Miti;* a copy of the portion dealing with Saparagamuva had been found and the King gave orders to enforce the services as recorded there, though they had long been discontinued. Ehelepola objected to their revival and would not undertake the responsibility unless the representations of the inhabitants affected were first considered by the King, who was stated to have been annoyed at his Minister's attitude.‡

At the end of December a verbal message purporting to come from the Adikar and Pilima Talavuva was received to the effect that they were in danger but were unable to escape to the British and hinting that they would like assistance. The King it would seem had expressed dissatisfaction at the former's actions in Saparagamuva, especially in connection with Elapata's estate. Two months later the King celebrated a *Kara Bendi Mangalya* or Marriage Festival, when according to the custom of his race he married two princesses, sisters, who were little more than children and had been brought from the Coast a year before. and Ehelepola was once again in favour.§ In

* D'Oyly's Diary, p. 149.

† For details see Portuguese Era, ii, 33-94.

‡ Ehelepola to H. M.'s Commissioners of Enquiry, forwarded from Mauritius where he was living in exile, dated 27th Jan., 1827. Ceylon Literary Register, Vol. IV.

§ D'Oyly's Diary, pp. 153, 172.

March, 1813 Brownrigg while suggesting that the failure to acknowledge his letter might be construed as a gesture of contempt which would warrant a demand for an explanation, concurred that he would not be justified in exciting angry discussion of problematical value so long as it was considered sound policy to be at peace with "this strange people." According to his information the King possessed much activity of body and mind* but was taking to spirituous liquors and sensuality; his recent marriage seems to have been the only ground for this last suggestion, which was somewhat out of place in a fervent admirer of the Prince Regent.†

Though perfect tranquillity had now lasted for nine years there were indications that the Governor was flirting with new ideas; "They are so contemptible as a military power that no serious consequences are to be apprehended from any change in their present dormant position" he informed Bathurst in a private and confidential letter on the 15th of March.‡ African slaves were being systematically purchased from the Portuguese on the Malabar Coast to complete two regiments with a normal establishment of 2,200 men, while there was also available another regiment composed exclusively of Malays.§ The spiritual welfare of the former was a cause of anxiety to the Archbishop of

* "He appeared to me to possess a very acute intellect and could penetrate with wonderful precision into the character of others. His mind in some respects was lofty and he could sometimes hold uncommon control over his feelings."—Grenville's Journal 10th Feb., 1816.

† In March, 1812 he was being openly lampooned as a "libertine" and "a corpulent gentleman of 50."

‡ C.O. 54/47.

§ Brownrigg to Liverpool, 25th Jan., 1813. C.O. 54/46.

Goa and it was arranged that Andrew Armour, who had given up his legal practise before the Supreme Court at Colombo to take charge of the Government school known as the Seminary and was employed to teach them English, should instruct them in the Christian religion as well.*

In April the Magistrate at Negombo arrested some British subjects who had broken into the house of a blacksmith within the King's dominions and murdered him and his wife ; evidence against them was available but as the opinion was expressed that the Magistrate had no jurisdiction to deal with the case, Brownrigg directed that the accused should be handed over to the King's officers. A letter was accordingly sent to the Uda Gampahe Adikar, the aged Unambuva, but contrary to the recognised practise the messengers, instead of waiting at the frontier till notice of their arrival was sent and arrangements made for escorting them, entered the King's territory without permission ; on this ground Unambuva after reference to Court refused to accept the letter and the messengers were sent back. It was thereupon forwarded again with a second letter ; the messengers now took the precaution to remain at the Kadavata, till an official arrived to ascertain the errand on which they were come. After a further delay of six days they were summoned to receive the reply which was to the effect that Unambuva had come to that district on other duties and could not accept the letter. The two letters with yet a third were next sent on to Ehelepola in Saparagamuva, but he too declined to receive them pleading that he was engaged on urgent business of the King.

D'Oyly was indignant at these rebuffs ; he had no doubt that Davie was dead and his explanation of the attitude of

* Wilson to Liverpool, 26th Feb., 1812. C.O. 54/42.

the two Adikars appears somewhat unreal; "For when it pleased Providence to snatch from the Tyrant's hands him who was regarded as the Hostage for the obsequiousness of the English Nation and the sole Pledge for the Attainment of his extravagant Demands, it was the next act of a sullen, haughty and unbending mind to reject in its disappointment all further overtures from a Power against which he was conscious of inability to prevail by arms, and must now despair of succeeding by negotiation. Hence the inveterate enmities of the Kandyan Court are more clearly displayed, the Path to Reconciliation has been intercepted, and the Prospect of a cordial Union between the two countries become more remote than ever." Nevertheless he was fain to admit that at no time had there been greater tranquillity, more devotion to the peaceful pursuits of agriculture, or more hopeful prospects of increased trade with the British Settlements. Brownrigg's own indignation at this further gesture of seeming contempt was only repressed, he declared, by his knowledge of "the duty powerfully incumbent on me to abstain from War, not so much with the Kandyan People, as with the pestilential Climate."* But he had information from his contract butcher who in the course of his business had opportunities of mixing with the King's subjects, that there was serious discontent and that several courtiers were anxious for British intervention.

*Brownrigg to Bathurst, 44 of 2nd Aug., 1813. D'Oyly's Report, 26th July; D'Oyly to Unambuva, 3rd June and 19th June; D'Oyly to Ehelepola 5th July. C.O. 54/48.

CHAPTER X

On the 25th of August a letter was received from Ehelepola in which he stated that he was so touched by the account given by a certain Silvestry of D'Oyly's affection for him, that as a personal meeting was impossible he proposed to send his confidential Vidane to discuss matters. Besides he would like "a good handsome small gun with which English gentlemen shoot birds, 4½ spans in length, not heavy, strong, which has not become old by use, good and handsome."* D'Oyly replied that he would try and find a suitable gun, adding that any communication sent through the Vidane would receive attention but that preferably matters of importance should be communicated in writing; he further inquired whether the Minister could not relieve the anxiety regarding the fate of Davie by definite information as to whether he was alive or dead.† The English Chief, Ehelepola replied, was indeed dead;‡ the rest of the letter, no doubt sufficiently cryptic in the original, has perhaps been rendered still more so by D'Oyly's translation, which alone has been preserved.§ Its significance can be judged from the following passage in his reply: "Ourselves also being anxious to promote in the

* Adikar to D'Oyly, received 25th Aug., 1813. C.O. 54/48.

† D'Oyly to Adikar, 27th Aug., 1813. C.O. 54/48. In view of this letter it seems strange that Brownrigg informed Bathurst that the Adikar's suggestion was rejected as being too indefinite, a supposed decision of which the Prince Regent disapproved. Bathurst to Brownrigg, 30th July, 1814. C.O. 55/63.

‡ Appendix G.

§ Adikar to D'Oyly, received 3rd Sept., 1813. C.O. 54/48.

Happy Island of Lanka the Prosperity of the World and Religion, I shall rejoice to receive from you an explicit communication by what means you propose to accomplish that beneficial object."*

That information was long in coming, for so strict was the surveillance maintained within the Kingdom that even Brownrigg's elaborate system of espionage was baffled; the rumours of disaffection were persistent but it was nearly impossible to ascertain the real views of any important Chief. At last Ehelepola revealed himself and his letter was frankly treasonable. "Before also we wrote many times because we could not support the Hardship which is come upon our country. We thought indeed that succour might be obtained for it, even from these Places. To that, however, we have not had occasion of learning an explicit answer. Since it is so, without thinking that our Inclination is doubtful, if we should learn even thus an explicit word, it is good. Now Women, Men and all other Persons residing on this side of the limits are disaffected to the Great Gate who governs our Country. If it be said, for what cause ? the Wrongs and Injustices which at this time have befallen the World are not things which it is possible to finish relating. If you have a desire for our Country it is good that anything which is done be done without delaying."†

D'Oyly's reply was non-committal : it was the nature of the British Nation, he said, to sympathise in the wrongs and oppressions inflicted on the world, but in the attempt to relieve them it was necessary to proceed without violat-

* D'Oyly to Adikar, 6th Sept.

† Adikar to D'Oyly, received 31st Jan., 1814. C.O. 54/51.

ing the principles of Moderation and Justice which ever prevail in its Councils. So long as the Adikar continued to hold the sentiments which he had expressed, his Government would sincerely desire to strengthen the bonds of mutual friendship, and to co-operate with him in promoting by just means the prosperity and welfare of all the inhabitants of the Island.*

Ehelepola understood from this letter that the English were in sympathy with him and no doubt it was intended to create that impression in his mind.† D'Oyly with skilfully ambiguous language had introduced the pretext of a possible commercial treaty and this was not calculated to make Ehelepola change his view.‡ Brownrigg now asked for instructions about the policy he was to adopt, for he expected developments which would not admit of indifference or neutrality; but while again protesting that he would act only " on the most obvious and cogent expediency " he also expressed the opinion, obviously the fruit of his secret hopes, that the recent attitude of the Court " did away every reasonable expectation that without a radical change in the Government of that Kingdom, any Commercial Treaty or more intimate connection can be established between the two countries."§

On the 2nd of March Eknelligoda Kodituvakku|| Nilame appeared with a confidential message from Ehelepola and

* D'Oyly to Adikar, 8th Feb., 1814. C.O. 54/51.

† Adikar to D'Oyly, received 24th Feb.

‡ D'Oyly to Adikar, 28th Feb.

§ Brownrigg to Bathurst, 68 of 10th Feb., 1814. C.O. 54/51.

|| Eknelligoda was born in 1783. *Kodi tuvakku*, Jingals, the small guns mounted on a wooden carriage with three feet: also known as " grasshoppers."

had two interviews with D'Oyly. He began by complaining of the wrongs inflicted by the King and when asked to be more precise, mentioned the additional duty recently imposed by him on all rice fields. Pressed further he exclaimed "If he plunder, if he murder, what other injustice is there ? Ever since he came to the Throne, the people have been suffering these things." Since the trouble of 1811 the Adikar had known that he was under suspicion and his spies at Court kept him well informed of any views expressed by the King. He now felt that he was in danger and if summoned to Court was determined not to go. Satara Korale, Udu Nuvara and Yati Nuvara were disaffected ; his emissary, a priest, was sounding the Chiefs of Sat Korale. Uva was at the moment doubtful. He asked for British assistance because he was confident that as soon as it was known that he was marching on the Capital with such support, the entire country would declare for him. If, however, it was considered preferable the British could restrict their activities to the occupation of Saparagamuva alone.

D'Oyly replied that the English could not act unless there was unequivocal proof of a general wish on the part of the people, for they wanted not conquest but peaceful friendship and commercial intercourse. Military action was out of the question until it was established beyond doubt that the people withdrew their allegiance from their King and sought refuge under British protection. As for occupying Saparagamuva that again would depend on the manifestation of a popular desire. "The British Nation" he said "will ever be ready to contribute Relief to a distressed People, as far as may be consistent with Propriety and Justice. But under the present circumstances, having no such grounds of action, and especially at a season when the rains are fast approaching, it cannot voluntarily and without provocation enter upon hostile operations." The Adikar, however, could be assured that a secure asylum was always available for him within British territory.*

Brownrigg was absent at Aripo in the desolate neighbourhood of the Pearl Fishery where Frederic North somewhat incongruously immortalised his hellenism in a Greek mansion with a Doric colonnade, from the roof of which the Governor could watch of an evening the pearling fleet as it hastened landwards with its cargo of living oysters. He wrote to D'Oyly that he had so much confidence in the correctness of his judgment and the maturity of his experience that he was ready to be guided by his advice at this crisis ; he himself, as a soldier, would see that timely precautions were taken to profit by circumstances as they arose.† In fact it was D'Oyly who represented the British side in the ensuing melodrama.

In reporting events to Bathurst the Governor while stressing the desirability of obtaining possession of the whole Island and the gratification which the attainment of this object during his administration would cause him, once again protested against any suspicion of aggressive intentions on his part, repeating that he would abstain from any act likely to create alarm, so long as no danger threatened His Majesty's possessions ; but he pointed out that the time was not far distant when the Chiefs would either openly resist "the oppressions of their Malabar

* Report by D'Oyly. Encl. to Despatch 71, dated Aripo, 20th March, 1814. C.O. 54/52.

† Brownrigg to D'Oyly, Aripo, 17th March, 1814. C.O. 54/52.

King " or seek British protection, and he was anxiously awaiting instructions for his guidance.*

Ehelepola was gratified with the result of Eknelligoda's mission and to satisfy D'Oyly regarding the disposition of the various provinces he forwarded three *talpat* from influential personages which he thought would sufficiently indicate the feelings of their inhabitants and which also revealed the fact that the removal of the members of his family who remained at the Capital as hostages for his loyalty, out of reach of danger, was being planned.† But in the light of North's experience D'Oyly was cautious, for it might well be that the Minister was acting with the King's knowledge, and he recommended a non-committal answer as before.‡ Ehelèpola understood the reason for the hesitation and to encourage the Governor he wrote to him a parable : " As any person wearing flowers does not cease wearing flowers again because the flowers which he wore two or three times have faded, this matter should be taken well into consideration."§

The King, however, was very well informed and by the 2nd of April, D'Oyly heard the rumour that in consequence of the discovery of Ehelepola's intrigues he would shortly be replaced in Saparagamuva by a new Dissava.|| Ehelepola

* Brownrigg to Bathurst, Despatch 71, dated Government House, Aripo, 20th March, 1814. C.O. 54/51.

† The letters were from Kattapitiye Vidane, Aturupane Mohottala, and Bambaradeniye Liyana Rala. C.O. 54/52.

‡ D'Oyly to Brownrigg, 23rd March ; Brownrigg to D'Oyly, Aripo, 28th March. C.O. 54/52.

§ Adikar to D'Oyly, received 22nd March, 1814. Also Eknelligoda to Hevagam Korale Mudaliyar, 23rd March ; D'Oyly to Adikar, 25th March ; Adikar to D'Oyly, received 28th April. C.O. 54/52.

|| D'Oyly to Brownrigg, 3rd April, 1814. C.O. 54/52.

also sent word that only his anxiety about his family was delaying action, but under any circumstances disturbances would break out within twelve days of the New Year, and if the British failed to assist at the start the Chiefs might object to surrendering Saparagamuva ; as matters stood all they had to do was to come and take possession, but they must maintain inviolate the established religion ; he therefore asked for an unambiguous declaration of their attitude. D'Oyly, however, did not think that the people had sufficient confidence in their own strength to rise without either an impulse from Colombo or some violent action on the King's part which would leave no alternative to armed resistance.* It was true that at Nivitigala† his officers were resisted and the royal granary plundered, but the Chiefs were hourly expecting the arrival of an armed force to arrest them and anxiously asked for a stock of ammunition ; this D'Oyly did not consider it desirable to supply till there was an open rupture with the King, though under certain circumstances arrangements might be made, he thought, for a secret source from which it could be furnished. He salved his conscience with the remark that the King's rejection of the British overtures rendered good faith unnecessary and that only motives of prudence need be taken into consideration. A rumour reached him at the same time that the Adikar in consultation with the Sapara-

* D'Oyly to Brownrigg, 4th April.

† D'Oyly to Brownrigg, 9th April. This great Gabadagama along with various other lands had been granted by Kirti·Sri Raja Sinha's sannas of 5th Nov., 1768 to Edirimanne Wijeratne Dissanayaka Mudaliyar of the Guard at Galle, who had deserted to the King during the war with the Dutch. On the Mudaliyar's death the lands were resumed by the Crown. See Colonial Secretary's Letters Received, Vol. 521. Colombo Record Office.

gamuva Chiefs had submitted a protest not only against the new levy but also against the Dissavani people being called upon to transport areka nuts from the King's stores to the river, a *Raja karia* or service to which the tenants of the Royal villages alone were liable.*

Brownrigg was greatly excited : were he free to follow his inclinations, he declared, he would not hesitate to strain every nerve to secure the whole Island for the British Dominion, but he was aware that the British public regarded the prospect of another Ceylon war with horror, and as his military resources were also insufficient he determined to wait and watch.†

On the 27th Ehelepola received secret news that his Dissavanis were transferred to Molligoda Nilame, on which with the approval of the Chiefs he made an appeal to the people, who promised him their support.‡ Eknelligoda was immediately despatched towards Korala Tuna§ and another chief towards Uva to stir up the inhabitants and guard the two sides of the province, and on the night of the 30th of April a *talpat* from Ehelepola and the Saparagamuva Chiefs reached D'Oyly. They inferred they said that no definite reply had been received to previous communications through doubt about the reliability of the offers they contained, but the time had come when there could be no further hesitation ; if they were informed when a British force would arrive at Sitavaka, all the levies of the Dissavani would be there to join them.||

* D'Oyly to Brownrigg, 29th April.

† Brownrigg to D'Oyly, Trincomalee, 18th April.

‡ D'Oyly to Brownrigg, 1st May.

§ Tuna, three; *anglice*, The Three Korales.

|| Adikar to D'Oyly, received 30th April, 1814. C.O. 54/52.

Another *talpat* arrived the next day : " On account verily of things prevailing in the World called the Custom of the World, when Fear and Danger have come upon any Person he procures assistance, strength and forces from a Place possessing Power" it said. The British were known to have rendered such aid to others and their help was now urgently needed to save the lives of the inhabitants who were willing to surrender that province.* Ehelepola also expressed surprise that at such a critical time D'Oyly should broach a new subject, a commercial treaty.† The reply to this was disheartening : no explicit answer was possible till the Governor's return to Colombo, but the Adikar could rest assured of his own unalterable friendship.‡

Eknelligoda urged the Hevagam Korale Mudaliyar§ to use all his influence to persuade D'Oyly to take active steps, explaining that Ehelepola's plan was to collect the men of Korala Tuna and move into the Uda Rata where the two Nuvaras were expected to join his standard, when he would be able to surround the " enemy." Even fifty British soldiers would be welcome ; they would receive pay and provisions and compensation would be given for all casualties, while a small stock of English powder, foreign flints, leaden bullets and cartridges, to be kept with Eknelligoda himself, was greatly needed.|| Ehelepola followed with pressing requests for even twenty Malays. The rebels were moving by way of Batu Gedera, Kuruvita and

* Adikar to D'Oyly, received 1st May.

† Adikar to D'Oyly, received 2nd May, at 10 p.m.

‡ D'Oyly to Adikar, 3rd May.

§ Balthazzar de Livera Wijewikrama Seneviratna, see Sinhalese Families, Pt. III.

|| Eknelligoda to Hevagam Korale Mudaliyar, 3rd May.

Panavala towards Ruvan Ella but Eknelligoda sent word that the position was desperate and if it came to the worst they would all cross into British territory. His countrymen, he said, were wanting in enthusiasm and not easily stirred by the sight of Sinhalese fighting men alone, whereas a few men in military uniform, even if they were not soldiers, would make an appeal to their imagination.* D'Oyly realised that a better chance for reducing the entire Island could hardly be expected, for undoubtedly there was disaffection and Ehelepola's authority and influence were such that a great part of the country would be on his side ; Saparagamuva was waiting to be occupied and Korala Tuna would submit without a struggle ; but he would take no responsibility without the Governor's express order.†

Molligoda had been appointed Adikar in Ehelepola's place and was expected any day with the armed forces of Hatara Korale.‡ Eknelligoda from Atulugama sent an entreaty for even twenty-five men : he had with him about 500 followers of whom nearly 400 were armed with guns but Molligoda was bringing some of the King's professional Malabar troops, of whom the Sinhalese stood in great fear ;

By whatsoever means, by whatsoever Contrivances or

* Ehelepola to D'Oyly, received 6th May ; D'Oyly to Ehelepola, 7th May ; D'Oyly to Brownrigg, 6th May ; Eknelligoda to Hevagam Korale Mudaliyar, 7th May. C.O. 54/52.

† D'Oyly to Brownrigg, 8th May. The difficulty of keeping in touch with the Governor by messenger will be appreciated from Brownrigg's statement of his attempt to accelerate public communications by establishing "one simple Rule, the Conveyance throughout the Island being by foot messenger, that the Progress of the post should be three miles per hour, including every stoppage." Brownrigg to Liverpool, No. 17, dated Trincomalee, 17th Sept., 1812. C.O. 54/44.

‡ Hatara, Four; *anglice*, The Four Korales.

Device, you must send fifty soldiers with equipment to meet us near Palangomuva Vatta* where we are staying, within two days of the sight of this. If it be true that there is affection, friendship, favour, towards all the People small and great, and to me and to Maha Nilame,† you must send them immediately." When Ehelepola joined them, he said, it would be possible to capture the King himself.‡

This appeal was supported by a letter signed by several Chiefs of Korala Tuna§ and was followed by one from Ehelepola "who before held the Great Dissavani of Saparagamuva and Pallegampahe Maha Adikaram Nilame" and other Chiefs, offering to surrender the banners, guns, arms and records of the Dissavani, and to render obedience to the British Government ; if that were not sufficient they were prepared to cross into British territory.|| Close on this came the offer of a lakh of money¶ for the services of 300 soldiers but D'Oyly's reply was the same as before.** Ehelepola was due to arrive shortly and D'Oyly was invited to be near the frontier to discuss matters with him ; Molligoda's army was steadily advancing, which would be an excuse for moving a British force in the same direction,†† and he therefore decided to go in person towards Hanvella.‡‡

* One of the King's gardens (*vatta*) near Ruvan Ella.

† A form of address employed for an Adikar.

‡ Eknelligoda to D'Oyly, received 10th May; D'Oyly to Brownrigg, 10th May.

§ To D'Oyly, received 11th May.

|| To D'Oyly, received 11th May.

¶ Ehelepola to D'Oyly, received 11th May. The coin contemplated was probably the silver *ridi* or *larin*.

** 12th May.

†† D'Oyly to Brownrigg, 12th May, 1814. C.O. 54/52.

‡‡ D'Oyly to Brownrigg, 13th May.

On the 14th news was received that Ehelepola was at Navugas Vatta, half a mile from the border, and that provisions for his household had been sent to the house of a Moorman at Galapita Madama within British territory.* On the following evening it was known that the King's forces were confronting the rebels and Ehelepola's baggage and elephant had crossed the frontier. At five o'clock two hundred men of his escort, with jingals and muskets, crossed the river while be boarded a *pada*, one of the large flat-bottomed boats used for the transport of goods on the river, and there he spent the night.†

On the 17th a deputation from him, led by Delgoda Atapattu Nilame and Eknelligoda, waited on D'Oyly. They complained that the King had failed to support their religion, appropriated two villages which from ancient times had been dedicated to the Dalada Maligava, imprisoned priests, destroyed their principal families and committed other acts of injustice of which a list could be supplied if desired. They had been driven into armed resistance but their efforts so far had failed and they implored military aid. They were ready to surrender their Dissavanis and if required would immediately hand over the records and Insignia of Saparagamuva ; they further explained what men and material were at their disposal. Molligoda had invited them to state their grievances promising them redress, but they declined to send a spokesman as a previous one had been imprisoned.

In accordance with Brownrigg's instructions D'Oyly questioned them closely about their prospects and resources‡

* D'Oyly to Brownrigg, 14th May.

† D'Oyly to Brownrigg, dated Hanvella, 15th and 16th May.

‡ D'Oyly to Brownrigg, 17th May. Brownrigg to D'Oyly, Batticaloa, 8th May.

but declined to send a British detachment to the frontier, as they earnestly pressed him to do. It was true that Brownrigg had ordered Major Kelly with 250 men to Avisaha Vella but this was only intended to "give countenance" to the rebels who, he said, must be made to fight their own battle though once actual fighting began they might be supplied with ammunition, which he suggested might be sent unofficially in charge of the Malay Mohundiram ; no open assistance however was to be given at least till Ehelepola had supplied the fullest details of his own resources as well as the King's. That Ruler he pointed out could have no cause for complaint so long as the movements of the British were confined to their own territory.*

The possibilities of the situation were great, but circumspection was essential. "All my hopes and wishes are naturally for its success, but I strongly feel that in order to warrant the future measures of Government, it is necessary that we should not appear to have been the fomentors of it, but that the work has been the genuine act of the oppressed people who in their struggle to rid themselves from the Rule of a Tyrant, call for our aid," he wrote to D'Oyly.† Indeed in eloquent language he had urged Earl Moira, the Governor-General, for "support and assistance in availing myself of opportunities which the existing crisis cannot fail to present of securing public advantages at all times ardently desired which it has hitherto baffled every endeavour whether of negotiation or arms to attain."‡ If the inevitable delay in taking effective action consequent

* Brownrigg to D'Oyly, Batticaloa, 8th May; Karrenkodativoo, 10th May ; Pierea Panaga, 12th May.

† Brownrigg to D'Oyly, Yalle, 14th May.

‡ Brownrigg to Moira, 11th May.

on his own absence rendered it impossible to take full advantage of the present opportunity, it should be suggested to the Adikar that he might base his calculations on what he knew was the disposition of the British and shape his measures accordingly.*

It was soon found that D'Oyly was under a misapprehension as to Brownrigg's instructions to the military and that more overt action would be justified ; a detachment was therefore hurried to the river which formed the boundary and the widest publicity was given to this movement. Molligoda with the bulk of his men had by this time turned towards Saparagamuva whereupon Eknelligoda followed him threatening his rear† while Ehelepola took up his quarters at Marambe Valauva, close to the frontier. In D'Oyly's eyes he was already " a man of fallen fortune " though Eknelligoda's men had set out " like men devoted to death."‡ Ehelepola consulted D'Oyly regarding his further course of action, obviously hoping that even at the eleventh hour the English would champion his cause ; § on Brownrigg's instructions he was informed that in the absence of a manifestation of unanimous feeling from the Chiefs and people the British Government would not be justified in commencing hostilities with the King|| and a definite refusal of military assistance was communicated to him ; it was his evil fortune, Ehelepola remarked, that his attempt which would have been of such great benefit to the British, had failed : as help was not forthcoming

* Brownrigg to D'Oyly, 14th May.

† D'Oyly to Brownrigg, Hanvella, 18th May.

‡ D'Oyly to Brownrigg, Kosgama Alut Ambalama, 19th May.

§ D'Oyly to Brownrigg, 20th May.

|| Brownrigg to D'Oyly, 21st May.

nothing was to be gained by staying where he was and he would meet D'Oyly wherever he desired.

D'Oyly was waiting for a reply to his last message when at midnight on the 23rd of May news was brought that Ehelepola had already crossed the frontier in his palanquin,* and one and a half hours later he appeared near the Rest-house at Avisaha Vella. D'Oyly advanced a hundred yards to meet him and ceremoniously conducted him within, where for two hours they sat, conversing at intervals on indifferent topics. Such was the etiquette of the Sinhalese Court.† He at last referred to himself; fortune he said had prevented his accomplishing what he had planned. On a former occasion the British had sustained much loss but their ambition might now be achieved with little expense and a small army. He had no object in going back without a military force, for he had lost his honours, family and property, and brought with him nothing but his life. He asked D'Oyly to accept his elephant as a present as he had no further use for it, but the offer was courteously declined on the plea that he would still have need of it for the proper maintenance of his dignity.‡

Ehelepola's removal to a safe distance from the frontier was the first consideration and D'Oyly arranged that he should stay at the house of the Vidane Arachchi of Kosgama, the only suitable residence in the Udukaha Pattu, and to this he agreed. The following day the two Dissave Mohottalas, Eknelligoda and Dolosvela, arrived, travelling

* D'Oyly to Brownrigg, Sitawaka, 21st, 22nd and 23rd May.

† Cf., the incidents of Prince Vijaya Pala's flight to the Portuguese: Ribeiro, Historic Tragedy of Ceilao, tr. Pieris, 3rd edition, p. 132.

‡ D'Oyly to Brownrigg, 24th May.

by way of Idangoda ; their plan for attacking the royal forces near Batu Gedera had failed as their followers had deserted. They brought with them the cane, encased in silver and curved at the top, which Ehelepola had received at his King's hand as the insignia of his great office, and had left concealed at Kuruvita ; Saparagamuva was now free of the insurgents.*

Under the ancient Hindu law a subject found guilty of instigating wild tribes or enemies against the King or of creating disaffection within his strongholds or in his army, could be punished by being burnt at the stake, though this was regarded as an extreme measure which should only be employed where the offenders were responsible for acts of special savagery.† The punishment for treason under Sinhalese law was well known and has been placed on record by authorities whose competency cannot be disputed, in the following words: "A law was also in existence by which it was decreed that when a King demanded the assistance of his Chieftains who held their possessions by Feudal Tenure, and they appeared remiss in their exertions or traitorous in their intentions, that not only the unfortunate man was doomed to expire by the most horrid and lingering of deaths (impaling alive) but also the whole of his family, his wives, his children, his nearest and tenderest connections, were doomed to suffer with him. even in his presence."‡

* D'Oyly to Brownrigg, 24th May, 1814. C.O. 54/52.

† Kautilya's Arthasastra, tr. by R. Shamasastry, Mysore, 1923, para. 229, p. 277.

‡ Pilima Talavuva, Mattamagoda, and others banished to Mauritius. Petition to the Prince Regent. Encl. to Governor Barnes' Despatch 28 of 18th Aug., 1820. C.O. 54/77.

Ehelepola well appreciated the risk to which by his traitorous acts he was exposing his family and before taking his irrevocable step had discussed the question with D'Oyly, minimising the danger in the light of the fact that the punishment of an innocent family was almost without precedent,* for in practise the death penalty was imposed only in the case of culprits of the highest status and then it was carried out by the sword. But Ehelepola's offence was of a peculiarly aggravated nature ; his immediate predecessor's fate had failed to teach its lesson and twice before the King's clemency had saved him from the death which by his offences he had merited. Now he had placed himself beyond reach of his Master's power, and abandoned his hostages, and the Law was that they must bear the penalty. His blood was attainted and could not be permitted to infect the race any further and the King pronounced the terrible sentence that his family was to be wiped out. The children, one said to have been an infant in arms, were put to the sword, and their bodies dragged through the streets to be thrown away, for burial was denied to those suffering capital punishment. Their mother, with three others, were led by female palace slaves to the brink of the lake at Bogambara, where their hands and feet were bound and a large stone secured round the neck of each, after which they were thrown into the water, the method of execution adopted in the very rare cases where a King of Ceylon sentenced a woman to death: they were spared the more terrible punishment of being consigned to the Rodiyas, the untouchables who according to the social scheme of the

* Ehelepola to Commissioners of Enquiry.

Sinhalese, were considered the vilest of the human race.*

At the Solemnity of the Investiture of a Sinhalese King with the Sword of State representatives of the three castes poured water on his head exhorting him to rule in accordance with the Ten Royal Virtues, but at the same time imprecating a curse on him should he be found wanting—he was the source of Justice, which he had to administer to his subjects according to Law without affection or ill-will, ignorance or fear,† and to that ideal Sri Vikrama continued steadfastly loyal. "The Kandyan laws are well known . . . Did I make those laws?"‡ That is Sri Vikrama's answer to the malignant libels of interested traducers.

* On 23rd May, the report reached D'Oyly that Ehelepola's wife, four children and nephew had been put to death "on Saturday or Sunday sennight." D'Oyly to Brownrigg, C.O. 54/52. Brownrigg wrote to Bathurst (87 of 31st Dec., 1814) "Nor is death even by torture the whole punishment which tyranny inflicts on its victims. The policy of a barbarous Court has a further provision against the possibility that a family of respectable connection might revive from the misfortune of losing its parent by delivering the females to degradation with men of the vilest and most despised condition." C.O. 54/53. See Appendix H.

† *Chanda, Dosa, Moha* and *Baya.*

‡ Granville's Journal.

CHAPTER XI

The King displayed no resentment against the English for their share in the outbreak beyond sending them a word of caution against placing reliance on traitors. This was contained in a letter which on the 24th of May, de Livera Mudaliyar received from the Korala Tune Dissava, advising the British when considering Ehelepola's overtures to bear in mind what had been the result of following the advice of runaways and traitors in the past. The British he said were notorious for creating dissension wherever they went. In their Settlements they had imposed new levies—even earthen pots had not escaped their greed—interfered with the supply of salt, artificially raised the price of pagodas and rupees, and substituted bits of paper for metal coin : indeed a sick man might no longer choose for himself the stick with which to support his steps.* In the time of Raja Sinha the Mudaliyars of the Littoral served the Great Gate with much fidelity as at the battle of Daladagan Wila,† but their power was now destroyed. Of old the Royal Ministers had waged war against foreign countries with their Sinhalese troops alone ; today only deceitful letters were received from the British : " there is nothing in the straight road productive of benefit to both parties " : that is why their letters were returned unread and correspondence with them had ceased. As for dispraise from

* The reference is to the Joy Tax imposed by North (1st April, 1800) on the wearing of ornaments " of Gold, Silver or other metal, Stone, Pearl, Ivory, Glass, Coral, Chank or Bone " which resulted in serious rioting throughout various parts of the country.

† When the Portuguese under Diego de Melo de Castro were destroyed in 1638. See The Portuguese Era, vol. ii., ch. x.

the mouth of an evil man, the Irshi* had said " the great Earth cannot support such an injurer of his Master"; the English would be well advised to avoid risk of injury to themselves on account of one who had injured his Master as the dismissed Adikar had done.†

The time for concealing Brownrigg's real views was over and he openly expressed his conviction " of the expediency of reducing this hostile and annoying power " whenever a good opportunity presented itself, though he professed that he would not allow himself to be drawn into a conflict which promised anything less than " an easy, certain and decisively important accession to the tranquillity, the revenue and general resources, as well as the secure possession of His Majesty's Colony."‡ An efficient tool was available in Ehelepola who was minutely cross-examined by D'Oyly about the King's military and financial resources, the hiding places of his treasure, his lines of retreat in case of invasion, the means of provisioning an army on the field, and the plan of campaign which he recommended—all matters of which no other Minister could have the same knowledge.§ Though this was information which Brownrigg had frequently urged D'Oyly to secure, he was still so nervous about the views of Downing Street that he laboured to dissociate himself from any connection ; it was quite

* Analogous to a " prophet " among the ancient Jews.

† C.O. 54/52. This warning the King repeated at a later date in the following words: " Ha, you had better take care of that man : he has betrayed me who was a father to him and will some day deceive you too. His soul is a compound of ingratitude and ambition . . . I twice gave him his life when he ought to have forfeited it to the laws of his country." Granville's Journal, 1st Feb., 1816.

‡ Despatch 75 of 28th June, 1814. C.O. 54/51.

§ Appendix I.

natural, he wrote, that this subject should have first presented itself to D'Oyly's mind, but it had no reference to his own plans and the incident was entirely casual with regard to himself.*

Ehelepola and his followers further submitted a memorial setting out their views; the Sinhalese had ever adored their King as a god, the treasures of the Great Gate were kept in secret places in charge of hereditary Chiefs and the Kings did not concern themselves with their safe custody, and that custom was maintained under the Malabar Rulers brought from Tondi, but a change had now occurred. The proclamations broadcast by North throughout the Kingdom had roused the people to a consciousness of the wickedness of the present Ruler; he had put to death not only seventy-three Chiefs but their relations, friends and servants as well. The few who had escaped were determined to hand over to the British that which they had once unsuccessfully attempted to acquire, together with the accumulated treasure of generations.†

Meanwhile the purging of the country after the recent outbreak of treason was continuing; executions were numerous and many were seeking shelter in British territory. Bathurst sent orders to afford every facility for the settlement of those whom the temporary convulsions within the kingdom or its general system of government drove out of their country, in those districts where the labouring population was insufficient.‡ Brownrigg was preparing his ground: he could not foresee, he said, how long the

* Despatch 76 of 16th Aug., 1814. C.O. 54/52.

† Address to D'Oyly. Encl. in Brownrigg to Goulburn, 5th Sept., 1814. C.O. 54/53.

‡ Despatch No. 18 of 10th May, 1815. C.O. 55/63.

violence of the Court would be borne by a people " who have no principle of union amongst themselves, no feeling of civil rights, nor under any circumstances the least idea of a common cause."*

The frontier was kept jealously guarded but in spite of this in August two bands of men from Mahara, an ancient royal village eight miles from Colombo, succeeded in penetrating within the King's dominions by a secret path in the guise of pedlars till they were detected and arrested in Sat Korale, a district which as the result of propaganda from Colombo had recently displayed signs of unrest, culminating in the execution of some of the chief inhabitants. After a preliminary inquiry the prisoners were sent on to the Capital, where they were formally tried on a charge of espionage on behalf of Ehelepola, before the *Maha Naduwa*, the highest judicial tribunal under the King. One of the Adikars presided at the assembly, which was held at a spot where four roads met ; with him were associated about twelve of the principal Chiefs, who were attended by several Mohottiyars and other officers. They formed one side of a square, while nearly 800 armed men occupied the other three. Questions were addressed to the accused through the medium of two Mohottiyars after which it was announced that they were found guilty and sentence was pronounced on them to the effect that one arm and ear and the nose of each accused should be cut off, and the arm hung round the offender's neck.†

Mutilation was once a well-recognised punishment in Europe and in mediaeval times included flaying alive and

* Despatch of 5th Sept.

† D'Oyly to Brownrigg, 30th Oct., 1814. Encl. to Despatch 86 of 30th Oct., 1814.

pulling out the eyes ; in England by an Act of Henry VIII striking in the King's Court was punishable with the loss of the right hand, and mutilation was frequently practised under the Stuarts, as well as by the officials of the Portuguese administration in Ceylon.* Among the Sinhalese robbing the King's treasury or striking a Chief might be punished by the loss of a hand or a finger, but for forty years this kind of punishment had been out of use, except when the noses and ears of some of Muddu Svami s followers were cut off. But now the very existence of the country was obviously at stake and no legal sentence could be too severe, and by Hindu law unauthorised entry within a fort was punishable with death.† A nice distinction was however maintained in the present case ; the guilt of those who entered the country first was the greater, and they would lose their right arm and ear, and the others the left.

The Chiefs forming the tribunal were responsible for the sentences being carried out, and they adjourned to the place of execution, another similar spot situated a short

* In 1630 Dr. Leighton who was convicted of vituperating against the bishops in a book which he published, was sentenced by the Star Chamber to be degraded from the ministry, fined £10,000, pilloried, whipped and branded on the face, after which one ear was to be cut off and one side of his nose slit. After a few days in prison he was to be pilloried again, further whipped, have the second ear cut off and the other side of the nose slit, and then remitted to prison for the remainder of his life. (R. Hist. Soc. Trans., series 4, vol. xxi, p. 120 in article by H. E. I. Phillips). Of that distinguished warrior, Gaspar de Figueira, the son of a Portuguese father by a Sinhalese mother, Knox has recorded "He would hang up the people by their heels and split them down the middle. Smaller malefactors he was merciful to, cutting off only their right hands. Several whom he hath so served are yet living, whom I have seen."

† Kautilya's Arthasastra, p. 275.

distance away. A cauldron was brought and a mixture of resin, jak milk, kekuna gum, coconut oil, and other ingredients, was heated in it. The Gahala Gambadayo, who were the executioners, seized each convicted person in turn, and stretching him out on his face, pressed him down by treading on his joints, hips and neck. The arms were extended in front of the head and a plank laid under one, which was held by two men, whilst a third cut it off at the elbow with an adze, as well as the ear and nose with a sharp knife. The bleeding stump was immediately anointed with the hot mixture and the severed limb hung from the neck by a cord. All this did not occupy half an hour. The prisoners were then made to cry out " After this punishment we will never again cross the frontier," and ordered to proceed to Colombo and show the severed limbs to the late Adikar.* Seven of the men were said to have died† as the result of the punishment, while the three survivors were escorted to the frontier by different routes.

Brownrigg in a lengthy despatch to Bathurst vigorously defended his Government against any suspicion of complicity in the alleged mission of the men ; he could only see in the punishment meted out to them " a wanton, arbitrary and barbarous piece of cruelty"‡ intended as a deliberate

* Evidence recorded by D'Oyly, 24th and 26th Oct., 1814. C.O. 54/53. Appendix J. The three survivors and the families of the seven others were provided with pensions by Brownrigg; see Accounts, C.O. 54/70.

† Appendix K.

‡ King on 17th Feb., 1816. " They came as spies and suffered as such. The Kandyan laws are well known. There was sufficient evidence to prove they intended harm, and they were punished in consequence." Granville's Journal.

The infliction of extreme human pain with little or no justification was frequent among the local English community, who as Brownrigg

insult to the British Government—the intention being unequivocally proved in his opinion by the men being sent back with the limbs hung round their necks. The public, he declared, were entitled to an explanation of the failure immediately to resent the insult. He abstained from recommending retaliatory measures, but was convinced that it would not be long before the security of the British possessions and the advantages of peaceful trade which the King's subjects desired, would have to be exacted from the King and his Councillors by the sword. Prompt action, he insisted, was needed to place relations on a footing of permanent security and he was only restraining himself till the views of the Prince Regent could reach him, but he was unable to say how long that restraint would last, for he felt that the King was now emboldened to take hostile action. He would therefore sedulously prepare for an eventual expedition.

The position, he pointed out, was very different from what it was in 1803 ; Sat Korale would join the British with alacrity and so would Saparagamuva, while Tun

indignantly remarked "regarded this with little interest as not particularly uncommon." A glaring case was that of Lieut. Dobbin of the 19th Regiment who suspecting his Sinhalese servant Daniel Appu of stealing some money, "caused him to be confined and afterwards to undergo repeated floggings with a cat o' nine tails by a Drummer of the Regiment both on his bare back and breach until the man was in such a state as to be obliged to be removed to the Regimental Hospital, and this with a view of extorting confession." Brownrigg pointed out that "such illegal and revolting proceedings which are in defiance of all law, highly repugnant to British feelings, and when exercised by an officer, degrading to the military character" and ordered Dobbin to be tried by the Civil Courts which found him guilty and sentenced him to six months' imprisonment. Brownrigg to Liverpool, No. 8, dated King's House, 29th May, 1812. C.O. 54/43.

and Hatara Korales would not be long in following. The Sinhalese generally were very friendly disposed and the influx of refugees had greatly facilitated pro-British propaganda amongst them. It would he thought be easy to get rid of the hostile Malabars, who were responsible for maintaining a correspondence with the other Europeans in India. Once this was effected he would feel bound to listen to any proposals advanced by the King for terminating the war, but he frankly admitted that he would not regret if its conclusion resulted in " the final emancipation of the Sinhalese from a dominion foreign and unnatural and tyrannically severe " and place them under the immediate protection of the British. He had already communicated with the Indian authorities and received from them the promise of 2,500 Sepoys when needed.* Like Frederic North, whom he rivalled in his ability to write specious despatches, he made the useful reservation that restraint would be exercised only so long as British dignity and territory were not jeopardised.

The Secretary of State replied to this on the 10th of May, 1815.† The Prince Regent he said appreciated the Governor's feelings and realised the advantages likely to accrue by putting an end to the King's authority, but he definitely forbad all hostilities not only under the existing circumstances but under any provocation short of actual invasion. War would mean heavy mortality from sickness among the European troops and an increase of expenditure quite beyond the Colony's resources. The policy of forbearance hitherto adopted was most in the real interest of the British ; if by any misfortune hostilities

* Brownrigg to Bathurst, 86 of 30th Oct., 1814. C.O. 54/53.

† Bathurst to Brownrigg, 19 of 10th May, 1815. C.O. 55/63.

had started before the arrival of these instructions, the earliest steps must be taken to bring them to a conclusion not dishonourable to His Majesty's arms.

On the 31st of December Brownrigg forwarded his version of the occurrences since the date of his last despatch. He had heard that Malabar troops were steadily making their way within the Kingdom, and that military movements were on foot there, though he admitted that these might be merely precautionary Many inhabitants of Sat Korale and Saparagamuva had been summoned to the Capital in connection with a festival, and strange tales were put in circulation about great pits which were waiting to receive their dead bodies. It was noised about that the inhabitants would all be removed into Uva and Malabars substituted in their place, and there was further the terrible threat that their women would be cast to the Rhodiyas. A similar summons was received in Korala Tuna calling on two men and two women from each family to attend at the festival, with an additional man to wait on the Dissava, and on the wake of this came an appeal for British protection and a *talpat* from the Dissava of the province, the younger brother of Molligoda, inviting Ehelepola to join them.

This was in November, and there was reason to believe that the new Adikar himself was in sympathy ; Brownrigg had therefore applied for the promised Sepoys while D'Oyly was sent to the frontier and on the 1st of December met the rebel Dissava and his supporters, who announced their revolt from their King and asked for help. On learning of this outbreak the King ordered Molligoda to take charge of his brother's Dissavani and he was reported to be collecting the Hatara Korale levies for that purpose, but a message was sent to him to join the rebels, backed by another from Ehelepola himself. An answer was received from him that he had been reprimanded by the King for his inaction, and that although he was anxious to join he could not do so as his relatives were in the King's power; he therefore desired to be taken prisoner. Ehelepola was satisfied that the loyalty of Hatara Korale was a mere pretence; some small bodies of men sent by the King to Saparagamuva were driven away by the inhabitants but Sat Korale still remained quiet.

Brownrigg said that he had so far refused to assist with soldiers, but arms and ammunition in small quantities were being supplied. He was also maintaining a close correspondence with all the disaffected Chiefs, and this had established, to use his words, "a kind of common cause and a feeling that if the dictates of political prudence should recommend the resolution of abandoning them to their fate, it must at the same time be reconciled to give up that principle of public generosity which forms so distinguishing a feature in British policy." Obviously he was the master-mind behind Ehelepola who had organised the entire conspiracy, and of whose influence, intelligence, knowledge and uncommon energy, the Governor was very appreciative: it was now possible, he was told, to take possession of the entire kingdom on the spontaneous invitation of the mass of the people at the cost of very little exertion against a Court which would command no support. Ehelepola offered to take the field in person and carry out everything with Sinhalese troops, provided he was given the moral support of a British force. Brownrigg said he had exercised the utmost restraint and carefully watched the proceedings of the Court and reached the conclusion that the mutilation of the British subjects was a deliberate act of defiance indicative of the King's confidence in his ability to challenge the British power.

He professed to be in a serious dilemma, for his instructions had been framed to meet an entirely different state of affairs and made no provision for the present political situation. If he followed these instructions it would be only in order to avoid the personal responsibility which he would incur by acting on his conviction of what the honour and advantage of his country demanded. Such a consideration was unworthy, and therefore he had determined to act under the novel circumstances according to the best lights with which it had pleased the Almighty to endow him. In reaching this decision he was also influenced by the realisation that unorganised villagers could not withstand the Royal power till instructions were received from Europe, and once they were reduced into submission they would not again contemplate negotiation with the British. Moreover the policy of forbearance was coupled with full liberty to resist aggression, and in his opinion the mutilation of the traders was ample aggression. Finally the change which had occurred since his instructions were framed were not nice or slight, but " a radical, essential and substantial change of relation, moral, political and military." It was no longer a question of reducing a people by force, but of accepting their voluntary submission; not of territory acquired and held by the sword, but of willing subjects and spontaneous revenue. Past attempts he said were directed against a King supported by a devoted people, and success could not have been anticipated unless a force of at least 10,000 men were employed ; today the army could with confidence expect to march unopposed to its destination, and in three months a British *talpat* would be obeyed in every part of the kingdom. He concluded this remarkable piece of special pleading by announcing that according to his arrangements the expedition would start by the middle of January.*

The plan of campaign was based on Ehelepola's advice. Two corps from Colombo were to advance to Ganetenna; two from Galle by way of Katuvana and Kataragama, into Uva; one from Tiru Kona Malai to Nalanda and a second to Meda Maha Nuvara, the usual place of refuge to which the Queens and treasure were reported to have been already sent; a seventh from Batticaloa also to Meda Maha Nuvara, while the expected Indian contingent was destined to occupy Sat Korale from Migamuva; at the last moment the despatch of these last was countermanded and the local plans were varied accordingly. The objective was to seize all the commanding points which encircled the bason known as the Kanda Uda Rata, at locations where the climatic conditions would not adversely affect the health of the troops.†

D'Oyly was on the frontier watching developments. On the second of January the Royal forces occupied Ruvan Ella and drove the insurgents across the river till on the 9th they crossed into British territory. A chance of striking a critical blow by wedging the King's forces between the insurgents and the British was anticipated and plans were laid to attack them in case they crossed the Sitavaka river on their expected advance into Saparagamuva, but D'Oyly sent word that they had followed the refugees within British territory, adding that they had also plundered a house.

This was the "aggression" that Brownrigg had waited for and on the 10th his Council "with sentiments of cordiality"

* Brownrigg to Bathurst, 87 of 31st Dec., 1814. C.O. 54/53.

† Encl. to Despatch 87.

agreed to the proclamation of hostilities. The British army promptly crossed the river and Molligoda after a show of resistance drew back allowing them to occupy Ruvan Ella where Brownrigg himself arrived on the 12th.* Three days later D'Oyly received a message from Molligoda, ostensibly engaged in erecting batteries to check the British advance, stating that as the people of Saparagamuva and Korala Tuna had been saved by their action, he desired to know in what manner Hatara Korala and himself could also be saved. D'Oyly replied that his only chance of salvation was to join the invaders and suggested a meeting. Molligoda immediately sent a *talpat* approving of the suggestion, and D'Oyly in replying declared that the British army had come solely with the object of securing the prosperity of the Happy Island of Lanka by removing the calamities which had befallen the World and Religion, and no hostility was contemplated against the Chiefs and the people; if Molligoda decided to follow his brother's example, D'Oyly was at the frontiers of Hatara Korala and would receive and conduct him in the customary respectful manner.†

To enable the Adikar to keep up appearances a feint attack on him was organised, with all precautions against

* Despatch 88 of 16th Jan., 1815. C.O. 54/55.

† Molligoda to D'Oyly; D'Oyly to Molligoda. Encl. in D'Oyly to Brownrigg, dated Mattamagoda, 16th Jan. C.O. 54/55. A matter to which in accordance with Sinhalese etiquette, the utmost importance was attached. In 1816 the Dissava of Uva visited Colombo and on his return journey by way of Matara and Katu Vana, he wrote to Sutherland while on the road from Veligama, "The two days of my stay at Galle . . . with respect to articles of provision provided and attention paid to us, there was no deficiency. Having tom-tom and flags and other honours with me, I walked in the Fort and saw the streets and was delighted with the views." Tr. Kandy Office, 8th Oct., 1816, C.O. 54/61.

the possibility of any injury being caused and due notice to him so as to forewarn his followers.* But the safety of his family had still to be considered; the British, he sent word, must approach the Capital so as to compel the King to withdraw and till then he himself with his army would fall back before them, maintaining the pretence of resistance. In accordance with this arrangement Balane, Girihagama and Gala Gedera were soon occupied by the invaders, and on the 6th of February Brownrigg joined them at Gane Tenna. Two days later Molligoda appeared there in state accompanied by the Chiefs of his Dissavani, and handed over its insignia, including the Great Flag with the blazon of the Sun and Moon, as well as the records. In the interval his family had been safely removed from the Capital.

Ehelepola now advanced to the chief seat of his former authority, Udu Nuvara, and in order to reassure the people of Hatara Korala, Saparagamuva and Korala Tuna against any fear of being abandoned by the British, a proclamation annexing these districts was issued on the 11th. The same day it was announced that Major Hook's division had reached Katugas Tota and that the King had fled, and this was followed the next morning by the news that the batteries commanding the Gannoruva Ford were abandoned, whereupon D'Oyly with a division entered the silent capital ; the inhabitants had disappeared, and only empty chests, baskets, and old mats were left behind. On the 14th Brownrigg, who with his Staff had spent the previous night in the King's granary between Gannoruva and the Capital, went into occupation of the Palace.

The King was reported to be in Dumbara and the British forces were so arranged as to cut off all chance of escape

* Brownrigg to D'Oyly, 17th Jan., 1815. C.O. 54/55.

from there, while Ehelepola was invited to carry out his promise to raise the people of that district. He started with D'Oyly and a military force, and on the evening of the 18th the King's hiding place was discovered at the house of an Arachchi at Galleyhe Vatta, and a vivid account of what followed has been preserved by D. V. A. Dias, a Sinhalese from the British Settlements who acted as interpreter to the English officers.*

Eknelligoda at the head of his men approached the house; the doors were closed and an Appuhami† of the *Setepena ge* or Bed Chamber, was on guard outside, spear in hand. He challenged Eknelligoda, whom he recognised, and followed the challenge with a spear-thrust aimed with such force that as Eknelligoda avoided the blow, the weapon was shivered to fragments against a stone. The Appuhami was immediately seized and hustled away and Eknelligoda walking up to the door called on the King with whom were two of the Queens, to open it; this he would not do although he replied to him, and handed out three silver-mounted guns and two daggers through a small opening. Nor did he produce the Golden Sword, the emblem of his

* Published in Sinhala Sanghrawa of April, 1861. Re-published in Sarasavi Sandaresa of 17th May, 4th June and 26th July, 1895; see also article by T. B. Pohath, R.A.S., Ceylon, vol. xiv. p. 107. The name of the writer appears in the second publication in Sinhalese as Don V. Dias and is quoted by Mr. Pohath from the first publication (to which I was unable to refer) as D. V. A. Dias. As the same Sinhalese letter reproduces the English V and W, it is hardly open to doubt that the writer was Don William Adrian Dias Bandaranayaka, who was one of the three Mohundirams of the Gate in 1819, in which year he was presented with a gold chain and medal by Brownrigg, at the same time as the Second Maha Mudaliyar, Eknelligoda, and others. *Gazette*, 5 June, 1819.

† Forty-eight such, sons of Chiefs, formed the guard in immediate attendance upon the King at the Palace

Kingship, though a demand was made for it. The door was therefore battered down and the men rushed in and a disgusting scene followed as the golden ornaments and the very clothes were torn off the persons of the royal captives, to each of whom a piece of cloth four cubits in length was tossed back to form their only covering.

Dias from outside shouted to the Queens to come out; he spoke in Tamil, addressing them by the respectful term *Ammayarum.* They came out reeling pitifully from side to side—"like fowls whose necks had been twisted" was Dias' graphic description*—and clung to him on either side in an agony of terror, crying out "Oh, protect us." Blood was streaming from the lobes of their ears which had been lacerated in tearing away their ear-rings, and crushing some medicinal leaves he stanched the bleeding. In the meanwhile Eknelligoda was reviling the King in the coarsest terms and ordering his men to fetch some wild creepers with which to bind him like a pig and drag him out. Dias could not restrain his indignation; "Your people" he hotly protested "up to this hour worshipped the King as father and god, but mine have long been under foreign governments and are not expected to show him the same reverence. All that is needed is his safe custody; why then insult, injure and bind him?" at the same time offering his own shawl if it was considered necessary to secure his limbs. Eknelligoda angrily retorted that his advice was not wanted; on his orders

*"The inhabitants have a queer way of killing fowls; they seize them by the head and twist it so quickly between two fingers that the head remains in their hands, whilst the body is thrown off, and runs about for a while until it bleeds to death and falls down."
Johan Jacobs Saar, 1647. tr. by P. Freudenberg, R. A. S. Cey., vol. xi. p. 243.

the King was tightly bound, and as he was unable to walk he was dragged and pushed along and thrown on the ground.

Dias, extricating his hands with difficulty from the grasp of the Queens, took pencil and paper from his pocket, and using the back of one of his companions as a table scribbled a hasty note to inform D'Oyly of what was taking place and entreating him to come at once with palanquins and clothes. Within a *peya*—the Sinhalese hour of twenty-four minutes—some officers and soldiers galloped to the spot. There lay the King, his large intensely black and piercing eyes shadowed with the physical pain which also showed itself in his singularly handsome features, though there was no expression of fear. The officers threw themselves from their horses and after uncovering, knelt before him and unfastened his bonds, while the troops with their whips drove away the Saparagamuva men to a distance. His beautifully formed limbs, massive in keeping with his height of six feet, and his delicate hands and feet, characteristic of the high-born Eastern, were covered with bruises to which, lowering the commanding voice which his subjects knew so well, he drew attention with the words "Is that the way to treat a King?" The grandeur and distinction of his presence did not abandon him even at this pitiful moment. As he complained of thirst some Madeira and water was offered to him and diluted claret to the Queens, all of whom gratefully accepted the refreshment. Palanquins now appeared with such clothes as could be hastily collected: the Royal Personages were robed in white and entered the former, the King before doing so turning to Dias with the words "Son, the English will doubtless put me to death but not the Queens.

ask you to take charge of them and protect them."*

The two chief officers† mounted their chargers and with drawn swords took their station on either side of the King's palanquin, the English soldiers, horse and foot, marched in front and rear, while Dias and his friends followed. Eknelligoda's mob was kept at a distance; and in this fashion Sri Vikrama Raja Sinha started on his last journey through his kingdom. All the members of the Royal Family were soon in British hands and on the 6th of March the King and the four Queens arrived at Colombo,‡ from where they were later transferred to the Fort of Vellore.

A Bulletin of Intelligence published by His Excellency's command on the 19th of February announced that "Devout thanks are due to the Supreme Disposer of events, who has enabled His Majesty's forces in this Colony in the short space of forty days, without the loss of a single individual, to overturn a tyrannical Government, which for several generations has oppressed the people of the interior Provinces in the Island of Ceylon." On a later occasion he generously admitted Ehelepola's "share in the late expedition, of which the success and in a great degree the

* Granville gives the only trustworthy account of the King's person, and he mentions that he spoke Sinhalese less fluently than Malabar. Journal, 13th Feb., 1816. The King's usual costume was only a white cloth edged with gold which was wrapped round the waist, the end being sometimes thrown over the left shoulder. Granville (21st Feb.) has preserved details of the King's elaborate costume, including vari-coloured satin trousers, when he landed at Madras.

† To one of these officers, Major Hook, who was appointed to command the King's escort, a ring was presented by the King, which is now exhibited at the Kandy Museum.

‡ Brownrigg to Bathurst, No. 95, British Head Quarters, Kandy, 25th Feb., 1815. C.O. 54/55.

origin, is known to have depended on him,"* as well as the services of "one of Ehelepola's most confidential, active and useful adherents, named Eknelligoda Nilame, under whose immediate conduct the King was arrested."† It could not be denied he said, that as a military feat the expedition was trivial, but he warmly insisted that it would be the height of injustice to estimate what the army would have done had the occasion demanded it, by the inadequacy of the opportunities for displaying its valour which presented themselves;‡ and Bathurst under the inspiration of the Governor's Despatches, while expressing his lively satisfaction at the liberation of the Sinhalese "from a foreign despotism as sanguinary and cruel as that under which the inhabitants of Kandy so long groaned," and recognising the additional security thereby obtained for the Settlements as the fruit of Brownrigg's wise policy, promptitude and vigour, placed on record his obligations to the army, though he said he realised that the nature of the hostilities did not "afford any opportunity for the display of their more splendid military qualities."§

At 4 p.m. on the second of March a Conference was held at the Magul Maduva, the Hall of Audience where the King had received Macdowal twelve years before. The British troops were drawn up in front of it, and as Ehelepola entered, first and alone, he was received by Brownrigg with much distinction and invited to sit down in a chair on his right hand. He was followed by Molligoda, who introduced the principal Chiefs, the Governor and Ehelepola standing up to receive them and remaining standing

* Despatch 169 of 5th Nov., 1816. C.O. 54/61.

† Despatch 129 of 9th Feb., 1816. C.O. 54/59.

‡ Despatch No. 95.

§ Bathurst to Brownrigg, 30 of 28th Aug. 1815. C.O. 55/63.

throughout the proceedings, in spite of the gout to which the former was a victim. After exchanging compliments a Treaty which had been prepared was read and explained to them ; by its terms the country was ceded to the British Crown, subject among other conditions to an undertaking to maintain the Religion and Customary Laws of the Sinhalese. To this the Chiefs gave their assent, after which they moved to the entrance of the Maduva, from where it was next explained to the assembled people.* The British flag was then hoisted for the first ti e at Senkadagala and British cannon announced that Sri Vikrama Raja Sinha had been replaced by George the Third, while Brownrigg's son hastened to England to lay the Lion Flag of Tri Sinhala at the feet of the Prince Regent.†

* The Convention was actually signed on the 10th of March by which time fair copies in duplicate had been prepared. *Gazette*, 15th March, 1815. The signatories, in addition to Brownrigg, were—

Ehelepola
Molligoda, First Adikar
Pilima Talawuwa. Second Adikar

and the following Dissavas :—

Pilima Talawuwa, Four Korales
Monarawila, Uva
Ratwatta, Matale
Molligoda, Three Korales
Dullewa, Walapane
Millewa, Welassa
Galagama, Tamankaduwa
Galagoda, Nuwara Kalawiya.

The signatures were witnessed by—

J. D'Oyly, Chief Translator to Government
James Sutherland, Deputy Secretary to Government.

A contemporary copy, certified by James Sutherland as Secretary to the Kandyan Provinces, is to be found in the volume "Letters and Proclamations, 1815." C.R.O.

† Despatch No. 95.

APPENDICES

APPENDIX A.

The two Pilima Talavuva Adikars

Sir A. C. Lawrie, in his Gazetteer of the Central Province of Ceylon (Colombo 1896, 1898), Vol. II, p. 728, has the following under *Pilimatalawwa* . . . " Pilima Talawwe, Dissave of Four Korales in 1769 A.D. and Pallegampaha Adigar in 1773. He died about 1783 leaving two sons and a daughter. The elder son, the Adigar Pilima Talawwe, was the greatest man in the Kandyan country at the end of the last and the beginning of this century. He was beheaded in 1812."

Mr. H. W. Codrington, in the "Pedigree of Pilima Talawuwe" attached to his edition of Sir John D'Oyly's Diary (Royal Asiatic Society, Ceylon Br. 1917) agrees with this and represents Pilima Talawuwe Wijayasundara Mudiyanse, First Adikar 1778-1784, as the father of P. T. Wijayasundara Rajakaruna Seneviratna Abhayakon Pandita Mudiyanse, First Adikar, exec. 1811.

Both these writers appear to be in error, for in Boyd's Report to North of his conversation with the second Pilima Talavuva at Avisaha Vella on the 6th of January, 1800, he puts the following words into the latter's mouth:—" that his brother who had been Adigar about 19 years ago had by his influence put a Prince on the Throne of the Malabar race, and about two years ago in the midst of civil discord he (the Adigar) had placed the present monarch on the Throne although he had no legal pretensions to it." Secret Diary, Colombo Record Office.

APPENDIX B.

List of Presents taken by Macdowal

For the King:

Cases

1–3	A glass temple.
4–18	Bengal sugar.
19	A coach.
20	Harness.
21–27	Coach
	3 (5?) horses.

28 21 ells gold cloth.
29 21 ells silver cloth.
30 2 pieces gingham.
31 5 pieces dariase.
32 5 pieces Bengal cloth.

For the First Adikar:

A gold betel box.
A kris.
A horse.

For the Second Adikar:

A piece gold cloth.
A horse.

For 2 Dissavas:

12 pieces gold cloth.
2 pieces plain white cloth.

For the Maha Mohottiar:

6 cubits gold cloth.
A piece white cloth:

For 4 Mohottiars and 4 Rate Ralas:

18 pieces muslin.

For 8 Mohundirams:

8 pieces muslin.

The gold betel box intended for the First Adikar was probably the " betel dish with ornaments of solid gold which had belonged to the late Tippo Sultan and was valued at eight hundred star pagodas " mentioned by Percival (Account of the Island of Ceylon, 2nd Ed., 1805, p. 385).

APPENDIX C.

The King and the Priesthood

The following documents are from copies found among Sir Alexander Johnstone's papers :—

No date, watermark 1805.

To His Excellency

The Right Honourable Thomas Maitland,

Governor of Ceylon, etc., etc.

The humble petition of Caretote Damma raume Naikey Teroon-nansey humbly sheweth

That the petitioner with the highest veneration begs leave to represent to Your Excellency.

That now about twenty-eight years ago the then King of Candy granted to the petitioner the three villages called Pallebedde, Baliwinne and Raume naikeygame, belonging to Candy, in order that the petitioner may enjoy the produce deriving thereby which may be about 1,000 rds. per year, and the petitioner continued to furnish with victuals and clothing to the ten or twelve desiples or priests to whom the petitioner taught Cingalese law.

That now the petitioner has been entered into the British Government's behalf and obtain salary from the same which having been reached to the knowledge of the present King of Candy, prohibited the petitioner from enjoying the said produce of the said three villages, and on that account the petitioner is unable to supply with food and clothing to the said priests as formerly.

Whereupon the petitioner very reverently and highest esteemably prays that Your Excellency will be kindly deign to take all of this matter into serious consideration and increas his batta in order that he may pass his time without any distress and in which case the petitioner will pray for your Excellency's prosperity and also himself will pass with the greatest pleasure without any disconsolate.

For which great favour and indulgence the petitioner with the sincerest thankfulness as in duty bound will ever pray . . .

No date, watermark 1802.

Petition to

The Hon'ble Thomas Maitland.

The humble petition of the Chief Priest Mahagoda Indesara sheweth

That your petitioner takes the liberty to inform your Excellency that the petitioner was appointed as Chief Priest over all the Upasampada and Samenere Priests residing in the Districts of Columbo and Gall under a Commission of His Majesty the King of Candy with such power that he may reproof the priests of the Boodoo religion agreeable to the Boodoo's law.

That your petitioner further begs leave to inform Your Excellency that it was always the custom that the Chief Priests within the European territories of this Island were appointed by the Kings of Candy according to the ceremony observed amongst them, and that always the Chief Priests so appointed were considered and respected as such.

That your petitioner although he was appointed as Chief Priest according to the custom of this Island, he being an inhabitant of this place thought it proper to have the confirmation of his appointment by this Government and therefore the petitioner humbly takes liberty to request that Your Excellency will be kindly pleased to grant him the confirmation of the said appointment under your Excellency's hand and seal, agreeable to the commission granted by His Majesty the King of Candy over all the Boodoo Priests as well as Upesampada and Samanera residing in the Districts of Colombo, Calture and Gall, with such power as that the petitioner may discharge from their priesthood such persons who shall not behave themselves according to Boodoo's law, upon enquiring the matter together with five other priests who behave themselves agreeable to the Winedarme or Boodoo's Commandments and such farther authority so that he may be able to maintain his duty as Chief Priest and also with such effect as that all such Upasampada and Samanera Priests residing in the said Districts shall acknowledge respect and obey the petitioner as their Chief Priest, and also to grant your petitioner that whenever he shall happen to go to the different Corles and Districts the Headman of such a Corle or District shall assist and respect him and provide him with coolies for his expense and farther permit your petitioner that he may pass in the palanquin by beating of tom-tom and carrying the Flag along with him without a hinderance of any person whosoever.

For which favour your Excellency's humble petitioner as in duty bound shall ever pray.

There is also a copy (watermark 1809) of a petition by the same Mahagoda Indasara addressed to Sir Alexander Johnstone, Chief Justice, where he repeated the statement that the Chief Priest over the priests in the European territory was appointed by the Sinhalese King. After the British occupation, Bodimalooway of Bentota was first appointed and on his death the petitioner himself was so appointed by the King over the nine Corles of Columbo and Gall Corle. His complaint was that a priest of Korotota, who was charged with various acts of *parajika*, had acted in defiance of his authority. He continued—

"That there are Boodoo Priests of two different orders which are Teroonnanseys and Ganinnanseys. A person could attain to the priesthood of Ganinnansey being within the Territories belonging to the English Government but it is always customary a Teroonnancy priest shall be appointed at the usual manner in Candy.

That the abovenamed pretended Teroonnansey Dammasidde though he could attain to the Ganinnancy priesthood being in the

English Territories he could not get the priesthood Teroonnancy without being appointed agreeable to the custom at Candy yet he pretends to be Teroonnancy which is the greatest of all the crimes that he has committed himself."

The procedure regarding the appointment of a Chief Priest was well recognised under the Dutch. There is in existence the Dutch translation, dated 13 June, 1789, of a letter addressed by Sange Rakkitte Nayeke Oennanse, High Priest of Mettepittiya, to the Commandeur at Galle, in which, after the usual compliments he informed the latter that "By appointment of His Majesty the Invincible Emperor of Ceylon the office of High Priest is held by me with the Maintenance lands and other marks of honour, such as gifts, flag and drums. I have given orders to the priests on this side of the Island and have come to Galle District with the same marks of honour and drums, to do my work here and thence on to Colombo."

Galle Records, vol. 1241.

APPENDIX D.

Senkadagala Nuvara (Kandy) in 1803.

From the "Journal of the Proceedings of the Trincomale Detachment, Commanded by Lieut.-Co. Barbut."

Tuesday (March) 22nd, 1803

This morning I rode into Candy and the following is my idea of the town.

It is situated in a bason and surrounded by steep hills on every side. The entrance to it from the road is through a rude attempt at a barrier gate, to which you ascend by a number of steps ; and advancing a few hundred yards, you come to another of the same kind ; you may then be said to be at the entrance of the town, which consists of one broad street, about two miles in length, from the second barrier to the palace, which is at the upper end, but in an open space, a little to the left of the street. From the main street a number of smaller ones branch off in various directions. The houses, or rather huts, are all raised ten or twelve feet from the level of the streets, and have flights of steps leading up to them, they are built of mud and thatched ; a few only, belonging to the headmen, are tiled and white-washed. Near the upper end of the street is a square choultry, supported by square wooden pillars most curiously carved and painted. There are also two large pagodas or temples, which are named the east and west temples, but I had not an opportunity of examining them.

The palace is a building of immense extent, though a good deal damaged by fire. It forms three sides of a square, and has a square enclosure in the centre, containing the tombs of the Rajahs, as I imagine; they are immense circular piles of brick and chunam, rising gradually to a point, something like the dome of a church; there were a number of very small buildings close to them, just big enough to contain a man, the walls of which were filled with figures of men and animals, the size of life, but most grotesquely painted. The first thing that attracts your attention on your entrance to the palace through the principal gate (for there are three or four) is an open hall supported by square stone pillars curiously carved; between the intervals of which are placed wooden spikes, about three feet high on which elephant's teeth were stuck on state occasions; through this hall you pass to the temple that contains a number of images of Buddha, all in a sitting posture, as large as life; some of white marble, neatly gilt, and others of brass. Upstairs, directly over this, is the throne, which is covered with thin brass plates, and set round with stones; the walls are covered with fine pier glasses; it is situated in a room without windows, and to come at it you are obliged to pass through two others, the doors of which are covered with brass and ivory; in short it appears merely calculated to make a very dazzling appearance at night, which is the only time the King ever gives audience to anyone.

The walls of the temple and the anti-chambers to the throne, are profusely covered with inscriptions and paintings. This appears to be the most ancient part of the palace, for it has evidently been built at very different periods of time.

In some rooms were immense quantities of bows, darts, spears, arrows, etc. beautifully painted; in others immense brass lamps of all kinds of fanciful shapes, such as men, elephants, birds, etc., one room was full of glassware in cases, and appeared never to have been opened since they were received from the Dutch; another room was hung round with Dutch paintings and mirrors, and the ceiling hung with lustres, globe lamps, etc.

Many brass guns were found, two or three pounders, the carriages of which were most curiously ornamented, and a number of ginjalls commonly called grass-hoppers; these are small iron guns carrying a ball of six to ten ounces, and mounted on three wooden legs, exactly like a common stool; these they carry from one bush to another with great celerity as occasion requires.

I saw a few of those whips that make such an uncommon noise and which they crack always before the King or Adikar, whenever they stir out. They are made of fibres of the aloe stained of various colours, the thong is near two yards and an half long, tapering gradually to a point from the handle, where it is the thickness of your wrist. The handle is about a cubit in length and made of the same material. The walls of many of the buildings attached to the palace were covered with grotesque paintings of giants, elephants, etc.

It would be an endless task to describe all the various apartments of the palace, which is, taken altogether, a mean-looking irregular building; suffice it to say that the King had removed everything valuable some time before our arrival.

The only living animals that I saw in the palace were five white deer.

The Journal forms an appendix to "Poems" by T. A. Anderson, printed by The Philanthropic Society, London, 1809, and was probably written by Lieut. Jewel, 19th Regiment, Major of Brigade.

APPENDIX E.

Barnsley's Account of Davie's Surrender

Corporal Barnsley's deposition as recorded by Captain Madge on 27th June, 1803, has been often printed and should be read with his fuller narrative dictated some days later at Tiru Kona Malai to Alexander Alexander. This shows that when the army reached the river it was joined by some of those who had been left in hospital with the news that the sick were being massacred. Rafts were prepared and when they were ready some of the native troops swam across with a rope and everything appeared hopeful till suddenly others of them cut the two lines before their eyes. Many of them who had deserted were seen in their uniform firing on the British, and at the same time the Sinhalese appeared on the other bank. Serious trouble was now anticipated. The demand for the surrender of Muddu Svami followed, and the Prince delivered up his sword to Davie, both being moved to tears at parting; on his surrender assistance to cross the river and guides on the way were promised but no help was received the next day Instead there followed a suggestion that the troops should give up their arms on the ground that this would relieve them on the march and at the same time remove any hesitation the Sinhalese might feel about assisting them. Davie summoned a Council of War to discuss the proposal, when a deputation from the soldiers came with a request that they might be permitted to hold their own council. Their request was refused and the council decided to act on the suggestion, to the great indignation of the soldiers, some of whom loudly protested. Davie gave the command " Ground your arms" and then recalled it for a short time while he destroyed all his papers. Then the order was repeated, the troops marched away from their arms, and the Europeans were separated from the native troops and after that the officers from the privates.

The Sinhalese now came up and stood round the Europeans gazing on them, while some tried to snatch away their possessions. They were then led away two by two out of sight and the fate that awaited them Barnsley learnt from personal experience. When his turn came he saw the dead bodies of his companions, while an executioner with a large sword struck him on the back of his neck, at which he fell down senseless. On regaining consciousness he found the Jingal bearers engaged in stripping the bodies, first striking everyone on the head : though this was no doubt intended to make certain of their being dead, and though a blow was dealt on his own head, he only lost consciousness a second time.

On again recovering he heard a great shouting and tumult and on cautiously peeping saw a great concourse pressed together and craning their necks to observe something. Pistol shots followed and he came to the conclusion that the officers, who had concealed these weapons, and some of whom he had heard threatening to shoot themselves rather than be chopped down, had acted on their threat. Of this incident in Madge's version he is made to say " he heard shots in the direction of the place where the officers were prisoners and which was followed by their massacre." Barnsley could hardly fail to distinguish the report of the officers' pistols from that of muskets, and his account makes it clear that the Sinhalese crowd was animated not by hostility but by curiosity : to quote his words " Those on the outside jumping up, stretching their necks as if to gain a sight of something that was going on in the centre." His surmise that the officers shot themselves rather than be taken prisoner might well be correct.

When daylight came Barnsley saw the raft which the troops had prepared being cut up and he succeeded with much caution in getting across the river. He was seen by a Sinhalese from whom he begged a mat with which to cover himself, for he had only a tattered shirt left, and he painfully continued on his way till he was met by some others who gave him what food they had to eat and led him to a Sinhalese Chief who was accompanied by a large number of soldiers. He prostrated himself before this official, an aged and kindly man, who had him well fed, and he accompanied the force of nearly 5,000 men till they came within sight of Fort Macdowal, when the Chief sent him on with two of his men to the foot of the hill on which the fort was built, charged with a message for Captain Madge. This officer was panic-stricken at Barnsley's terrible news, and by ten o'clock as the moon sank behind the hills, he spiked his guns and, leaving his lamps burning, stole out of the fort. The sick who were being abandoned to their fate, discovered what was taking place, and as many as could walk followed the line of march till they dropped helpless on the road, while the more fortunate, along with Barnsley, harassed only by the howling of the village dogs, succeeded in reaching the Cottiar shore, where they were taken on board by some man-of-war boats; Barnsley himself was promoted to be Sergeant but was subsequently tried by court martial for drunkenness and reduced to the ranks.

(The Life of Alexander Alexander, written by himself and edited by John Howell, London, 1830).

APPENDIX F.

Purchase of Caffre Slaves for the Army

Statement of expenses incurred in purchasing Slaves at Bombay and transporting them to Colombo.

79 men capable of bearing arms at rxd 145 each ..	11,455
19 boys capable of bearing arms at rxd 125 each ..	2,375
2 women	250
	14,080
Freight of 100 Slaves from Bombay to Colombo at 40 rxd each	4,000
Insurance, Commission and provisions laid in for the voyage	2,139
	20,219

Expense in the purchase of Caffres at Goa and their transport from there to Colombo.

70 men at an average price of about rxd 175 per man and 8 women at 150 each	13,070
Provisions issued to them previous to embarkation ..	820
	13,890
Freight from Goa to Colombo and Insurance ..	3,500
Commission, Provisions, etc.	2,564
	19,954

Agreement entered into with Mons. Fortin for the supply of a certain number of slaves for the Ceylon Government.

His Excellency the Governor agrees to receive from Mons. Fortin a number of able-bodied Caffres to the extent of five hundred to be brought from Mosambique and landed either at Galle or Colombo at the rate of one hundred and twenty-five Spanish Dollars for each. One-third part of the said price to be paid in Cinnamon to be valued at three shillings sterling the pound weight and the other two-thirds in Bills on Bengal or Madras as it may suit the convenience of Government at the time. The exchange of the Spanish Dollars to be 16 to 10 pagodas and of the sterling money to be 8*s*. per pagoda.

The Cinnamon must be warranted under Bond to be for the Eastern Market and must not be sent to the Westward of the Cape of Good Hope. C.O. 54/14.

"Both the natives of India and the Candians have a greater dread in encountering the Caffres than even Europeans. From the latter they expect mercy, if conquered; from the former they look for nothing but cruelty and death."

John Wilson, Colonel, 4th Ceylon Regt., to Bathurst, dated 39, Albemarle St., 4th March, 1815. C.O. 54/58.

APPENDIX G.

Date of Davie's Death

" From examinations taken with great care by Mr. D'Oyly it is collected that Major Davie died in the town of Kandy between the 12th of December, 1811 and the 12th of January, 1812. Among the varying depositions on this subject respecting which no written record exists I have preferred the account given by Milawa, Dissave of Velassy, a Chief well acquainted with all the occurrences in Kandy and eminent amongst his brethren for intelligence and accuracy. Great pains have at various times been taken, particularly when I was last at Kandy, to find the remains of the Major in order to render to them the honours of military interment, but every endeavour failed."

Brownrigg's Despatch 177 of 18th Nov., 1816. C.O. 54/62.

Davie left a son by one of the women who were given to him. See Mrs. Heber's Journal for 18th Sept., 1825.

APPENDIX H.

The Tragedy of Ehelepola's Family

The first reference to the fate of Ehelepola's family which has been traced among the English official records is contained in a letter addressed by D'Oyly to Brownrigg and dated Sitavaka, May 23rd, 1814, which runs as follows :

" There is a general report that the wife and 4 children of the Adikar and his nephew have been put to death as well as Puswelle late Dissave of Nuwara Kalawiya, with his wife, children and relations. Puswelle is said to have been treacherously seduced to Kandy by the promise of the office of Adikar and the King's increased favour but was cruelly cut to pieces. These executions are said to have taken place in Kandy on Saturday or Sunday sennight." C.O. 54/52.

Writing again the following day he has reported Ehelepola's first conversation with him thus :

" The power of his adversaries had now prevailed and he had no object in returning to that country without an auxiliary force. For he had lost his honours, family and property and had brought nothing but his life with him into our territory." C.O. 54/52.

In his Despatch 75 of 28th June, 1814, Brownrigg reported the events connected with the rebellion :

" On the news of his (Ehelepola's) defection reaching Kandy the King degraded him from his office of Adikar as well as from that of Dissave of the Province of Saffragam and appointed a successor who was immediately despatched towards Saffragam to quell the insurgents. Although the persecutions on the occasion of this revolt have been extensive in their range and dreadful and even barbarous in their severity there has not . . . been the least indication of any intention on the part of the King to attack His Majesty's territories. The cruelties he has exercised seem to have spread general terror throughout his country." C.O. 54/51.

In his next Despatch, 76 of 16th August, 1814 he again spoke generally of " tyranny and oppression, suffering, violence and injustice." C.O. 54/52.

The Address presented to D'Oyly by the Chiefs of the Korale Tuna and Saparagamuva offering their services to the British Government, which was annexed to Brownrigg's Despatch to Goulburn of 5th Sept., 1814 (C.O. 54/53) was intended to be the strongest possible indictment of the King's actions. It ran thus :

" The wickedness committed by the King who has now attained to the Great Gate is this : Having got into his Power by sweet words, as innocent persons, Men who had done no fault, he has caused thousands of men to be put to death. To cause such things to be done is not becoming to the Royalty and to the name of God. If you say, for what cause ? When it appears in our Buddha Religion that we must not kill a small animal or a beast, the destruction of so many Souls who have done no fault, ought to be considered further. Because the Great Gate perceived that they had not good dispositions to submit to the Command of that unrighteous King, subjecting to death 73 Chiefs of legitimate Family, he cut them off, causing various pains to be inflicted. That resentment not being abandoned merely by cutting off those 73 Persons, he killed and destroyed Relations, and Kinsmen, great and small, descended from them, and friends together with Servánts and Maid-servants, a numberless Singhaleze multitude. The two or three Persons who remained, having seen the things abovementioned, becoming thence more and more inclined, disobeying with great fortitude the order of the unrighteous, unwise, King, deserting that Government, have come because they desired, becoming the subjects of wise righteous Sovereigns, to continue performing the Service ordered. From that circumstance our Wives, Children, Relations and Brothers, Riches and Property, Gardens and Fields, having lost these many things mentioned . . . we all request with our assistance to procure and grant succours for accomplishing the Objects abovementioned."

Ehelepola's memorial to His Majesty's Commissioners of Enquiry written shortly before his death from his place of exile, Mauritius, was very detailed and intended to make out the most impressive case he could of what he had suffered as the result of taking the British side. The references to the fate of his family which it contained were as follows :

" In consequence of my becoming a friend to the English Government the lives of my wife, my children and relations were destroyed and all my property taken by the King."

" As I have received no favour from Government and as the King destroyed all the lives of my family and took all my property."

All these documents though strongly biassed against the King were written with a sense of responsibility ; they all mentioned the infliction of a punishment of the extremest severity but which admittedly was in accordance with the law of the land, but they contained no suggestion that the judicial sentence was accompanied by any circumstance of extra-legal barbarity.

D'Oyly in his Constitution of the Kandyan Kingdom dealt with the recognised legal punishments, and he was assisted in his task by the best knowledge available among the Chiefs. He wrote "The instances of capital punishment inflicted on women are rare and these have generally been executed by drowning." And again "The execution of innocent wives and children for the crime of the traitor, and torture previous to death, were acts of barbarity, wantonly inflicted by an enraged and sanguinary tyrant and for the honour of human nature have scarcely a precedent in Kandyan History." The warmth of his language might be excused in view of his own share in the events which led up to the tragedy of Ehelepola's family; the suggestion of torture had no reference to that incident. He further dealt with mutilation as a punishment and mentioned that some of Muddu Svami's adherents were thus punished, but he made no suggestion anywhere of any specially revolting feature in the Ehelepola case; had he been aware of any such he could not have failed to mention it in speaking of the punishments inflicted in the King's time.

It is, however, the commonly accepted belief that by the King's orders the heads of Ehelepola's children were put into a mortar and that the mother was compelled to pound them with a pestle. No other similar incident has been recorded in the long history of the Sinhalese Kings and no such punishment was recognised by their law. At the same time such an act was always present in the minds of the people as representing the limit of cruelty to which a ruthless oppressor could attain, and village talk was full of such deeds by Siman Kure Rala, the Sinhalese Christian who once was the doughty supporter of the Portuguese. As the Londoner Robert Knox, who was a prisoner among them from 1659 to 1679, has recorded their talk, "He would make the women beat their own children in their mortars wherein they used to beat their corn."

Siman Kure, however, merely imitated the Captain-General, Jeronymo de Azavedo, of whom Manuel de Faria y Sousa* has rerecorded the following:

"When he was acting in Ceylon as Lord of War, he used to oblige women to throw their own children into stone-troughs and pound them in them, as they would spices in brass mortars, without any

*Asia Portugueza, iii. 321. Lisboa 1566-1675. The translation has been kindly furnished by the Revd. P. Lucian Jansz, M.A. The original is as follows:

Quando en Ceylam andava tan dueno de la guerra, obligava las mugeres a que echado a sus proprios hijos en pilones: Alli los machacassem como especies en almirezes, sin que le aplacassen los estallidos que davam aquelles innocentes por los golpes, y los pechos de las Madres por ver se he chas verdugos horribles de seus mismas Almas. Luego que ellas los avian hecho pastas el las degollava como si no le uvieron obedecido.

mitigation of the cries uttered by those innocents under the blows that fell and without any pity for the hearts of mothers who saw themselves made the cruel executioners of their own souls. As soon as they had reduced (the children) to paste, he had the women beheaded as if they had not obeyed him."

Once at any rate the Dutch had recourse to similar conduct, and with circumstances of added horror. This was when at the siege of Colombo in 1656 they found it necessary to take extreme steps to prevent the exodus of famished non-combatants from the beleaguered city. "When a woman came and brought small children, we forced her to put her child into a wooden mortar and to pound it to death with the pounder and then go away again with the dead child" is the account of one who was present on the occasion.*

The first suggestion of such an atrocity on the part of the King was contained in Brownrigg's Despatch No. 95, dated Kandy, 25th Feb., 1815. C.O. 54/55.

"Amongst a variety of acts of atrocity on the part of the King which have come to our knowledge or received confirmation since our arrival here, one is the fact and manner of his destroying the family of the Adikar, related by one Thoen, a native of Leyden, who enlisted at Colombo in the Bengal Artillery and who having accompanied General Macdowal's expedition, at the evacuation of the city by Major Davy in 1803 remained a convalescent in hospital, and survived almost miraculously the horrid carnage of that day. He states that the four children of Ehelepola Adikar had their heads cut off, the yongest being torn from its mother's breast for that purpose: that the bodies were dragged thro' the streets and the heads put into a mortar, the pestle of which was forced into the mother's hands and she was obliged to pound the mangled heads of her own children. She was then with three more women relations of the Adikar led to the brink of a large tank by some female slaves of the palace, and their hands and feet being bound and a stone tied round the neck of each, they were thrown into the lake where their bodies still remain. The gentleman who took this examination, Captain Cleather, Dep. Judge Advocate, had the curiosity to make inquiry of Molligodde Adikar as to the truth of these circumstances, by whom they were fully confirmed."

This passage is intimately connected with the following from Brownrigg's Official Declaration of the Settlement of the Kandyan Provinces in which he has drawn the most lurid picture possible of

*Johann Jacob Saar: tr. by Ph. Freudenburg, in R. A. S. (Ceylon) xi, 299.

the King's misdeeds. Among the words employed by him are massacre, blood, mutilation, murder, perfidy, animosity, defiance, horrible, treacherous, awful, implacable, daring, unprovoked, barbarous, unparallelled and destructive.

" The wanton destruction of human life comprises or implies the existence of general oppression : in conjunction with that no other proofs of the exercise of tyranny require to be specified ; and one single instance of no distant date will be acknowledged to include everything which is barbarous and unprincipled in public rule, and to pourtray the last stage of human depravity and wickedness, the obliteration of every trace of conscience, and the complete extinction of human feeling.

In the deplorable fate of the wife and children of Ehelepola Adikar, these assertions are fully substantiated ; in which was exhibited the savage scene of four infant children, the youngest torn from the mother's breast, cruelly butchered, and their heads bruised in a mortar by the hands of their parent, succeeded by the execution of the woman herself, and three females more ; whose limbs being bound, and a heavy stone tied round the neck of each, they were thrown into a lake and drowned."

The Declaration was published on the 2nd March, the day on which the Convention was accepted.

Brownrigg frankly explained in a later Despatch that the preamble to his Declaration was intended " to bring to view certain facts more strongly illustrative of the character of the late Government than any which had been made public, and of such a nature as I conceive would supersede the possibility of my justifying any attempt towards the re-establishment of such a Dominion." (No. 96 of 15th March). In other words the story of the pounding of the children's heads was till then not known to those whom the preamble was intended to influence, and its publication was expected to counteract any popular feeling in favour of the continuance of the King's Government. As early as the 4th of April, 1814 D'Oyly had pointed out to Brownrigg that the King's subjects would not rise against him without either being instigated from Colombo, or exasperated by such an act of violence on the King's part as would leave no alternative to armed resistance. C.O. 54/52.

In the same year there was published in London " A Narrative of Events which have recently occurred in the Island of Ceylon written by a gentleman on the spot." This was obviously inspired by Brownrigg and it gives the following account of the execution:

"The mother and five children, the eldest of whom was a lad of eighteen and the youngest an infant at the breast, were bound and led into the market place. The infant was first torn from the arms of its mother and its head being severed from its body the parent was compelled to pound it in a mortar. The others were murdered in succession, the eldest being reserved for the last victim : and this scene of wanton and savage butchery was crowned by what every feeling mind will contemplate as an act of supreme though unintentional mercy, the sacrifice of the mother herself."

The authority for the information is not stated, though the writer devotes three pages of the booklet to details about Thoen.

John Davy arrived in Ceylon in August, 1816 and in the preparation of his work "An account of the Interior of Ceylon" received much assistance from Brownrigg. His tenth chapter deals with the history of the Island and is based on information supplied by the aged and greatly respected Millawe Dissave, but "As this chief's interest was closely connected with that of the late King of whom he was a favourite and in several instances the agent of his nefarious designs, the particulars given of this monstrous reign were collected in general from more unbiassed sources." In other words he rejected what was likely to be favourable to the King. His narrative of the execution cannot be reconciled with the previous account. According to him the eldest son, who was eleven years old, was called upon first but as he was terrified his brother, aged nine, stepped forward and was decapitated, his head being then thrown into a mortar which the mother was compelled to pound, and this was done with all the other children including a girl, in turn.

Henry Marshall arrived in Ceylon in 1808 and was senior Medical Officer in the Kandyan Provinces 1816-1821. He was familiar with both the above accounts on which he makes some critical remarks, and states that it was the eldest who was first executed, the head of each being pounded in turn. He too does not mention the authority for his information. His "Ceylon" was published in 1846. It was to Marshall that Thoen presented himself first and it was from Thoen that he obtained details of what took place at the hospital in 1803, but he is not mentioned as having given Marshall any information regarding the alleged atrocity : had he done so it would have been natural for Marshall to state the fact.

There is to be found in the Library of the Colombo Museum a curious palm leaf MSS. of 29 foll. which is catalogued as 2371 *Ehelepola Daruwan Marima* and is illustrated by crude drawings. The following is the translation of the relevant portion of the narrative.*

"Molligoda Adikar advanced with his soldiers but learning that Ehelepola Mantri had escaped returned and reported "O King, Ehelepola has escaped to Colombo with the intention of seizing the country with the help of the Ingrisi." The King was enraged like a cobra struck with a stick and exclaimed "How can I trust the Sinhalese Ministers ?" and inquired from the Diyawadana Nilame what the Sinhalese law was in respect of those who were guilty of treason against the King but had escaped. The Nilame read out the law as follows : "In the case of those who have committed treason against the King the remaining members of their family shall be arrested and the males beheaded and the females put to death by drowning : such is the law" he said.

Thereupon the King sent for the executioners and ordered them to go speedily and fetch Ehelepola Kumari and her children as well as Puswelle Kumari and her daughter. They went and fetched them all to near the *Wal bodhiya* where the Diyawadana Nilame read out the law. On hearing it the Kumarihami beat her breasts and imprecating the gods cried aloud "Am I and my children to answer for the wrong of my lord and husband !" To this the King replied "Thy husband is an ungrateful and despicable dog. As the fellow is not here the penalty will be exacted from thee and thy children." Thus saying he entered the Patirippuwa and looked on. Loku Banda, frightened at the sight of the executioners, and falling at the Kumarihami's feet began to sob. The nine-year old Madduma Banda exclaimed "Elder brother, there is nothing to be gained by tears. They disgrace the Sinhalese race. Therefore it is right to give up our lives for our father." With these words after performing his religious duties he advanced to the executioners and said "Fellows, you may strike off my head," and lowered his neck. Loku Banda seeing his brother's head struck off began to scream in deadly terror whereupon the executioners rushed forward and seized him and struck off his head. Thereat the Kumarihami fell with imprecations on the King upon the ground, when the executioners rushed and snatched Dingiri Menika who was at her hip and struck off her head and put it into a mortar, whereupon the King ordered the Kumarihami to pound it, but she continued to lie prostrate and lament. They then snatched the infant child which was in her arms and when they struck off the head the milk it had drunk trickled out. The King exclaimed to the mother "If thou wilt not forthwith pound the children, I shall order thee

*I have to acknowledge the assistance of Mr. Julius de Lanerolle in its preparation.

to be given over to a Paduwa." At that Molligoda Adikar said to her "Younger sister, do so and avoid the disgrace to your birth." She took the pestle in her hand and let it fall into the mortar and immediately collapsed. The King shouted out and commanded that the women should be forthwith removed and drowned in the Wewa. As the executioners came near, the Kumarihami would not permit them to touch her person and she and the other three proceeded to Bogambara Wewa. There she exclaimed "May the blessing of the gods be with my lord and husband, Ehelepola Adikar. May the country pass before long from the wicked cruel and worthless King who now rules over it to another Government" and all three plunged into the Wewa. On that day the whole country became as one funeral house. The radiance of the Divine Sun was diminished. The entire land was drowned in tears."

The writer's name does not appear; but he was not skilful in the use of the stylus and was ignorant of grammar. The language employed is not that of a Kandyan Sinhalese, and his substitution of David for Davie indicates a knowledge of English names. While the list which he gives of the Sinhalese military officers connected with the 1803 fighting seems to preserve a genuine local tradition, the omission of the more important details of that period is noteworthy. He does not profess to have been an eye-witness of any portion of the events recorded by him, and a striking confusion in their sequence suggests for the compilation a date sufficiently far removed from the incidents themselves to render such confusion natural to one who relied on hearsay. He has placed the arekanut incident of 1802 and the spy incident of 1814 together in point of time, as leading up to the war of 1803; with regard to the second of these he lays the responsibility on Pilima Talavuva, who was executed three years before, adding that that Minister had the men mutilated and sent them to Colombo to announce that this was done by the King. He further repeats as a fact the monstrous story that Muddu Svami was sentenced to be flayed alive. The work would seem to be a comparatively recent compilation by one who had some acquaintance with the printed English narratives as well as village tradition; its most valuable contribution to our knowledge is the fact that the King consulted his advisers as to the law before passing sentence on Ehelepola's family.

Two other Sinhalese versions which are frequently quoted should be noticed. One is the *Ehelepola Hatane*, an anonymous ballad in eighty-two verses by an unknown author who in the last verse states that the eighty-two verses were completed on the fifth day of the waning Moon of the month Bak (April) of the Saka year 1738

(1816 A. C.). This statement cannot be accepted because among the verses are several dealing with events subsequent to that date, including the King's death at Vellore in 1832. A critical examination of the contents of the ballad leads to the almost irresistible conclusion that it is little more than a versification of the narrative published by Davy and is of no probative value. This was printed in Colombo in 1921. The second was also printed in Colombo (4th Ed. 1923) under the same name of *Ehelepola Hatane*, with the sensational sub-title of *Daru Ketavima* (The Pounding of the Children). This consists of 169 verses and the correct title as mentioned by the author whose name appears as Tembilipola, is *Perali Hatane*. It displays neither literary nor technical skill and is a medley of disconnected verses in which the writer has obviously given free rein to his imagination, and is not entitled to serious consideration.

Still other versions are current and one familiar to the Wahumpurayo of Panavenna in Saparagamuva introduces a love motive which also figures in the first Hatane.

Excluding Thoen's for separate consideration the other narratives are mutually so contradictory that they cannot be based on the truthful evidence of witnesses of one incident. It may not be unjust to class them in the same category with the portrait of the "Queen of Kandy" and the details of the interview with her at Kandy published in 1834 (Oriental Annual) by the artist William Daniell—who never was in Ceylon.

The Narrative of John Albert Thoen is printed as an Appendix to "The Wanderer in Ceylon," a Poem by T. A. Anderson, London, 1817 with the statement that "It was taken down from the mouth of the narrator and as near as possible in his own words, by the Deputy Judge Advocate of Ceylon in February, 1815."

The portion referring to the execution is as follows: "About six or seven months since three or four children of Ehelepola the Adikar or Chief of the Province of Saffragam, were put to death in the city, his wife was there also; her young child was taken from the breast and its head cut off before her face, the child's body was thrown on the ground, the head was put into a mortar and the pounder put into the mother's hand, and she was obliged to pound the head of her child (the heads of all the other four children being in the mortar also) the bodies were then dragged about the streets, and this woman and three other female relations of the Adikar were led to the tank side (the lowest of the three tanks) by some slave women of the King's, who tied there hands and feet, and then fastening a stone round their necks, they threw them into the water. The King was looking out of a window at a distance all the time, and from whence he gave his orders."

Thoen at the time and for many years before was living practically as a beggar in a hut at Kandy, along with a Moorish woman whom he had married after first becoming a Mohammedan. His knowledge of English was very limited. He did not suggest that he witnessed the execution, which he said he did in the case of the Sinhalese spies, and from his uncertainty about the number of the children it is not unreasonable to conclude that what he narrated was hearsay.

The object of the law in laying the penalty of death on the hostages left behind by an escaped traitor was not revenge but the intimidation of possible imitators, and publicity was essential to its attainment. In this case it was alleged that in order to increase the efficacy of the punishment an atrocity revolting to every human instinct and hitherto unknown in connection with the Sinhalese administration of justice was introduced. The whole country should have been ringing with the news of the horror, and yet Thoen's story caused Cleather so much surprise that according to Brownrigg he appealed to Molligoda who confirmed the charge against the Master whom like Ehelepola he had betrayed. It was left to Brownrigg to enlighten a public which for nine months had remained in ignorance.

Waging war through the Printing Press is no new device even in Ceylon. As the Saparagamuva Chiefs said on the 5th of September, 1814 "Afterwards the Governor North, who came to the Kandyan Country by order of the Great King of England, promulgated in our Countries also several printed proclamations. The minds of all people great and small who saw those proclamations being inclined, he appeared an unrighteous King." Brownrigg's propaganda was frankly directed to create the impression of "an oppressed people who in their struggle to rid themselves from the rule of a tyrant, call for our aid." His propaganda had spread the stories of open graves awaiting the Saparagamuva men and the embraces of untouchable Rodiyas their women. He deliberately intended that the preamble to his Declaration should contain new material which would render the continued existence of the King's Government impossible. Perhaps Brownrigg and Cleather alone were competent to explain the discovery of that material at the psychological moment after its long concealment from those who were most interested in ascertaining the truth. Apathy towards elucidation of fact and the all too human weakness to accept without reserve anything that savours of sensationalism rank among the most helpful allies of political propaganda, and speaking of these horrors Bennett* who arrived on the Civil Establishment of the Island in 1816 has remarked "Were the facts hypothetical or not founded upon official reports of the highest authority, and subsequently proclaimed as such by the British Government of Ceylon (they) would be altogether incredible."

How the popular imagination, once roused, can embroider a tale is well shown in the series of vignettes illustrative of the execution which are reproduced by James Campbell, who arrived in the Island in 1820, and ascribed by him to "a native artist."† One bears the legend "The King commands one of the sons to be chopped with an axe" and another the still more effective one "The mother is made to eat the flesh of her second son." These details had escaped the notice of Brownrigg, but are recorded in the two so-called Hatanes.

There were other similar acts ascribed to the King which failed to command the same acceptance from a horrified public. One was recorded by Lieutenant Richard Blakeney who was in Colombo at the time Sri Vikrama was brought there, in his Journal of an Oriental Voyage, under date the 18th of March, 1815. "The cruelties practised on the British captives were horrifying. The eyes of many were taken out and the remainder put to death. Major Davy was preserved as a footstool for the King and shortly after, his eyes being taken out, died." Another was preserved by Bennett. "This monster of depravity was treated as a Sovereign Prince (and) with his numerous wives conducted to Colombo, his dagger still incrusted with the blood of one wife whom he had murdered." Perhaps it would not be unjust to attach to the more lurid details of an already sufficiently terrible incident the same degree of credibility as these atrocious libels merit.

The evidence available is insufficient to establish the assertion that the heads of Ehelepola's children were put into a mortar and that their mother was compelled to pound them with a pestle. The probability is that the story was fabricated as a piece of political propaganda of the type so familiar today and was intended not merely to estrange the minds of the Sinhalese from their King, but also to counter the declared policy of Downing Street against territorial expansion.

*"Ceylon and its Capabilities" 1843, p. 383.

†Excursions, Adventures and Field-sports in Ceylon, by Lieut.-Colonel James Campbell, 2 vols. London, 1843

APPENDIX I.

The King's Resources

Questions put to Ehelepola by D'Oyly and his answers.

Q.—What is the number of the King's constant military force? Of what description of people does it consist? Who is their Chief? What pay do they receive? Besides this regular force, in time of War in what manner and from what parts are his additional military forces collected? What number is he capable of assembling from each country or Dissavany?

Ans.—The military force at this time constantly on foot near the Great Gate consists of about 300 Moormen and about 100 Singhalese. In a time of War forces are assembled from the Five Countries of the Upper Country, strong stout young men, supernumeraries, but men are not pressed from the Four Dissavanies. People may be collected from the Five Countries for soldiers as follows :

From	Uda Palata	about	25 men
,,	Udu Nuvara	,,	50 ,,
,,	Yati Nuvara	,,	50 ,,
,,	Tunpane	,,	70 ,,
,,	Harasiya Pattuva	,,	300 ,,
,,	Dumbara	,,	300 ,,
,,	Hevaheyta	,,	80 ,,
,,	Walapana	,,	40 ,,

Besides these the whole number of Malabar soldiers from the Dissavani of Uva, from the Dissavani of Saparagamuva, from Kandy, is—

In Uva residing	32 Malabars
In Saparagamuva	14 ,,
In Kandy	36 ,,

These Malabar soldiers receive no pay. Lands are delivered to them. The Singhaleze and Moormen abovementioned receive pay. The person who is Muhandiram of soldiers according to Singhaleze account 15 ridi

The Aratchy	10 ridi
The Kankanama	7 ,,
The soldier	5 ,,

These Malabars and Moormen, Yonnu, are under charge of the Nayakkara, the King's Malabar relations. The Singhalese are under charge of the Singhalese Chiefs. There is no single great Chief to the soldiers. Besides all persons who have villages and lands in the Upper (*Kattuwa*) Country and the Low (*Kattuwa*) Country when they come having provided with guns for the service of these lands, lead and gun-powder are given from the Great Gate. The Chiefs who have obtained the several Countries and Dissavanies make War, but there is no other method.

Q.—What quantity of arms and ammunition, cannon, matchlocks, musquets, lead, gun-powder, saltpetre, sulphur ? What quantity foreign and what Singhaleze ? In what places are they deposited ?

Ans.—There is altogether no manufacture of cannon in our country. The cannon which are now in Kandy are of the guns which were carried to Kandy at the time when the Fort of Gurubeybele was destroyed. There are—

2 cannon at the Kadawata of Nalanda in Matale.

2 cannon at Balani Kadawata in Yati Nuvara.

There is 1 gun in a mud hole in the village Diwela in the Four Korles.

2 guns are buried in the village Hatoluwa in the same Dissavani.

There are 2 guns at Girihagama Kadawata in Harasiya Pattu.

There are 9 guns in Kandy.

There is a small gun at Batugedera.

There are 22 matchlocks or Ginjaals (Kodituwakku) belonging to Kodituwakku Lekam.

18 in the Dissavani of the Four Korles.

16 in the Dissavani of the Seven Korles.

9 in the Dissavani of Uva

8 in the Dissavani of Matale.

13 in the Dissavani of Saparagomu.

Of these 8 guns will have been delivered at Hitawaka ; whether the other five are in the middle of the country or in charge of what persons I do not know. There are—

7 Kodituwakku in the Three Korles.

5 Kodituwakku in Uda Palata.

6 Kodituwakku in Walapana.

5 Kodituwakku in Nuvara Kalaweya.

5 Kodituwakku in Taman kada.

5 Kodituwakku in Wellasse.

Besides those there are no others.

The hand guns (musquets) belonging to the Great Gate will be the Dutch, French, English and Singhaleze guns, about 2,000 or 3,000, not more. Lead and gun-powder are distributed to all the people of the provinces, but gun-powder is deficient to make war many months. There will be some sulphur ; the sulphur is in Bintenne. There will also be some saltpetre in Kandy, it is in the village called Hairuvelli.

Q.—From what several sources do the King's Revenues arise ? What amount is collected annually from each source*?

Ans.—The revenues received by the Great Gate : of the things produced in the Dissavanies, the Countries, the Lekam, Badu, Widhana, Gabada Villages—of the things produced in all these places there is nothing which is not received into the Great Gabadawa. Those I have not written separately because the things which are profitable to men are numerous, but not intending (or entertaining) any disingenuity. Of the things accruing to the Great Gate at the lowest even plantain leaves are fixed to be given. For whatsoever thing is produced there is no expenditure.

Q.—Where are the King's Treasures deposited ?

Ans.—The King's Treasures are concealed at Uduwela, Sanguranketa, Manakola, Walapane, Meyde Maha Nuvara, Teldeniya, Hairuvelli (Hiruwala) Kosgama, Arattana, Mawela, Kotmale, Gabbela, Pupureyssa, Ramukeneylli.

Q.—In what Chiefs does the King at present place most confidence ? What Chiefs are most attached to him ? What Chiefs are of greatest ability for Counsel or for War ?

Ans.—Of all the Singhaleze people great and small I do not believe that even a single person is friendly to the Great Gate at this time. He who both lived most friendly and was received into his confidence was Puswelle Dissave and there is intelligence that that person has been put to death. The persons now living perform the things which they are told because of their inability to satisfy but it is not that they are friendly. Besides either for Warfare or for Counsel in all affairs and matters except the few Chiefs now living there is no other person. Besides since the King is little pleased with such persons of understanding it does not appear to me to state that such a person is a favourite, a man of Counsel.

Q.—In case of attack from hence to what places would the King retire from Kandy ? What are the means of obtaining possession of his person ? If War were undertaken, what plan of operations would he recommend ? By what roads should detachments march and what numbers by each ? What are the means of subsisting them ?

Ans.—If you should proceed from here to war the King leaving Kandy will not go to a new foreign country. The English Government surrounds our country. Because he is living as fish encompassed by a net, in a time of War he will retire to a village or the jungle but there is not a place which does not appear to men. If in the same manner as you made War the former expedition, although you go again two or three times, you will fail. If you should proceed from hence to War, a military force of about 500 men, going across Madakalapuwa to Bintenna Nuvara should stop there. About 500 men proceeding from Katuwana going by the road of Idalpitiye to Badulla should stop there. If a small number should go by Hitawaka to Saparagamuva and Korle Tune, and by the road of Tiru Kuna Male to Matale and to the Seven Korles, without allowing much trouble to take place, your intention may speedily be accomplished.

If arrangements be made for about 200 of the force which went to Bintenne to come to Meda Maha Nuvara, and for a few of the force at Badulla to come to Mulnuvara in Walapane, and for a force to be stationed at Sanguranketa Nuvara and Maha Nuwara (Kandy) and for a few of the force which went to Matale to stop at the places Kosgama, Naranpanawa, even the places in which the property is are in these places which have been mentioned. Still there are remaining about 2 villages called Nillamba, Kotmale on the side of Kandy on which is Samantakuta. There is no other quarter to go to. If he should go to Nillamba it will be near to the people stationed at Sanguranketa. If he should go to Kotmale there are roads to go thither either from Korle Tune or from Saparagamuva. If it should be arranged in that manner, there is no other place to go to. If it be done in this manner it may be in a much better method than going by one road only. I can assemble and furnish forces so that there shall not be any failure of all the people dwelling in the Countries or the Dissavanies and in Kandy.

With respect to the circumstance stated, in what manner can the force which goes to War obtain provisions, it cannot be obtained by trade as in this Country. They may be supplied from the paddy and rice which is in the Gabada Villages. There is altogether no occasion to doubt that the Warfare will fail as the last time. It failed the last time both because the manner of Warfare was not good, and because the principal Chiefs living at that period were adverse but it was not that he escaped by entering a secret place, which does not appear to men. Hereafter also if there is an intention of making War, if you inquire at that time the manner of going and coming, and the methods necessary to be adopted, I can inform.

C.O. 54/52. Date does not appear.

Annexed to the Despatch 96 of 15th March, 1815 is the following memorandum of the revenues of the Kingdom by D'Oyly:—

Sources of revenue in the Kandyan provinces:

1. Presents to the King from the Adikars and Dissavas and other superior officers to obtain or upon obtaining their several appointments, which have of late years been annually and sometimes more frequently exacted.

   This revenue is abolished by H.E. the Governor as unworthy of the British Government.

2. Deykum, or Annual Tribute of fixed amount collected by the Dissavas and other Chiefs from the general provinces and paid soon after the New Year in money.

3. Kat Rajakariya: An annual duty from all provinces in the nature of a land tax paid partly in kind (rice and coconuts) and partly in cash.

4. Rice or paddy, the produce of the Royal villages.

5. The produce of the Royal gardens.

6. The monopoly of areka in the Four Korales, Saffragam and the Three Korles. Also a small annual duty on areka in the Three Korles.

7. The exclusive right of the Crown to precious stones.

8. Labour in the service of the State according to the general castes and occupations of the people, in consideration of lands held on such conditions. C.O. 54/55.

It is not without interest to compare this list with the revenues of Dharmapala (1551-1597): see The Portuguese Era.

APPENDIX J.

The Trial and Punishment of the Spies 1814

Depositions enclosed in Despatch, Brownrigg to Bathurst, No. 86 of 30th Oct., 1814. C.O. 54/53.

Colombo, October 25th, 1814.

Pulukkutyge Louis Appu of Mahara,

I left my village one month and seventeen days ago, in company with four other persons of my village to trade in the Kandyan country, *viz.*, Jayamannege Gabriel, Korallage Sinno Appu, his sister's son and Neykatyge Hacha. We carried cloths and two or three plates and about a parrah of salt. We went about one day's journey beyond the Deydura Oye, to the villages Indiwinna gama, Kurundugas Weywa, Angunakoli, Olpitigama and others. We exchanged our goods for ghee, and a few medides of tala, mun and mustard seed. We proceeded on our return one day's journey on this side of the Deyduru Oye and lodged at the village Meyllipotte that night. The next morning having proceeded a league further to Imbulani gama, a washer village, as we were stopping there and cooking our rice, five men of our village came with cloths to exchange for ghee. Their names were Jayamannegei Koni Appuhamy, Kaiappuge Migiel Appu, do Soesaya, Korallage Juannes Appuhamy, his sister's son Korallage Bastian. They told us that on the way a person called Ganati Vidan had taken from them three white *katchies* of 20 cubits and two *Urama* (handkerchiefs) and as the washerman said that if they complained to the Dissave who was residing at Magulagam they would recover them, we also stopped to see, because they were people from our village. The same afternoon about 4 o'clock four persons, *viz.*, Kaiappuge Migiel Appu and Korallage Juannes Appuhamy, the joint owners of the stolen cloths and of our party Jayamannage Gabriel and Korallage Sinno Appu, went to the Mohottali who lived near the Dissave's residence and made their complaint, and were told to come there the next morning.

The next morning about 8 or 9 o'clock four messengers came from the Dissave and called away two of us, *viz.*, Korallage Juannes Appuhami and Korallage Sinno Appu, saying only that it was the Dissave's order. A short time after, about half an hour, three more messengers came, desiring by order of the Dissave, that two more intelligent people amongst us who could converse, would come for the purpose of causing some good clothes to be brought for the Dissave. Jayamannage Gabriel Appuhamy and myself went and joined there our two companions who had gone before, and all four persons remained together a long time under the coconut trees in the garden where the Dissave resided. In the afternoon at four or five footsteps after noon our other six companions were brought bound to the garden and the two washermen of the two houses where our two parties lodged, unbound, and they said that their goods had all been placed in a room and the room closed and sealed.

Before these persons arrived a Mohottiyar asked us by what road we had gone and what merchandize we had brought. To this Jayamannage Koni Appuhamy replied that we had come across Negombo and the Seven Korles and had brought cloths and that on the way the cloths had been plundered by Ganati Vidan. He also said Ehelepola Adikar is residing at Colombo, are you come with secret *olas* and to learn intelligence ? We replied that we came for no such purpose. He enquired, do you know that he is at Colombo ? We replied we have heard that he is there but we have not seen him. He enquired no more and then ordered us four persons to prison.

(On desiring him to explain how Koni Appuhamy could have answered not being one of the four then present, he says first) Koni Appuhamy told me that they enquired in this manner (again apparently recollecting himself) I was mistaken. I meant to say that Jayamannage Koni Appuhamy accompanied me, not Gabriel. We were imprisoned and put in the stocks in a *Mandoo.* Late in the evening before sunset about 5 o'clock, our six companions and the two washermen were brought and all including the washermen were put in the stocks in the Mandoo with us and our arms bound. They told us that they had been brought bound and that their goods had been shut up in a house and sealed. Three days after this Korallage Juannes Appuhamy and Korallage Sinno Appu, his first cousin were called from their confinement, to attend the Dissave, they returned shortly after and related that Ganati Vidan had been brought and being asked whether he took the cloths, denied it. That thereupon Juannes Appuhamy said We will swear in Badabeyddi Dewale (a temple in Seven Korles) that Ganati Vidan took from us three cloths of 20 cubits and two *Urama*—upon which the Mohottala and Korales present reproached the Vidan saying " You are telling falsehoods. Give up the cloths "—and the Vidan thereupon restored them.

We remained ten days in prison and Kodituwakku Vidan told us that *olas* had been sent to Kandy informing that people of the Low-Country had come, five with ghee and five with merchandize, that we might remain without fear, that we should incur no blame, and should be released as soon as *olas* came from Kandy. Ten days after we were imprisoned we were all ten persons conducted to Kandy bound in two places under charge of sixteen men, and with us were sent the cloths recovered from the Vidan, and one 20 cubits cloth which remained in the hands of Juannes Appu. No other enquiry was made from us at any time during our confinement nor at the time of despatching us to Kandy than what I have above stated. After being bound in readiness to be despatched to Kandy, we were brought into the Court of the Dissave's house where we made obeisance to the Mohottiyars and cried and complained of the injustice done to us and begged a little of our money which had been shut up in the house, for our expense on the way. They gave no answer but ordered us to be despatched quickly.

We arrived in Kandy after a journey of five days at dusk in the evening and were lodged that night in a kind of prison *Mandoo* at the house of a Dissave, said to be the elder brother of Dodumpani Dissave of the Seven Korles. No enquiry was made and nothing was said to us that night, except that a person called Walauwe Vidan came in the dusk and ordered us to be well bound and guarded.

The next morning early we were conducted by the Walauwe Vidan with guards to the Walauwe formerly belonging to Migastenna Nilami, and now, it is said, obtained by another Dissave. We were there confined in a *mandoo* next the street and the Walauwe Vidan of this house enquired from us, by what road we came and what merchandize we brought. We replied, we went across Negombo and Giratalan Pattu and Kolamunni Oye and we brought cloths and salt and had exchanged them for ghee and tala and mun, that on our return we met five men of our village, who complained that their cloths had been plundered, that we were called to the Dissave's house and imprisoned. The Vidan then asked, Why did you come, knowing that it is forbidden to come to this country ? We replied, we met with no hill or gravet in our way and we did not know it was forbidden. Besides, the people of the Seven Korles and of this country go to Negombo and carry away salt and salt-fish, and we likewise go for trade to this country. The Walauwe Vidan having made these enquiries went away and shortly after the Dissave came out of the house and without enquiry from us said " Well, I will communicate your affair " and went away, as we understood, to the Palace. This happened about 6 or 7 in the morning.

We remained there all day and in the evening the Dissave returned and calling to the Mohottale and Vidan bade them order the messengers to take away these people and guard them properly. He would communicate (the affair) to-morrow. The messengers conducted us away to the *mandoo* where we were confined the preceding night.

The next morning early the messengers conducted us to another large *mandoo* in the street, saying that it was the place where complaints are heard. At about noon the messengers conducted us to a place where four streets meet. We were stationed in the middle surrounded by a number of men, armed with guns, lances and swords. I think 700 or 800, and within stood the Dissave and other Chiefs, Mohottiyars and Vidans to the number of 60 or 70, at a little distance from us. Two Mohottiyars or Vidans approached us and enquired on what business we had come ? We replied that we had come for ghee, tala, mun, pepper and such merchandize as we met with. Korallage Juannes Appu said, all the Korale Vidans of these villages knew that since 10 or 15 years I am accustomed to come and trade in this country. I came for no treacherous business. All the Headmen and people from Deyduru Oye to Mi Oye, and from Mi Oye to Kala Oye know that I am accustomed to live by trading there. They then enquired, Did you come to seek intelligence for Ehelepola Adikar, or did you bring articles of merchandize ? We replied, we knew nothing whatever of that matter, we came on trade for our livelihood. The two Chiefs thus questioned us and reported our answers to the Dissaves two or three times and shortly after came and said "It has been ordered by the Supreme Great Gate that you are found guilty."

We replied "We have done no fault, we came on trade for our livelihood, therefore we pray in the name of the Golden Sword of the Great Gate, to release us for charity that we may go to our villages begging." To this no reply was made. We were immediately conducted from thence to another place where four streets also meet, at about a call distant, said to be the place of execution. The armed men stood arranged on three sides and the Dissaves and Chief on the fourth.

A large cauldron was brought, and fire and firewood, and ingredients were put into it and heated and two or three adzes, a saw, two or three swords, two or three planes, and two or three knives. A long time elapsed whilst these things were in preparation ; we knew not what punishment was about to be inflicted on us but expected to be put to death.

At about five footsteps after noon the punishment began. The five who went first on trade and the five who went last, were stationed separately and the punishment began with us, who went first. Seven or eight men, executioners, called Gahala gammans, first seized one man, laid him with his face on the ground, trampled on all his joints, hips and his neck. The two arms were extended in front of the head ; a log of wood was placed under the arm and whilst two men held it another cut off the arm at the elbow with an adze and immediately after the ear and nose were cut with a knife, and then the stump of the arm was anointed with the hot mixture in the cauldron. I do not remember which man was mutilated first. I was taken the fourth, and one man after me, I do not remember who. Next the other five who came last were treated in like manner. The right arm and right ear of the five first were cut off ; the left arm and left ear of the five last. The punishment of all ten was finished in much less than half an hour, and immediately the Dissaves and other Chiefs went away. We were left lying on the ground, the armed men remained, and the people of the streets came in charity with water, apas, plantains, jaggery and cakes, and put them into our mouths. My arm was cut off with two blows of the adze. I lost my senses at the time and recovered them late in the evening when a little jaggery and some water were administered to me. Nearly as the sun was setting a Dissave came again to the spot and said to us " You are released in the name of the Great Gate for charity and have permission to go begging to your villages." He then gave order to the Korales and Vidans that we should be raised up and taken to houses this evening and be fed with congee and rice and taken care of, and said it was the order of the Great Gate that these ten should be delivered to the ten Dissaves, to be carried, if they could not walk, to the limits, to go to their villages. The people then raised us up and assisted us on our way. My companions were taken different ways and I did not see what became of them.

I was conducted by four men to the work house of a potter in. Kandy and rested there that night and was supplied with congee. Soon after dark the same evening I heard that four of my companions had died, and the next morning that three more had died during the night. In the morning I saw four dead bodies carrying along the street and I was told that seven bodies had been carried away for the purpose of being hung at Hunu Kotuwa.

At about noon, four men who I understood were people of Saffragam returning to their villages after expiration of their term of service, came and said that they had received orders to conduct me to the limits and that the other four who before attended me must return to the Walauwa. On coming into the street a Chitty gave me some food and after eating I set off under charge of these four men. In passing Hunu Kotuwa my conductors pointed out to me seven bodies hanging, three on one jak tree and four on another, and said that they were my companions. I recognised them to be my companions and saw their arms which had been cut off, suspended to their necks, and tears came into my eyes.

As soon as our arms had been cut off they were tied round our necks and we carried them thus suspended. I was told the next morning by my conductors that it was the order that we should carry them in that manner to the limits. I carried it as far as Saffragam but on account of its putridity cast it away before I came to the limits. I came under charge of these four men in seven days from Kandy to the residence of a Dissave near the Dewale of Saffragam. My arrival was communicated to the Dissave and I was despatched the next morning towards Sitavaka. I stopped one night on the way and reached Sitavaka about noon the next. The four men who conducted me from Kandy to Saffragam were called *Galladdo*, and two *Kula Hewayo*, low caste lascorins, I believe Jaggererers, were sent from Saffragam by the Dissave in the place of two of these Gallado to Sitavaka. They left me at about a quarter league's distance from the limits, saying they feared they should be seized.

(He explains his identification of the seven corpses). He is informed that it is not credible that such punishment would be inflicted on them unless they were guilty of some offence, inasmuch as many other inhabitants of our territory have been and are still trading in the Kandyan country and nothing has happened to them, and he is repeatedly warned to declare the truth, and whether they committed any offence or were accused of it.

He positively declares that he has spoken nothing but the truth that they were guilty of no offence, and no other was laid to their charge than above related by him. Enquiry may be made from the Vidan Mohandiram of Maharre and others whether they are people of evil conduct.

Question.—Did you meet with a man named Kirige Andries.

Answer.—When we were imprisoned by the Dissave of the Seven Korles, we found there a man in irons who said he was of Kosinne. He was not of our party. He told us that he had struck his wife one blow with a small stick, upon which she in anger went into a room and hanged herself. Other people said that he had killed his wife by beating. He said he had taken his wife from Kosinne and had been resident a long time in the Kandyan country. When we were despatched to Kandy he still remained in irons.

Q.—It appears that the Dissave first called four of your companions in kindness. What was the cause of his change of disposition towards you ?

A.—An inhabitant of the village named Delgoda Rala, a Vellale, had come to the house where the other five lodged and looked at the 20 cubit cloth which remained and wished to buy it and take it away. But the washerman of the house desired to have it and as Juannes Appu two months before had left two *pingos* of ghee under the washer's charge, he refused the cloth to Delgoda Rala and took it away. Delgoda Rala went away saying " We will enquire and see the power of the washerman and my imbecility and inability to buy a cloth for ready money." I learnt this after we were imprisoned and people said this would not have happened if the cloth had been given to Delgoda Rala.

The above is read over to Pulukkuttyge Louis Appu and admitted to be correct.

Before me,

October 27th, 1814. J. D'OYLY,

Chief Translator to Government.

(*Extracts from the evidence given by Kai Appuge Migel Appu on 26th October*, 1814).

" On the fourth day we reached Kandy at dusk in the evening and were carried that night to the house of Diyawadana Nilame the younger brother of the Dissave of the Seven Korles. The next morning at daybreak we were conducted under charge of the same persons to the house of Siya Pattuwe Adikar. Shortly after the sun rose the Adikar came out saying " I am going to make communication to the Great Gate. You stay till my return." We were confined that night at the house of the Diyawadana Nilame and early the next morning were conducted to a place near the new tank where a new building is erecting. After remaining there about two hours we were conducted to another spot where four streets unite. (After the examination) " We pray in the name of the Great Gate in the name of the Dalada Maligawa in the name of the Golden Sword, to be released for charity " " That cannot be done. You have been pronounced guilty. It has been ordered to inflict thirty-two tortures, of those a part will be inflicted. It has been ordered that for the crime of having come first the right arm and right ear and nose be cut off and the arm hung round the neck."

As soon as all had been punished whilst we were lying on the ground a Mohottala came near and said " It is commanded that you cry out 'Having seen this torture we will never again go beyond the limits ' and hanging your amputated arm on your neck, without casting it away on the road, go to Colombo and show it to the Adikar and Dissave." About 4½ in the afternoon the Walauwa Mohottala of Siya Pattuwe Adikar came with two Durayas and raised and supported me and led me to the house of the Adikar. The Walauwe Mohottala gave me assistance in stopping the blood of my arm by incantations and by applying cotton soaked in oil. I remained there the two following days being unable to move, and was well fed and taken care of by the Mohottala. At the place of punishment it was one Great Chief alone who spoke and questioned us. I heard afterwards from the people of the street that it was an Adikar. I forget his name ; it was not Siya Pattuwe Adikar."

APPENDIX K.

Exposure of Dead Bodies

Severe comment has been often made on the fact that the bodies of the seven spies who died were hung up on trees by the King's orders ; that was a common method of disposing of the body of a convicted criminal and was considered less disgraceful than impaling it. A similar custom prevailed under the English criminal law. In 1816 the local Supreme Court on sentencing a man to death further directed that his head should be severed from his body and exposed in an iron case. On 18th September, Brownrigg remitted the latter part of the sentence explaining that his action " arises solely from my feelings of repugnance to adopt that which appears horrible and is not sanctioned by the customs of our country. It also seems to me to be forbidden by the 6th Clause of His Majesty's Instructions to Mr. North as well as by Mr. North's Proclamation of the 23rd September, 1799."

To this letter the Chief Justice, Sir Alexander Johnstone, and the Puisne Justice, Sir William Coke, replied the next day, pointing out that the Instructions and Proclamation referred " only to torture, breaking upon the wheel, and other modes of punishment which often preceded the infliction of the punishment of death upon criminals under the practise of the Dutch Government " and not to the disposal of the body after death ; " a similar sentence having been passed on Seesau by the Supreme Court and carried into effect under the Warrant of the Governor in 1807." They added " On referring to the sentences which are usually passed in England in aggravated cases of murder Your Excellency must be aware that a part of the common sentence passed on such occasions is, that the body of the offender be hung in chains. In consequence, however, of the difference between this climate and that of England, the Judges on the occasion of passing sentence upon Seesau thought themselves justified in ordering the head only of the offender instead of the whole body to be hung in chains." They further pointed out that in England in atrocious cases of murder another direction was that " the body of the criminal after execution be anatomized. Your Excellency will do us the justice to believe that we as well as

Your Excellency are not without our private feelings as to the horror which such a spectacle, involving the entire mutilation of the body, must naturally incite in such a case and we are not without similar feelings in regard to this case" but the very horror created by such a sight was the reason it was ordered.

Hardinge Giffard, the Advocate Fiscal responsible for preparing the Warrant, expressed his opinion that "the able and benevolent Judges who pronounced the sentences" merely copied the earlier sentence in execution of which the criminal's head still remained exposed.

Brownrigg's Despatch 166 of 2nd Nov., 1816. C.O. 54/61. By Lansdowne's Act (9 Geo. 4 c. 31 sect. iv) it was enacted—

That every person convicted of murder shall be executed . . . and the body of every murderer shall, after execution, either be dissected or hung in chains, as to the Court shall seem meet."

APPENDIX L.

The Maintenance of the Captive King

Sundry applications of the King respecting which His Excellency requests D'Oyly's observations.

Colombo, 4th April, 1815.

He wishes it to be informed to the Governor that he is ashamed to see his wives without the ornaments most necessary for women namely :

In gold 4 pair of ear ornament called Caudoly.
,, 4 pair of ear ornament called Coppu.
,, 4 pair of ear ornament called Ouneppu.

The King says that there are several Golden and other state hats in Kandy which he used to wear there—of which he requests the Governor will be pleased to give him two :

1 made of pure Gold.

1 made of superfine cloth mounted with Gold and feather along the edge.

2 jackets, *viz.*—

1 of superfine white cloth.

1 of superfine embroidered.

1 flat Gold neck ornament called Mante.

14 Tupaddies bordered with Golden Lace.

1 small knife like a dagger mounted of Gold, some rings and lockets of stones.

The above ornaments the King says are necessary to be with him to be dressed with when any gentleman wants to visit him.

He wants the following articles to be furnished with for the use of his table :—

5 silver salvers.
6 silver dishes to eat rice in.
6 silver cups to drink milk in.
6 silver chembus.
1 golden box to keep beettle leaves for the King.
5 golden chunam boxes.
6 arekanut cutters mounted of gold.
6 combs of ivory mounted of gold.

He reminds of several sets of ornaments belonging to his wives of which he had lately spoken to Colonel Kerr.

As the King is used to bathe himself once a week that is to say on every Wednesday, he requests that the Padicary Mohondiram be instructed to issue to him on the evening of every Thursday, (Tuesday ?)—

1 bottle of leneseed oil.
1 bottle of castor oil.
100 limes.
1 pound of arrepper, a stuff to rub over head.
1 pound of cheeyakka, a stuff to rub over head.
5 measures of country gram.
3 measures of leneseed.
7 pounds of saffron called castoory for women.
4 measures of unboiled patche* rice.
4 coconuts.
1 measure of grain called oelundu.
10 pounds of sandal wood per month.

* "The most nutritious and the most palatable rice, although considered common and known by a reddish film, is the sort called Patcherie by the Singhalese." (J. W. Bennett, Ceylon and its Capabilities, London 1843 p. 40). "Its grain when boiled is nearly twice the size of the Patna rice and more oblong and egg-shaped . . . it is of a more mucilaginous nature, and has a fine and peculiar flavour, which makes it worthy of notice." p. 245.

The King says that the allowance of rice now issued to himself and family consisting his four wives and mother, namely :

8 seers to him
4 to each of the women } per diem.

is insufficient—he therefore requests the Padicary Mohondiram be instructed to issue him every day 12 country measures of rice, which will be about 16 seers for himself and six measures to each of his wives and mother which will be 8 seers each. He further requests that all other articles of vegetables, currystuff and so on be issued to him and his four wives and mother, once as much more as they give now.

He wants 10 pagodas a day besides, for trifling expenses.

The King observes that as a Royal prisoner he considers himself entitled to the above allowances.

Letters and Proclamations, 1815, C.R.O.

Schedule of allowances for the maintenance of the deposed King.

	Rxd.	F.	P.
8 seers of mootoo samba rice	1		
½ measure butter		4	2
1 dry fish	1		
6 kombelmas (small dried fish)		1	2
6 coconuts for curry		1	2
8 sorts of vegetables		10	
Curry stuff		4	2
Beetel, tobacco and areca nut		3	1
1 calinjee or 1 oz. of cardamons			2½
½ calinjee or 1 oz. of cloves		1	
½ calinjee or 1 oz. of mace		3	
3 bottles of milk		3	
5 king coconuts		2	2
8 oranges		4	
5 pomplemos or shaddocks		1	3½
½ pound soft sugar		3	
½ pound sugar candy		6	
1 seer fish	2	10	
4 coconuts as fruits		1	
Daily ..	9	1	1
Monthly ..	273	1	2

	Rxd.	F.	P.
Extra monthly allowance :			
1 coast pot or chattie		1	
2 cingalise chattie		2	
10 bundles of thread		2½	
5 cingalise knives		6	
10 common mats		10	
2 large earthen pans and 1 pot		5	
2 brushes		1	2
2 coast pots		6	
Chatties		9	
Flowers	1		
1 winnow or sieve		1	
7 common mats		7	
1½ pounds of sandalwood	1	6	
4 bundles of coir rope		1	
2 bottles of rape seed oil	2		
1 bottle of rape seed oil including bottle ..	1	6	
Total ..	10	3	2½
Pecuniary Allowance ..	200		
Grand Total Rix Dollars ..	483	5	0½

Despatch 107 of 26th September, 1815. C.O. 54/56.

APPENDIX M.

Some Treasures of the King

" Amongst other articles we are in possession of a rich and curious piece of ancient workmanship and State, in the Throne and Foot-stool of Rajah Singa, an ancient Malabar King of this country, whose remarkable reign is treated of in the works of Baldius and Vallentine. The King's Seal has also been brought to me and the Royal Banner."

Major Brownrigg is taking this Despatch to England. " He will be charged with the Banner or Standard of Kandy to be laid at the feet of His Royal Highness the Prince Regent. The Throne already mentioned and all other Insignia of Royalty that can be recovered will be forwarded for the gracious acceptance of His Royal Highness."

Despatch 95 of 25th Feb., 1815, C.O. 54/55.

Memorandum of the Delivery of the King's Jewels, etc.

British Headquarters,
Kandy, 13th March, 1815.

On Monday the 13th March the Adikar Ehelepola sent to request an audience of H.E. the Governor, which being agreed to he arrived at the Palace about half past five in the afternoon and was received by Mr. D'Oyly in the Great Hall where the Governor soon after joined him.

He requested the screen of the doors might be let down that the conference might be entirely private. This being done he made a signal for some of his people, and three bundles were brought in and laid on the table, which he proceeded to open himself.

One proved to contain a complete suit of Gold Armour, with the exception of the shoes which were afterwards explained to have been forgot at his house, and of the head pieces which probably consisted of the Crown and Cap about to be mentioned.

Pieces:

1 for the back.

1 for the front.

1 tippet for the neck and shoulders.

1 each hand.

1 each leg.

1 each ankle.

The second bundle contained a Gold Crown and a Cap of the Cingalese form, the upright part of which was a band or circlet of gold and the top plaited linen according to the custom of the country. Some ornaments, appendages of the Crown, either unscrewed or broken, were separate. One was in the form of a Plume resembling in some degree the feathers of the Prince of Wales' arms except that the number of divisions was five instead of three and were said to be Snakes' heads of the species called Cobre Capelle. This jewel was of gold set with stones. The remaining appendages consisted of several changes of tufts for the top of the Crown and one or two ornamental pieces of gold set with stones.

The third bundle when unfolded proved to contain a silver box of globular form and considerable size, which being opened a variety of rich ornaments were produced of gold and precious stones. There being no opportunity to take a particular Inventory of them at the time and as the whole of the articles were immediately sealed up in a trunk, the following particulars are put down from memory and must be considered to be very incomplete as well as deficient in point of accuracy.

1 Breast ornament attached to a gold chain, very large, of massy gold set with rubies, the centre stone of a great size.

1 Breast ornament, smaller, also with a gold chain, having a very broad square emerald in the middle, also set with rubies.

1 Breast ornament, small, with a chain, having a smaller emerald in the centre, set with rubies, very bright.

1 Breast ornament, the centre comprised of rows of table diamonds forming a square, the rest rubies.

1 very long and heavy chain of fine workmanship.

1 Catseye of extraordinary size richly set in gold and with a massy gold chain. The form of the stone a little oblong but the upper surface a fine uniform convex and of considerable height. The long diameter about 1½ inches, the short one about 1¼. The ray double and very fine dividing the length exactly. The ground sea-green.

13 Medallions in the form of stars, gold set with rubies.

3 pairs massy gold bracelets set with stones.

1 pair smaller in the calibre but deeper in the band.

1 Necklace of massy gold Bezils closely pointed, set with diamonds, the front part made to fall on the breast and much enlarged.

1 piece of an ornament unknown, of the same construction.

1 gold necklace set with blue stones.

1 tuft of white and green fibres.

1 right hand Chank mounted with gold.

1 gold box containing an Ear of Paddy with a small pearl attaching to one of the grains and said to have grown upon it.

1 Dagger carried in the hand, gold set with stones. The sheath of the Blade Velvet.

There were several other articles which cannot be remembered. It was stated that the most valuable and curious had belonged to Rajah Singa, and the Catseye, the Chank and the miraculous Ear of Paddy were mentioned as instances.

When the Adikar had exhibited the contents of the bundles, he stated that they were the King's jewels and ornaments (the Regalia) which had been deposited at Dombera and that he having heard there was a design on the part of some of the natives to plunder the deposit had sent confidential persons to bring the things away.

Present: His Excellency the Governor,
The Hon'ble John D'Oyly, Esqr.,
Mr. Sutherland.

Additional Memorandum

Kandy, 15th March, 1815.

This forenoon some of Ehelepola's people came with the King's Palanquin (details of the pieces follow). C.O. 54/55.

The *Ceylon Gazette* of 5th April, 1815 stated that Major Brownrigg who was sailing in H.M. Frigate Africaine " takes with him the Royal Kandyan Standard and two other flags also the Throne and Sword of State of the Kings of Kandy."

(*N.B.*—The reference to the Sword seems to be an error. Lieutenant Blakeney, who was on Board, states in his " Oriental Journal " that what was received on board were " the throne and sceptre of the captive King." Blakeney's dates are all incorrect, as he places the ship off Ascension on 10th October and at Spithead on 2nd December. The package was delivered at Woolwich about the 10th or 11th October).

Despatch 105 of 21st July, 1815 (C.O. 54/55) deals largely with captured property and states that "The Throne and Footstool of the King Rajah Singa (since sent to England) the Seal of State and the Royal Banner were also mentioned as being amongst the valuables taken."

Instructions for the Prize Committee, 22nd June, 1815

" The King's jewels delivered to H.E. the Governor by Ehelepola Adikar and certain other articles of which a list will be furnished, being Regalia or Appendages of State, are excepted from the Prize Fund now to be divided by the Governor's authority and reserved for the disposal of H.R.H. the Prince Regent." C.O. 54/56.

Woolwich Dock Yard,
11th Oct., 1815.

Sir,

In addition to my letter of this date I beg leave to acquaint you for the information of my Lords Commissioners of the Admiralty that on the arrival of the Newcastle in the River Captain Lord George Stuart forwarded a large case to my care, addressed as follows, *viz.:*

His Royal Highness The Prince Regent
"The Throne of Rajah Singa"

which I immediately caused to be put into a place of safety in this yard and wrote a note to General Bloomfield requesting to receive the commands of His Royal Highness how and where it should be forwarded, to which I have not yet received an answer, consequently it is still remaining here.

I have, etc.,
C. Cunningham.

John W. Croker, Esqr. C.O. 54/58.

The Throne was first kept at Carlton House and subsequently removed to Windsor Castle.

In a *puskola* of the year 1815 in which Ehelepola set out his claim to various lands, the following occurs :—

"The land called Henepola was descended from generation to generation of the great Levuke Dissave and that Dissave caused to be constructed the Great Throne, took it to the Great Gate when he obtained Sannas to the land called Heylemada Weregoda. The great Dissave had a grandson who was Dissavá of the Four and Three Korales and who having been beheaded at Guruwewilla saying that he without fighting against the English at Guruwewilla wanted to surrender up the King, confiscated those lands." (Board Papers, Miscellaneous, 1815. 1828. C.R.O.). For further information about the great Dissava see Notes on Some Sinhalese Families, Part II. The Throne referred to was one presented to Kirti Sri Raja Sinha and may well have been the one mentioned in Appendix C.

D'Oyly to Brownrigg, Received 3rd Aug., 1815

"Ehelepola has just sent to me some parcels of the King's property consisting of a few gold ornaments, silver vessels, cloths, gold and silver bands, a low table (not a stool) plated with silver, and the King's sword."

"His Excellency will authorize the said articles to be delivered to the Prize Agents with the exception of the King's sword which will be classed under the head of Regalia of the Crown to be transmitted to His Royal Highness the Prince Regent." C.O. 54/69.

The sword here mentioned was not the State Sword and may have been the silver hilted one which was sold in London on 13th June, 1820.

By Despatch 168, dated King's House, 3rd Nov., 1816 Brownrigg forwarded a descriptive list and valuation of what Ehelepola had delivered over, in accordance with Bathurst's Despatch 44 of 4th May, 1816. The opening of the parcels, inventorizing, appraising and packing was chiefly carried out in Brownrigg's own presence by the Joint Committee of Civil and Military officers who signed the list.

King's House, 29th Oct., 1816.

Present:

H.E. the Governor

Committee of Civil Officers:	*Committee of Military Officers:*
Alexander Cadell, Esqr.	Col. T. W. Kerr
Edward Tolfrey, Esqr.	Col. Brooke Young
Thomas Eden, Esqr.	Lieut.-Col. H. Evatt

James Sutherland, Esqr.
Secretary for the Kandyan Province.

List of Jewels Packed Up

No. 1. A Suit of Golden Armour in five pieces:

- A. One for the back.
- B. One for the breast.
- C. One for each arm.
- D. One for each ankle.
- E. A tippet for the neck and shoulders.

No. 2. In two pieces:

- A. One Gold Crown with ornaments of diamonds and rubies revetted on. One space for an ornament is vacant, supposed to be for a plume. No. 17. Two tufts appearing to belong to it are taken from another parcel.
- B. One Cap of Cingalese form, the upright part being a band or circlet of Gold and the top plaited linen according to the custom of the country.

No. 3. One pair ornaments (*Kaikattoo*) made to clasp round the wrist and cover the back of the hands, Gold set with diamonds, rubies and emeralds.

No. 4. One pair smaller ornaments (*Moorish Kaikattoo*) of the same kind; gold set with blue sapphires and rubies.

No. 5. One other pair (*Kaikadakum*) set with sapphires and small rubies.

No. 6. One other pair (*Kaikadakum*) sapphires and rubies.

No. 7. One pair in the same manner, but with small stones.

No. 8. One large massive arm ring called *Baaje Bandoo* set with ?

No. 9. One Gold box containing an ear of paddy with a small pearl on one of the grains.

No. 10. One waist ornament (*Ernakody*) for a man, Gold set with rubies, garnets and sapphires.

No. 11. One Padakkum or breast ornament circular, 5½ inches in diameter, Gold set with rubies, emeralds, and diamonds, a large ruby in the centre, with some small pendent ornaments and a massive Gold chain.

No. 12. One Padakkum, smaller, circular, 3¼ inches diameter, Gold set with rubies and diamonds with pendent ornaments of shell, pearl and a Gold chain.

No. 13. Another Padakkum, circular, 3½ inches diameter, Gold, set with round diamonds and rubies and having a large emerald in the middle with a long Gold chain.

No. 14. One Padakkum, Gold set with diamonds and a few rubies, pendent ornaments of shell pearl.

No. 15. A woman's neck ornament (*Olkattoo*) three rows of emeralds with small rows of pearls, one on each side.

No. 16. Thirteen medallions or women's ear ornaments (*Todoo*), Gold set with rubies and emeralds, twelve to match and one of a different pattern. These are found to belong to the Suit of Armour and screw on.

No. 17. Two pieces:

A. A jewel in the form of a Plume apparently for the Crown, Gold set with diamonds, emeralds and rubies, with a large pearl at the top.

B. A small one set with rubies, emeralds and sapphires having some pendent ornaments. This piece is valued with the Crown.

No. 18. An ornament for the forehead (*Nattiputtum*), Gold set with stones of various kinds, appears to belong to the Crown.

No. 19. The ornament described in the original memorandum as a Plume of snakes heads. It is called *Shindoo* and appears to be the resemblance of a Bird with an expanded tail. A large emerald in the breast, the rest set with rubies, sapphires and diamonds.

No. 20. A Dagger with Gold handle and set with small stones. An ornament at the pummell screws on.

No. 21. A Catseye of extraordinary size set in Gold studded with rubies and with a massive gold chain. The stone as appearing out of the setting is nearly semi-spherical but longer in the direction of the ray, measuring across in that direction 2 inches.

No. 22. A Gold chain about 22½ feet long.

No. 23-24 Two odoriferous balls mounted with Gold, one having a small chain.

No. 25. Two massive rings said to be ear ornaments, Gold set with sapphires.

No. 26. Fragment of a massy waist ornament, Gold set with rubies and sapphires.

No. 27. A right hand Chank Shell mounted with Gold.

No. 28. A pair of ear ornaments called *Todoo.*

No. 29. Fourteen small ornaments set with different stones.

No. 30. Four small medallions and ten buttons, white sapphires, set in Gold.

No. 31. *A Chelink* or Turkish tuft.*

No. 32. A polished uncut ruby.

No. 33. A Sardonyx or snake stone and some small fragments of little value.

No. 34. Eleven slips of Gold with Cingalese inscriptions used in conferring titles—being for that purpose bound on the forehead.

No. 35. A large silver box in the form of a globe opening in the middle.

N.B.—The diamonds are all flat or table diamonds except a few rose diamonds.

* A Chelink, or Plume of Triumph, was presented by the Sultan of Turkey to Nelson after Aboukir Bay and to Sidney Smith after Acre.

107—H 1

Valuation in Rix Dollars

No. 1 & 2.	24,669	No. 20.	1,672
No. 3.	4,043	No. 21.	8,200
No. 4.	826	No. 22.	3,140
No. 5.	806	No. 23 & 24.	56
No. 6.	517	No. 25.	135
No. 7.	524	No. 26.	822
No. 8.	1,372	No. 27.	100
No. 9.	180	No. 28.	122
No. 10.	1,116	No. 29.	155
No. 11.	6,881	No. 30.	120
No. 12.	3,76	No. 31.	10
No. 13.	4,1822	No. 32.	1,500
No. 14.	2,230	No. 33.	40
No. 15.	2,180	No. 34.	144
No. 16.	3,050	No. 35.	286
No. 17.	1,607		
No. 18.	433	Total	76,205
No. 19.	1,325		

Particular Valuation of Nos. 1 & 2.

		Standard of Gold	*Weight in Star Pagodas*	*Value in Ceylon Currency*
No. 1.	A.	1·2 Gold mohur	816 at 8 rxd	6,528
,,	B.	1·2 Gold mohur	884 at 8 rxd	7,072
,,	C.	Star pagoda	426 at 7 rxd	2,982
,,	D.	Gold mohur	130 at 8 rxd	1,040
,,	E.	Gold mohur	277 at 8 rxd	2,216
				19,838

N.B.—A and B each two pieces.

Number 2 allowing for the weight of the cloth.

A.	Star pagodas	228 at 7 rxd each	1,496
B.	Gold mohur	80 at 8 rxd each	640
	The two tufts with the Crowns		50
	The jewels on A at ..	..	1,145
	The pearls, 77, on B at ..	..	500
		Rix Dollars ..	24,669

Signed as at the head.

Despatch 189 of 19 Nov., 1816. C.O. 54/62

"I have now the honour to transmit to your Lordship two Bills of Lading signed by Captain Burford of the *Eclipse* Packet, one for the box of the Kandyan jewels."

Huskisson to Goulbourn, 11th April, 1818 . . . Forwards account of charges on the chest containing the Kandyan jewels brought from Ceylon and deposited in the Bank of England, amounting to £61-8-8 including ½% commission on £6,000 . . . £30. C.O. 54/72.

"Mr. Howard presents his compliments to Mr. Goulbourn and requests he will move Lord Bathurst to authorise the Chief Cashier of the Bank of England to deliver to Mr. Howard the case of Kandyan jewels deposited there in his Lordship's name" . . . Treasury, 24th March, 1820. C.O. 54/78.

Despatch 169 of 5 Nov., 1816. C.O. 54/61

"Millawa Dissave of Wellassy, a man of very advanced age and much looked up to for his learning, experience and abilities . . .

A third instance of the Public Service relates to the Kandyan Crown and Sword of State which have long been known to have been secreted, but every endeavour to trace them had proved ineffectual. When I was in Kandy the Wellassy Dissave stated to Mr. Sutherland that the Regalia certainly was either in the custody or within the power of Ehelepola. He enlarged with warmth upon the consequence of getting possession of them and did not scruple to own that the Chiefs and people never would believe that the Government definitely was transferred to the British Crown until those Insignia were secured. The information was immediately conveyed to Mr. D'Oyly with the names of persons referred to by the Dissave, who had himself been present when the Regalia were packed up and sent away from Kandy. It has known that they had been sent to Ouva and the persons under whose charge they were placed were also known, but although every inquiry was made on the part of Mr. D'Oyly to ascertain what had become of them, fear and influence for a long time suppressed the truth and no satisfactory account could ever be obtained.

When Ehelepola came to pay his last visit at Colombo on the occasion of His Majesty's Birthday, the loss of the Crown and Sword was made the subject of conference with him, and he was requested to exert his means of information and influence to recover them. He undertook the search but urged the probability of their being destroyed. If they were in existence he thought he should certainly be able to find them out.

The Dissave of Wellassy who was at Colombo at the same time renewed his assertions that they must be concealed under Ehelepola's own orders.

A fresh reference was made to Mr. D'Oyly and further enquiries set on foot but for a long time without effect, and Ehelepola showed no signs of any intention to produce them. At length the Dissave brought witnesses forward to prove that the box had been sent for out of Ouva by Ehelepola and brought to his house at Kandy, that it had remained a night there, and was then sent back to Ouva where the box was supposed to have been afterwards found along with other property of no particular consequence ; there was reason to believe that it was the same which had been brought to Kandy in November last containing some suits of royal but very plain apparel, which were afterwards sent down to Colombo and presented to the King.

As the strongest suspicion now existed that the Regalia had been taken out while the box remained at Ehelepola's house, Mr. D'Oyly communicated to him the facts which had been stated and represented how extremely discreditable the imputation was and the displeasure which would be felt by the Governor if the Royal Insignia were not forthcoming.

He protested his innocence of the charge made against him and said that since he had been spoken to at Colombo he had been using every effort to get possession of the articles in question, that his relation the Dissava of Ouva then on a journey into his Dissavani had it in charge to take that opportunity of making a personal search, and that he was not without hopes of being successful. Next came an ola from the Dissava in which he mentioned in a hesitating way that he had got some clue to discover the property and had good hopes of succeeding in finding it, and now by a letter this day received from Mr. D'Oyly I fin• the Dissave has returned to Kandy and brought with him the Crown and Sword and some other Appendages of Royalty said to have been found along with them, and the whole are safe in Mr. D'Oyly's possession."

Enclosure . . .

Kandy, Nov. 2nd, 1816.

My dear Sir,

I have much satisfaction in acquainting Your Excellency that the unrecovered Regalia are safely delivered into my possession.

Ehelepola to whom I sent a message on Wednesday, excused himself that day on account of sickness and attended yesterday. He informed me that the articles had been brought, and that the

Dissave of Uva would wait upon me with them in the evening. He added that certain persons had ruined them by calumnies in the King's time and would do so now, if it were not for the goodness of the officers in authority, who do not give credit to them without inquiring nor act precipitately, that he is guilty of no infidelity towards the English Government, and that I should learn further from the Dissave of Uva.

The Dissave of Uva came late in the evening with the following articles . . .

A Sword with Gold hilt studded with small red stones and a diamond at the end.

Sheath of wood covered with blue velvet very much worn, with some Gold work.

Red velvet band with Gold embroidery.

Three cloths enfolding it.

A Gold four-cornered Cap or Crown with carved work at top. The four faces and four corners studded with stones, principally red—a few emeralds and blue sapphires. The centre ruby is fallen from one face, but in the box.

A large brocade cloth.

A Gold crest or top knot.

A four-cornered black beaver hat, Gold laced, surmounted with white feather all round the brim.

Two cloths.

The Dissave in answer to my enquiry after the band or belt studded with precious stones which is said to belong to the Sword, stated that the band was not in the box, that there were 11 or 12 *peti* or plates set with precious stones, which are sometimes attached to the band, but sometimes not, and those plates he believed were amongst the valuables delivered up by Ehelepola to Your Excellency. He stated further that these Regalia were found deposited in a case in the forest between Uva and Kotmale, and were under the charge of Agale Kumbure Sattamby, who was half inclined not to produce them, and the Dissave discovered them by means of other persons.

The Dissave renewed his expressions of fidelity to the British Government on the part of Ehelepola and himself and stated their request that the Regalia which they hold in great respect, should not be exposed to sale or exhibited to common persons, or to those Chiefs who under the King's Government were never admitted to see them. I promised that they would not be exposed to sale and in general terms that they should be treated with every respect by the British Government.

I propose with Your Excellency's permission to notify to the Kandyan Chiefs the recovery of these valuables and assure them that Government is well aware of the high honour and estimation in which they are held by the Nation, and that having become the property of the King of Great Britain, they will be preserved with the same respect as the Regalia of the British Crown.

I have, etc.,

J. D'Oyly.

Of these the Crown, Sword, Sheath and Velvet Band, as well as Raja Sinha's Throne and Footstool have been returned to the Island, through the gracious consideration of King George V and King Edward VIII. With them was also returned the Golden Staff, miscalled "Sceptre." Of the Crown, Staff and Sword a three-quarter size oil painting is preserved at White Waltham House, Berks, and the attached legend records the fact that they were presented to the King by Sir Robert Brownrigg in person at Carlton House in 1821 (*The Kandyan Throne* by Beatrice Brownrigg).

The *Gazette* of 13th Nov., 1816 contained the following :—

"It is not we believe known to our readers that the ancient Royal Crown and Sword of State of the Kandyan Government had until lately remained secreted and that every endeavour to recover them had long proved ineffectual. A Golden Crown was indeed found and a Sword mounted with Gold, but neither proved to be of the Regalia used on occasions of public solemnity. The latter were held by the Priests, Chiefs and people in great veneration and considered as symbolical of the Sovereign Power. We have therefore much pleasure in stating that the zeal and fidelity of certain Chiefs have, by much pains and enquiry, discovered the place in which these Insignia were concealed and that they are now safe in the possession of the Resident."

At an enquiry, Puswelle Mohottala *v.* Eknelligoda Nilame, held on 20th Jan., 1816, it was mentioned that Puswelle had protested against the writing of a certain palm leaf document "in the name of the King and the Five Swords, saying the land could not be alienated being held on a grant from the King of Sitavaka." C.O. 54/59.

Further information regarding these Five Swords is not yet available.

Not all the King's treasures were surrendered to the British, and Ehelepola has admitted that a part was retained by himself, and in that connection the following are of interest :—

Brownrigg's Despatch 299 of 24 July, 1818. C.O. 54/71

"In addition to the above are articles as mentioned in the enclosed list which on the day subsequent to Ehelepola Maha Nilame's arrest (3rd March, 1818) were taken by the guard at Gonarua Ferry on a person of his establishment, attempting to carry them into the Four Korles for concealment. This circumstance naturally attracted suspicion and they were detained in the treasury here and lately exhibited to the First Adikar (Molligoda) who declared they were jewels which with the exception of those numbered 4 in the list, no wife of a subject could possess or wear, and that they were the Queen's jewels which had been long searched for in vain. Their value I have no means of judging of but should estimate them at about £2,000. In Ehelepola's baggage which was sent from this the day after his arrest was a large assortment of most valuable jewels which he was in the habit of wearing since the establishment of the British Government, although the greater part never, according to the Customs of the country, could have been exhibited by him during the former administration of the deposed King."

Annexed . . .

A list of property belonging to Eheylepola Maha Nilame taken from Pehenne Rala who was removing the same by desire of Henwittiponne Mohottala to conceal in the Four Korles.

1. 1 ornament consisting of 25 Gold balls strung on black cord and ended by one large Gold tassel cup and three small do. Weighing 100 pagodas, at rxd 6½ a pagoda, rxd 650.
2. 1 ornament consisting of 25 balls, 1 large tassel cup, and 4 small. 75 Star pagodas at 7 rxd . . . 525.
3. 1 necklace of large coral and Gold beads of 25 each, 1 necklace, smaller, 21 Gold and 22 coral, 1 necklace, smaller, 19 Gold and 20 coral. Total weight 175 pagodas at 7 rxd . . . 1,400.
4. 1 necklace of 27 Gold beads, 1 Gold worked chain, weight 52 pagodas at — rxd . . . 312.
5. 1 pair bird bracelets richly set with rubies, 5 rose diamonds and 2 small emeralds in each . . . rxd 2,500.

6. 1 pair of three-ribbed Gold bracelets richly set with emeralds and rubies and 3 table diamonds to each . . . 1,000.

7. 1 pair of serpentine Gold lights with clasps set with emeralds, rubies, catseyes, etc. . . . 750.

8. 1 necklace of Gold beads and pearls, four rows, pearls about size of a peppercorn, 1 necklace of Gold beads and pearls. Value rxd 2,500.

9. 2 rich head ornaments representing the sun and moon entirely studded with rubies, emeralds, table diamonds and pearls, 2 rich head ornaments but much smaller and inferior in value. Value rxd 1,000.

10. 1 rich bandeau for the head richly studded with rubies and a few table diamonds and emeralds and pearls . . . 600.

11. 1 armlet set with rubies, emeralds and few diamonds . . . 350.

12. A necklace consisting of a string of small Gold beads ending in 4 large Gold and coral beads and a small Pedegam consisting of rubies and rose diamonds. A necklace of glass beads and Gold (20) beads set with rubies.

13. 13 coral and 1 Gold bead . . . rxd 50.

14. A Royal whip set with Gold and some precious stones, crystal knob.

Geo. Lusignan,
Secretary,
Kandyan Board.

N.B.—No. 14 was found among Eheylepola's property in his house and immediately recognised as the whip the King used.

The values are added from Barnes' Despatch 57 of 3rd Jan., 1821. There is a Note: "recognised to be the King's property by the Kandyan Chiefs."

Jewels taken from Ehelepola after his imprisonment and declared to be the King's "as being of a quality no subject could wear."

Gold Box, 280 Star pagodas at 6 rxd	1,680
Gold Chain, 128 Star pagodas at 7 rxd	896
Gold Padecum set with precious stones with a Gold chain ..	3,000
Do do do do do do ..	1,300
Gold Buckle, with rubies and sapphires	190
16 Gold Buttons, emeralds	400
20 Gold Buttons, rubies	1,100

1 large Dagger, velvet scabbard	640
1 Gold Handled Dagger, set with rubies	750
1 do do do do	950
1 Ornament for the top of a Cap	50

C.O. 54/78.

Regalia* of the King of Kandy.

A CATALOGUE

of

A Splendid and Valuable Collection of Jewellery forming the Regalia of the King of Kandy,

The whole of the purest massive Gold comprising the Crown, a complete Suit of Embossed Armour, a great variety of armlets, bracelets, breast ornaments (*called Paddakums*), plumes of jewels for the head, chains for the neck, particularly one 23½ feet in length, a magnificent dagger, and various other costly articles of regal decoration, all of them of elaborate workmanship and richly studded with diamonds, emeralds, rubies, sapphires, pearls, etc., many of which are of an extraordinary size and beauty ; a catseye of matchless grandeur, an immense mass of ruby in the rough, etc. presented by His Majesty to the captors for whose benefit they will be sold without the slightest reservation by Mr. King, at his great room, 38, King Street, Covent Garden, on Tuesday, the 13th day of June, 1820, very punctually at one o'clock.

May be viewed on Monday, 5th June, till within two days preceding the sale in their present state, after which they will be unset and lotted out. Catalogues, price 2*s*. 6*d*. without which no person will be admitted may be had at the Auction Room.

Conditions of Sale

Which must be rigidly observed

First. Each person bidding to advance one shilling per oz. for the Gold, and one shilling per carat for the jewels.

Second. A deposit made by each purchaser (without distinction of persons) of £25 per cent. in Bank of England Notes, or cash, and each purchaser to give his real name and place of abode.

*This reproduces the Sale Catalogue preserved at Downing Street, a copy of which was generously supplied by the Colonial Office.

Third. Every article purchased, to be paid for and taken away within three days from after the sale, or the deposit money forfeited, and the lots re-sold at the Buyer's expense who must make good the deficiency, if any.

Fourth. It is believed that each article (not otherwise mentioned) is of the purest gold, and the jewels all of them real; but the purchaser must exercise his own judgment, as all faults and errors of description, T. King will not be responsible for.

Such gentlemen, as cannot attend the sale, may have their commissions faithfully executed, and free of expense by their obedient humble servant

Thomas King.

A CATALOGUE

&c., &c., &c.

On Tuesday, the 13th day of June, 1820 *punctually at One o'clock.*

Kandyan Regalia

Lot		
1	Ten buttons, Gold set with crystal, a chelink, or Turkish tuft, silver mounted, and a sardonyx pebble	All at
2	Four larger buttons, Gold, with 5 crystals in each ornament	do
3	Two fragments of chain, screwpin, 5 buttons, and various fragments, Gold	do
4	Two odoriferous balls,* mounted in Gold ..	do
5	A pair of ear ornaments (called *Todoo*) Gold, set with rubies	do
6	Fourteen small ornaments, in the form of a cross, Gold, set with rubies and sapphires	do
7	Eleven slips of Gold, with Cingalese inscriptions; used in conferring titles, being for that purpose bound on the forehead	At per oz.

* *Ambiri Bola*, the European Pomander.

Lot		
8	Two massive rings, Gold, set with rubies, and sapphires	At per oz.
9	A fragment of a massive waist girdle, Gold, set with large rubies and sapphires	do
10	Various fragments, Gold	do
11	A small elegant ornament (called *Nattiputtum*) worn on the forehead; Gold, set with rubies, emeralds and pearls	All at
12	A larger ornament, Gold, set with diamonds, emeralds, rubies, sapphires, etc. with 5 large pearls on the outer edge, in the form of a Tiara	do
13	A reverse Shell, called (*chank*) elegantly mounted in Gold; and held in great veneration by the Cingalese, who imagine medicine administered from it, a cure for all diseases; and to the Conchologist it is highly interesting, and probably unique.*	do
14	A pair of ornaments to clasp round the wrists, (called *Kaikattoo*) elegantly wrought in Gold, set with sapphires and small rubies	do
15	A pair of larger ornaments (called *Kaikadakum*) Gold, set with sapphires and small rubies ..	do
16	A pair of larger ornaments (called *Kaikadakum*) Gold, set with sapphires and small rubies ..	do
17	Various large sapphires, from the above, weighing	At per carat
18	A pair of ditto (*Moorish Kaikattoos*) made to clasp round the wrists and cover the back of the hands, of elaborate workmanship, Gold, set with sapphires and rubies	All at
19	One large massive armlet (called *Baajee Bandoo*) Gold of elegant workmanship, set with large rubies and small turquoises	do
20	One large massive waist girdle, for a man (called *Ernakody*) Gold, of a curious and beautiful pattern, set with large and small rubies, sapphires and garnets	do

* One such is to be seen at the Dalada Maligava.

Lot		
21	Sundry rubies from the above ornament, weighing	At per carat
22	A Gold box, containing an Ear of Paddy (rice corn) having a pearl attached to one of the ears ; held in high veneration by the Cingalese, the Box	At per oz
23	The ear of paddy, with the pearl	All at
24	A massive chain of exquisite workmanship, 22½ feet in length, Gold	At per oz.

N.B.—The above chain will be sold in such lengths as may be most convenient to the buyer.

Lot		
25	A most magnificent and exquisitely finished pair of ornaments (*Kaikattoo*) made to clasp round the wrists and cover the back of the hands, richly studded with rose diamonds, rubies and emeralds	All at
26	Various large rose diamonds, from the above, weighing	At per carat
27	Various smaller rose diamonds, from the above, weighing	do
28	Various rubies	do
29	Various emeralds	do
30	A splendid and elegantly designed ornament, (called *Shindoo*) in the form of a bird, with an expanded tail, to which are attached pendant ornaments of table diamonds, pearls, sapphires, and rubies ; on the breast is an emerald (rose-cut) of extraordinary size and beauty. The whole of this magnificent decoration is of Gold, richly studded with large and small rubies, sapphires, &c.	All at
31	Various sapphires from the above, weighing	At per carat
32	The pendant ornaments of diamonds, &c. ..	All at
33	The emerald, centre stone, weighing ..	At per carat
34	A woman's neck ornament (called *Oolkattoo*) Gold, set with 3 rows of emeralds, 102 in number, and 2 outer rows of strong Pearls, 132 in number ..	All at

Lot

A splendid ornament, worn on the breast (called *Paddakum*), 3¼ inches diameter, Gold, set with rubies and table diamonds, of a large size, having also 13 large pear-shaped pearls pendant to it, the whole suspended by a chain.

35 The setting and chain attached to it — At per oz.

36 Nineteen large rubies from 35, very rich in colour, weighing .. .. — At per carat

37 Twenty-nine large table diamonds, from ditto weighing .. .. — do

38 Thirteen large pear-shaped pearls — At per pearl

Another *Paddakum*, 3½ inches diameter, Gold, set with table diamonds, rubies and emeralds, of great size and beauty, having 13 pearls pendant, and attached to a chain 8 feet in length.

39 The setting of the above .. .. ..At per oz.

40 The chain .. .. do

41 Two emeralds .. .. All at

42 Thirteen pearls .. .. .. At per pearl

43 Thirty-seven rubies, large and fine, weighing — At per carat

44 Thirty-seven table diamonds, large and fine, weighing .. .. do

Another *Paddakum*, of an elliptical form, Gold, set with rubies, rose diamonds, and emeralds; in the centre is an emerald of extraordinary size and beauty, an emerald bead is also pendant to this magnificent ornament, the whole of which is suspended by a massive Gold chain of exquisite workmanship, 4 feet in length.

45 The setting of the above ornament . ..At per oz.

46 Various rubies, large and small weighing.. At per carat

47 Forty rose diamonds, large and small, weighing do

48 The emerald bead, one table daimond, various emeralds, &c. .. .. All at

49 One large and fine emerald (the centre stone of a pentagonal shape), 1 inch diameter, weighing — At per carat

Lot		
50	A massive Gold chain, 4 feet in length	At per oz.
	Another most magnificent *Paddakum*, 6 inches diameter, of an oval form, Gold, set with diamonds, rubies, and emeralds ; in the centre is a ruby, 1 inch in length by about half an inch in breadth, of fine colour, surrounded by 10 rose diamonds, of very great size and fine water ; the circle beyond is studded with table diamonds, the next circle with table diamonds and emeralds and the outer circle with very large and fine rubies, and a table diamond at the top ; there are 9 pear-shaped pendant ornaments of Gold, set with small rubies, the whole of this costly decoration is suspended by a massive Gold chain, of beautiful design, 4 feet in length.	
51	The setting of the above ornament	do
52	Emeralds of the above ornament, weighing	At per carat
53	Rubies of the above ornament	do
54	Large ruby, the centre stone weighing	do
55	Nine pendant ornaments, Gold, set with rubies ..	All at
56	Table diamonds, weighing	At per carat
57	One large rose diamond, weighing	do
58	Do do do	do
59	Do do do	do
60	Do do do	do
61	Do do do	do
62	Do do do	do
63	Do do do	do
64	Do do do	do
65	Do do do	do
66	Do do do	do
67	The massive chain, 4 feet in length	At per oz.

Lot

A catseye of extraordinary grandeur and matchless beauty, set in Gold, with small rubies. The stone as appearing without the setting is nearly semi-spherical, but longer in the direction of the chatoyant ray of light, in which it measures 2 inches. It is presumed to be the largest and finest known. A massive Gold chain (bit pattern) suspends this jewel.

*68 The catseye, in the mounting and a small chain attached .. .. All at

69 Massive Gold chain .. .. At per oz.

70 An enormous rough ruby, 2 inches in length by 1 inch in breadth, through which run in various directions a number of small hair-like tubes—a most interesting specimen to the Mineralogist.

A splendid dagger, Gold handle, with an ornamental guard of beautiful design, which covers the back of the hand, richly studded with table diamonds, emeralds, and rubies; a Gold device, set with rubies, and surmounted by a large pearl, screws on the pummel; the scabbard is also richly decorated with table diamonds, rubies and emeralds; a small Gold chain is attached to it.

N.B.—It is to be hoped that this matchless weapon may not be broken up, but should the public think it advisable to do so, it will be sold in the following detached portions:—

71 The table diamonds, weighing At per carat

72 Emeralds .. .. do

73 Rubies .. .. do

74 The handle, chain and setting At per oz.

*For the subsequent history of the great catseye, No. 68, till its sale at the Winan Collection on 13 June, 1928, see Letters to Ceylon, Note 102. Dr. G. F. Herbert Smith in his Gem-stones. p. 237, has recorded the size of the stone as 35·5 by 35 mm. An application to the Ceylon Government for some financial assistance to enable me to continue the search for the rest of the King's jewels, made on 14th Oct., 1935 while Trade Commissioner for Ceylon in London, was unsuccessful.

Lot

75 The screw ornament at top, with the pearl, the scabbard and jewels which ornament it, the blade, etc. .. .. All at

76 A very large silver globe-shaped box, which appears to have contained the Crown .. ..At per oz.

The Crown

The King of Kandy's Crown, of a very singular, but tasteful form, Gold, with projecting angles, from which are suspended ornaments of table diamonds, small rubies, etc. (two only remaining); round the circle, which embraces the forehead, are fifteen ornaments of Gold, set with rose diamonds, and rubies which screw on, on the top is an ornamental tuft of Gold and pearls, and in front attaches an enamelled Gold ornament of great beauty, in the form of a plume, covered with table diamonds, emeralds and rubies, the centre ruby of a very large size, forming altogether a singularly splendid, and costly mark of Royalty.

77 The Gold of the Crown will be sold .. ..At per oz.

78 Table diamonds of the plume weighing At per carat

79 Rose diamonds of the ornaments to the Crown, weighing .. .. do

80 Rubies of the ornaments to the Crown .. do

81 Top tuft of Gold, and pearls, with the two pendant ornaments of table diamonds, and rubies All at

82 A ruby the centre stone of the plume, weighing .. .. At per carat

83 Emeralds of the plume, weighing .. do

84 Setting of ditto with the large pearl drop, and various small rubies, and emeralds, which decorated it .. .. All at

A Sinhalese Cap, the upright part being a band or circlet of Gold, with a double border of leaves, to the inner row of which are pendant 78 pearls of a uniform size, and fine colour; the Cap is of plaited linen, according to the custom of the country.

Lot

85 The Gold circlet .. .. At per oz.

86 Seventy-eight pearls .. .. At per pearl

N.B.—This cap is probably worn without the Crown.

The Armour

A complete suit of richly embossed Gold armour, consisting of the following parts :— One piece for the front reaching from the neck to the waist, one piece for the back, which joins when on the wearer with the former, two richly embossed Vandyke ornaments, which attach in the form of skirts to the above, surround the hips, and partly cover the thighs; it is so connected with the body part as not to impede the wearer's movements, and is fixed on by the means of thirteen elegantly designed ornaments, studded with rubies and emeralds.

87 A plaited Gold tippet, 9 inches in breadth, with small pendant ornaments, which goes round the neck, and covers the shoulders, and is worn over the armour.

88 A pair of plaited Gold ornaments for the wrists, in the form of triple ruffles, 6 inches broad.

89 A pair of leg ornaments, or boots of Gold, singularly formed, and reaching from the knees to the ankles with small pendant decorations, the whole of these parts forming a most gorgeous specimen of Asiatic magnificence.

N.B.—The Gold of the above suit of armour will be sold at per oz. either in one lot, or in such portions as may best suit the purchaser's wishes.

90 The thirteen rosettes, which attach the skirts to the body of the armour, Gold studded with rubies and emeralds, the Gold .. .. .. At per oz.

91 The emeralds from the above, weighing At per carat

92 Rubies from the above, weighing .. .. do

93 Another parcel of emeralds, weighing .. .. do

FINIS.

Amounts obtained at the sale of jewellery forming the Regalia of the King of Kandy, held in 1820.

Lot No.	*Amount*			*Remarks*
1	1	18	0	
2	3	14	0	
3	3	3	0	
4	4	14	6	
5	3	13	0	
6	6	6	0	
7	8	4	0	4 oz. 1 dwt. at 80/- per oz.
8	7	10	0	
9	21	10	0	(Emanuel)
10	4	0	0	
11	2	17	0	
12	19	19	0	
13	14	3	6	
14	16	5	0	
14a	10	0	0	Sapphires from Lot 14
15	17	17	0	
15a	5	15	0	Sapphires from Lot 15
16	18	18	0	
17	6	15	0	
18	38	17	0	(Benthy)
18a	7	10	0	Sapphires and rubies
19	42	0	0	(Emanuel)
19a	11	0	0	Rubies from Lot 19
20	55	13	0	(Emanuel)
21	29	8	0	(Charman)
22 & 23	13	2	6	
24	31	5	0	(Dent) 5 oz. 14 dwt. 18 grains at 109/- per oz.
24a	30	15	0	(Dent) 5 oz. 10 dwt. 21 grains at 111/- per oz. Parts of Lot 24.
24b	32	4	9	(Dent) 5 oz. 17 dwt. 6 grains at 110/- per oz. Parts of Lot 24.
24c	29	14	0	(Baker) 5 oz. 16 dwt. 12 grains at 102/- per oz. Parts of Lot 24.

Lot No.	*Amount*			*Remarks*
24d	31	1	9	(Pringle) 5 oz. 17 dwt. 8 grains at 106/- per oz. Parts of Lot 24.
24e	29	1	8	(Davies) 5 oz. 16 dwt. 8 grains at 100/- per oz. Parts of Lot 24.
25	70	7	0	(Emanuel)
26 & 27	115	10	0	(Cohen) 26½ carats at 88/- per carat
28 & 29	10	17	10	(Levi) 20¾ carats at 10/6 per carat
30	18	7	6	(Devisne)
31	5	5	0	
32	—	—	-	
33	41	0	0	(Gilmore)
34	26	15	6	(Davies)
35	6	15	0	
36	8	1	3	10¾ carats at 15/- per carat
37	43	4	0	(Devisne) 27 carats at 32/- per carat
38	25	4	0	(Bouchy)
39	7	7	0	
40	19	10	7	(Davies) 5 oz. 8 dwt. 12 grains at 72/- per oz.
41	—	—	-	
42	21	11	6	(Isaacs)
43	127	16	0	(Fletcher) 71 carats at 36/- per carat
44	—	—	-	Sold with Lot 78
45	9	0	0	
46	39	7	10	(Chapman) 47¾ carats at 16/6*d*. per carat
47	75	8	0	(Devisne) 26 carats at 58/- per carat
48	2	12	6	
49	69	0	0	(Fletcher)
50	33	4	5	(Sharpe) 6 oz. 19 dwt. 21 grains at 95/- per oz.
51 & 52	57	0	0	(Davies and Bouchy). In Lot 52 there were five emeralds
53	44	2	0	126 carats at 7/- per carat
54	45	3	0	(Bouchy)
55	—	—	-	Is crossed out
56	36	19	0	(Devisne) 20¼ carats at 36/6*d*. per carat
57 to 66	137	5	0	(Levy) 45¾ carats at 60/- per carat

Lot No.	*Amount*			*Remarks*
67	50	7	0	(Bentley) 13 oz. 5 dwt. 18 grains at 76/- per oz.
68	450	0	0	(Fletcher for Rundell)
69	56	11	0	(Fletcher for Rundell) 14 oz. 8 dwt. 5 grains at 78/6*d*. per oz.
70	110	0	0	(Charman) 1 oz. 12 dwt. 12 grains
71 to 75	52	10	0	(Bentley)
76	16	2	0	(Delaunay) 65 oz. 10 dwt. at 4/11 per oz.
77	84	5	0	(Delaunay) 20 oz. 6 dwt. 12 grains at 79/- per oz.
78	14	1	6	12½ carats at 23/- per carat
79	4	0	0	
79a	18	18	0	(Devisne) rose diamonds of rosettes 9 carats at 42/- per carat
80	17	17	9	38¾ carats at 9/3*d*. per carat
81	—	—	-	
82	18	10	0	(Gilmore) 18½ carats at 20/- per carat
83 & 84	10	10	0	
85	38	0	6	9 oz. 15 grains at 78/- per oz.
86	61	8	6	15/9*d*. each pearl
87 to 89	1,017	19	6	(Massey) 277 oz. at 73/6*d*. per oz., includes back and front pieces and skirts
90 to 93	91	7	0	(Davies)
				Not in Collection
94	40	8	6	(Delaunay) Sardonyx star set with turquoise
95	2	12	6	(Engled) poignard silver sheath
96	12	12	0	(Mony) silver hilted sword
97	8	18	6	(Delaunay) Ivory hilted poignard
98	5	0	0	(Jointer) Beetle box
	3,837	7	10	Total amount of sale

The supplement to the *Gazette* of the 4th August, 1815 contained a catalogue of the prize property captured in the Kandyan territories which was sold on 18th September in the Long Room, No. 4,

Prince Street, Colombo Fort. The articles are enumerated under the following heads :—

1. Gold articles
2. Silver articles
3. Pearls and precious stones
4. Ivory and Tortoise-shell articles
5. Gold and silver lace
6. Brass and copper articles
7. Swords, daggers, spears, etc.
8. Piece-goods of various kinds
9. Brocades, velvets, carpets, etc.
10. Spices
11. Plated articles
12. Enamelled Chinaware
13. Miscellaneous articles
14. Additional articles.

The Gold articles varied from goblets to earrings. There were 112 finger rings set with precious stones. Also 11 pieces of the King's State Carriage "the whole cased with Gold mohur, Gold and Bombay rupee silver, most exquisitely enchaised, representing the late King's arms, figures and various ornaments executed in the most masterly manner." Among the silver articles appeared 43 cups and 33 bowls, 126 wasit belts, 145 chunam boxes. 34 rice dishes, 28 palanquin ornaments, 12 table spoons, 2 dessert spoons, 1 drum, book written in Sinhalese characters, 1 hunting watch, 1 plain watch with seconds. Of pearls there were 5 double rows and 116 strings of coral. Ivory articles included 422 chessmen, models of a Portuguese Governor and family, a Dutch Governor and family and various other racial types, as well as 404 combs, some plain and some curiously carved. Of elephant tusks there were over 6,000 lbs. in weight. There were two Persian carpets and another in Gold-embroidered velvet. The brass articles included 92 rice plates. The most important piece of household furniture was an ebony cabinet inlaid with ivory and calamander doors supported upon four wooden figures. European influence appeared in a lady's miniature picture in a locket, two spying glasses, 27 pairs of damaged spectacles, a plated tea-pot stand and a bed-room candlestick.

For a detailed account of a jewelled Firelock belonging to the King, see "A King of Ceylon's Gun" by J. F. Pieris, *The Connoisseur*, Sept., 1936, where the ring presented to Major Hook is also illustrated; the same writer has described one of the King's daggers in the issue for January, 1938.

The following extract dealing with the manner in which the treasures were disposed of on the approach of the British, has been very kindly supplied to me by Mr. H. W. Codrington, sometime of the Ceylon Civil Service.

Kandy, 31st January, 1829.

Before George Turnour, Esqr., Revenue Commissioner.

Informations taken touching the Lekamitiyes found in the Revenue Commissioner's Office of the Jewels and other movables the property of the deposed King which were divided and distributed among different Headmen and others to be concealed at the time the interior was invaded by British troops.

Madugalle late Basnaike Nileme of Katragam Dewalle examined.

I was one of the two Wanooko Nilemes of the Maha Aramudele at the period the King was deposed : the other was the late Dodangwelle Attepatoo Lekam. The King's Treasures in money were chiefly kept in the Maha Aramudelle. But the Jewels, Gems and Articles of the greatest value were kept a small part in the Hettapangawa Aramodelle and mostly in the Ulpengawe Aramodelle. The above Dodangwelle Wanakoo Nileme was also Lekam of the Hettapangawa Aramodelle. The Lekam of the Ulpengawa Aramodelle was the late Tallagooni Wanakoo Nileme—Mirihawatte Dissawe now in Ouwah was Kankanema of the Hettapanne and Wellegedera Satamby now in Kotmale was the Kankaneme of the Ulpengawe Aramodella.

When Ehelleypolley Maha Nileme fled from Saffragam to Colombo an intimation was received by the King, that the interior was likely to be invaded by the Englsh, His Majesty ordered that his Jewels, etc. should be packed up and distributed among trusty persons to be concealed. The distribution of the Treasure in the Maha Aramudelle was managed by Dodangwelle Wanakoo Nileme and myself. We had five Lekams under us of whom I can only recollect one at this moment, *viz.*, Wallawatte Lekam and five Kankanemas of whom I recollect three Marookana of Dumbera, Dellewitte of Seven Korles and Wellewitte late Ratey Mahatmeya. Any of these Chiefs as they happened to be present wrote out the Lekamitiye of the property consigned to the different people. The gold and silver coins were regularly counted over. I recollect delivering myself a box containing 6 or 7,000 සකාඃච්වරාගනත් Scot Pagodas to Asweddume Ratey Koralle. The copper money was chiefly measured out with a coronie measure each averaging to contain 100 ridis. The money was put into bags and was removed partly by bullocks and partly by men. I superintended the burial of copper money in two places. I buried at Teldeneye one lac and eighty or ninety thousand ridis—a copper sannas having engraven on it the amount and the names of the persons entrusted with the concealing the money was buried with it. At Doreleyadde I buried 80,000 ridis. Both these spots were disclosed to the troops, into whose hands the money fell, a great part of which is said to have been delivered up to the Government. Lekamitiyes were written at all three Aramodelles. They specified the articles contained in each box and the mark placed on each box. I assisted in preparing a part of the Ulpengawe Lekametiye also. All these Lekamitiyes as well as the Lekamitiyes of lands and other important records were put up in boxes and sent to the Royal Villages—Teldeneya, Damberave and Oudewelle. I cannot say to what particular village any particular Lekametiye was entrusted. It is understood that the Lekametiyes in general fell into the hands of Sir John D'Oyly. But I never heard before this, that the Lekametiyes now in question had come to light, certainly no enquiry ensued in regard to them. I do not at this moment recollect any other considerable sum being entrusted to any one but Asweddume Kalley Korale, but the Lekamitiye will specify every item of any amount. I recollect asking Kalley Korale about a year after the accession what had become of the money entrusted to him. He said he had delivered up the whole to Ehelleypolley.

About three days before the King fled the Capital for Dombera, he sent for me into his room, to assist in putting up his regal ornaments preparatory to his departure. I found in the room one of the King's relations Aigeloo Naiyaka Unanse and Welleygedere Sattamby. The King told me that I would find a list of the articles in the box containing the articles themselves and desired me to see if all was right. The box was about 2 feet high 3 long and 1½ broad. Inside of it was a smaller box which contained the Maha Padekan and seven or eight smaller ones with the chains, three or four daggers, two or three pairs of නවරුවංබැඳි හසථකඩවලළු Hasta Kaddu bracelets. These were the most valuable of the Royal Jewels; about 15 or 20 rings of different sizes. These articles were found to be right. I was desired to make out another list; I did so, and the box was sealed up. In the larger box there were four Caps, one gold set with gems, and another of embossed gold the third of burnished gold and the other was made of plate of gold with a cloth top, the tippet of gold. Two or three pairs of trousers of cloth of gold. The boxes containing the gold and silver jackets were not shewn to me. The small box was replaced in the large one and sealed up. I saw nothing more of these boxes till I attended the King in his flight to Meda Maha Neura. When the King heard that Ehellepolle had crossed the river with a detachment of troops and had defeated the Malabar Princes who were to defend a pass, he desired me and Tallagoone Wanekoo Neleme to remove the box to the rock cave at Potdalgodde in which the carriage was concealed, and to deliver it to the Headmen of that village; they were the late Haimagahagedere Dukgene Ralle, Kapukotowe Dukgene Ralle, Horimulle Kalley Korale and Attapattogedere Aratchy. The King desired that these headmen should remove all those Articles to some other place as the circumstance of their being concealed there had transpired. They replied that the removal could not be effected at that moment for the want of people. We staid there till the next morning. Hearing that the detachment was approaching we went to Oudawella in the Gampaha of Doombare and waited for the King there who was hourly expected. We heard soon after that he had fallen into the hands of Eknellegodde, Tamby Mudiyanse and others. The King had by him a box of jewels, consisting of necklaces, rings, &c. intended for rewards to people who might assist him in his flight. These fell into the hands of his captors.

I did not come into Kandy till I heard that the King had been sent to Colombo. A rumour was then in circulation that the British Government intended to raise Ehellepolle to the vacant Throne and people were secretly bringing in Articles to him. This rumour was afterwards publicly contradicted and people began to give information to the Resident. In about 20 days after my return to Kandy, I found that the Headmen of Potdulkande were imprisoned by the Resident in the present Rice Store for the purpose of recovering concealed valuables. I heard from them after their release that all the Articles were delivered to Ehellepolle, who had given many of them up to the Resident. I think the Lekamitiye of Ulpengawa Aramodelle was in the King's possession at the time he was taken and that it fell into the hands of the captors. Neither the Resident nor Ehellepolle ever inquired from me regarding the King's effects.

I now recollect that there was also a golden sword set with stones in the larger box.

Kandy, 4th February, 1829.

Resumed from 31st ultimo.

Welleygedera Apoohamy Sattambi examined.

I had been from my childhood about the palace and was already a household Servant at the time the deposed King came to the Throne. I was appointed Kankanema of the Ulpengawa Aramodelle about three years before the deposition; at the same time Tallagoone Wanekoo Neleme was appointed Lekam. About a year prior to the accession the Hettepenagawa Aramodelle was also placed under Tallagoone Wanekoo Neleme. As his Assistant I had in fact the management of the department. A relation of the King Aiyaloo Nayeka Unanse was always present at the opening and closing of these Treasuries. As soon as we heard that Ehellepolle Adikar had thrown off his allegiance and gone over to the English an invasion was apprehended. and I think about three months before the invasion actually took place the King ordered that his Treasures and other movables should be distributed among headmen and others to be concealed and this distribution was carried with great secrecy. I was the person who chiefly packed up the Articles. If they were too bulky I used to call in the Sattambies in the Ulpengey. Tallagoone Wanekoo Neleme wrote the account of the distribution in Cingalese and Aiyaloo Nayake Unanse in Malabar. In each box a List was deposited of the Articles contained in it, and it was marked and locked and sealed.

Besides these lists a Lekamitiye was kept specifying the numbers of boxes, the mark on each and to whom entrusted. If the articles formed any part of the Regalia, or were of great value they were also specified in the Lekamitiye but of cloths and other valuable goods no further account was made out than the list thrown into each box. The people who were to receive charge of the boxes, used to be ordered to assemble at the Saanchy Mandape after night fall and the boxes were given out after the people in the town had retired to rest. The parties receiving the boxes could neither ask or be afforded any information as to their contents; they are only told that they are to take care of the boxes and be responsible for them till called for. But as the boxes containing the Regalia and other costly Articles are packed up in wax cloths and ropes and sticks for removing them are fastened on within the Aramodelle before they are given out (which is not the case with the other boxes) it was pretty well known which of the chests contained the most valuable things. The Articles of the Regalia, the carriage and the Throne were entrusted to the Headmen and people at Potdulgodde and a box of jewels was entrusted to the people of Palaate. The Silver Articles were chiefly entrusted to the people of Manakalla; the Kalley Korale had the concealment of these things and from the nature of their office which are that of ranger and preserver of forests only confidential and trustworthy people were selected for it. I could by referring to the Lekamitiye give detailed information which from memory alone I could not do.

The personal ornaments of the King were kept in the apartment adjoining the bed chamber. Those Articles were not packed up till news came that the troops had crossed the borders at Sitawakke. The state dresses were sent off to different villages. The ornaments of gold and jewellery were packed up in two boxes. Those two boxes were packed up by the late Pahallewelle Deve Neleme, Tallagoone Wanekoo Neleme, Aiyaloo Nayake Unanse and myself and its contents were also written in the Lekamitiye. Madugalle Wanekoo Neleme was certainly not there, though he did assist on other occasions—the deponent describes the Articles to be nearly the same as those specified by Madugalle. These two boxes as well as two boxes of the richest dresses were kept to be taken when the King left the capital. Two days before the King started he sent off two boxes of treasury Lekamitiye and among them the Lekamitiye of the division of the treasure, &c. to Teldeneye. A memorandum taken from that Lekamitiye Tallagoone kept in his hands that he might send for any particular box if called for by the King for rewards. At Teldeneye the King gave the two boxes of Lekamitiyes and two large copper bathing chaldrons to Pettawelle Vidahn—a box of gems was despatched from thence to Palata. The King started for Meda Maha Neura taking the four boxes of ornaments and dresses with him, as well as immediately about him a box of pagodas, and trinkets to be given away in rewards. At Meda Maha Neura we found that detachments of troops were approaching us in different directions. The King gave the two boxes of ornaments to Tallagoone and Madugalle Wanekoo Neleme, telling them that the carriage, &c. were concealed in the neighbourhood, but the place of concealment had become known. They were therefore to get them removed further and the boxes placed in safety. Before those Chiefs could return the King was captured having by him only the box of pagodas and of trinkets and a gold mounted sword. I was not present at that moment having been sent to reconnoiter in another direction.

I concealed mysef in Dombere till I heard that the King had been sent beyond the Kandyan limits. I then came into Kandy and made my appearance to Ehellepolle. I think that was six days after the

King had been captured. Ehellepolle said that he had got information where the King's ornaments had been concealed and that I must assist in bringing them; on that very day I Petteyegedere Aratchily Teldeneye Radda Bade Vidahn and half a dozen Madowe men started. We called on the Kalley Korale to show us the cave at Potdulgodde. He went with us attended by several of his people, by chool light it being night. We found the two boxes of jewels, the gold and silver jackets, and the carriage—a golden chair (not the Throne) was also said to be there but I did not see it. We were desired to break open the boxes and bring the Articles clandestinely —we did so but the two silver heppoos in which the Articles were contained were not opened. We tied them up sealed as they were in bundles with cloths, some smaller heppoos (I think five) also containing jewels and the two jackets. Three golden ornaments a foot long each of the chair and some trifling articles consisting of gold mounted canes. These things were brought into the town secretly tied up in the form in which අඩුක්කු පෙට්ටියක් මෙන Adookoo (provisions) are brought to the Adikar. It was day light by the time we reached the town; they were delivered to Ehellepolle who removed them unopen to an inner room. I was desired not to leave the house. At night I was called into the inner room. There were there the Adikar; his beetle bearer Pinnawelle Appoo and myself only, by candle light the heppoos, &c. were opened and the articles examined. The Adikar put the golden hat and jacket on himself. I noticed to him the impropriety of that act; he replied that in a few days I should hear him proclaimed King by the British Authorities. In the morning I asked him to appear before the Resident lest I should hereafter be criminated for bringing these valuables without apprizing the English Authorities thereof. He said that it was not necessary, that he would report the circumstance. He gave me a silver heppoo and a chunam box and a couple of cloths and sent me off to my village in Kotmale. In about 10 days I got an order from the Resident to appear before that gentleman. I did so. He enquired if I knew how the King's property had been disposed of. I told him to the best of my recollection and mentioned that the Royal ornaments had already been delivered to Ehellepolle. I could not discover from that gentleman's manner, whether he had been already apprized of that circumstance. He made me state the Articles which he wrote down in a separate piece of paper. He also took down a general statement of the distribution of the property; by this time I understood that the carriage and many other articles had already been recovered and that Tallagoone Wanekoo Neleme had given to the Resident the memoranda he had by him of the more valuable articles. The General Lekamitiye was not attended to at all beyond my saying that such a document had been formed and left at Teldeneye. I was permitted by the Resident to return to my village and was never after that questioned by that gentleman. About a year thereafter Messrs. Gay and Sawers sent for me and told me that I ought to be able to assist in recovering the King's effects. I replied that I could do little without the Lekamitiye. They said that it was not to be found but that I should search. In about ten days I searched the houses of Potdulgodde and the caves of the adjacent mountains attended by the Judicial Commissioner's Aratchy and Peon. We found the gun and powder horn, etc. of King Rajasingha (which were plated with gold) contained in a box. Those things must have been concealed on some former reign. We also found some silver mounted arms of the deposed King deprived of the silver ornaments and in use among the villagers. Also a number of boxes and utensils.

I am quite certain that many of these goods remain in the hands of the persons to whom they were originally entrusted. Owing to so great a length of time having elapsed the fear of a search must have long been allayed. I would recommend an immediate search of the houses of the principal persons entrusted with these goods. The people themselves might afterwards be brought into Kandy and for any Articles not forthcoming be made to state to whom they were delivered up.

APPENDIX N.

Note on the Frontispiece

This reproduces a drawing found in the collection recently purchased from the representatives of William King by the Colombo Museum, to the Managing Committee of which I desire to record my obligations for permission to make use of it in this Book. Of King himself Brownrigg wrote on the 2nd of August, 1819 to the Secretary of State as follows: "My Aid-de-Camp Captain King of the Royal Staff Corps having suffered much lately from the effects of his continued exertions at Attapittia, I have found it necessary to admit of his resigning the Civil and Military duties of that Station. I have directed the Fort to be called by his name, in which I hope to meet with your Lordship's approval." (Desp. 358, C. O. 54/74). The picture shows Ehelepola, Molligoda and Kapuvatta discussing with D'Oyly the appointment of new officials, an incident recorded in D'Oyly's Diary thus "March, 19th. Dined with the Governor at 3 p.m. Sundry complaints, applications, and visits of Kandyan Chiefs in the morning. At 5 p.m. Eheylepola and the two Adikars attend at the Magul Maduwa. Long conference with them to arrange the remaining offices."

No other likeness of the Sinhalese Chiefs exists so far as I am aware, and even of D'Oyly the only portraits available are those taken when he was a little child. The reference in the notes for the artist's guidance to green in the costumes is of interest, as green velvet could only be worn by an Adikar, and in January, 1811 Ehelepola purchased at Colombo a web of forty cubits for 500 rix dollars (Diary, p. 52). The standing figure is the Sinhalese Mohottala recording the conversation with a stylus on a strip of palm leaf. The glasses perched on his nose need not necessarily have been European, as similar articles were made locally by the *Navandanno* who ground the lenses from crystal. The chairs it will be noted are covered with white linen in accordance with Sinhalese etiquette.

Addendum to Note on Vimala Dharma, p. 118

It appears from the Proceedings of the Political Council of Colombo (vol. 28, p. 318) that a letter dated Candy, 6th Sept., 1699, was brought from Court by Dodangoda Mohottiar and Oedoeowitte Modelyar, containing the news that the King had conferred on Pyl the honorific name of *Karoenadipatti*, which the Dutch interpreted as "well loved, as he had treated the Court well." The name is of the class which would be given to the highest Officers of the Court, of a status corresponding to a Privy Councillor; the connotation of the word is that the recipient was "the most worthy of the Royal Favour." Pusvelle, Pilima Talavuva, Migastenna, Levuke and Molligoda all bore the name Raja Karuna.

INDEX